When Hate Groups March Down Main Street

When Hate Groups March Down Main Street

Engaging a Community Response

Deborah Levine and Marc Brenman

ROWMAN & LITTLEFIELD
Lanham • Boulder • New York • London

Published by Rowman & Littlefield
An imprint of The Rowman & Littlefield Publishing Group, Inc.
4501 Forbes Boulevard, Suite 200, Lanham, Maryland 20706
https://rowman.com

6 Tinworth Street, London SE11 5AL, United Kingdom

Copyright © 2019 by The Rowman & Littlefield Publishing Group, Inc.

All rights reserved. No part of this book may be reproduced in any form or by any electronic or mechanical means, including information storage and retrieval systems, without written permission from the publisher, except by a reviewer who may quote passages in a review.

British Library Cataloguing in Publication Information Available

Library of Congress Cataloging-in-Publication Data

Library of Congress Control Number: 2019949039
ISBN 978-1-5381-3264-7 (cloth)
ISBN 978-1-5381-3265-4 (pbk.)
ISBN 978-1-5381-3266-1 (Electronic)

Contents

Preface — vii

1 The Local-Global Context — 1
2 Hate and Neo-Nazis — 11
3 Hate and White Supremacists — 17
4 The Hate Message Online — 25
5 Hate Crime Connection — 37
6 Corporate and Legal Context — 53
7 Community Organizing — 63
8 Recruitment and Radicalization — 79
9 What Is Our Moral Obligation? — 89
10 Globalization and Economic Disparities — 99
11 Bias, Prejudice, and Hate — 107
12 The Special Responsibility of Schools — 117
13 Holocaust Education — 127
14 Interfaith Efforts — 135
15 Conclusions — 141
16 Postscript — 145

Glossary — 151
Resources — 169
Appendix 1: Know Your Enemy — 185

Appendix 2: National Socialist Rally: Press Release	191
Appendix 3: Compassionate Witnessing and Rehumanizing the Enemy	193
Appendix 4: Example of Anti-Nazi Resolution	195
Appendix 5: Sample Hate Crime Policy	197
Appendix 6: Sample Bias Incident Response Protocol	199
Appendix 7: CRS Efforts to Defuse Hate Crime Activity	205
Appendix 8: Holocaust Ethical Implications	213
Appendix 9: Human Rights First	221
Appendix 10: Financial Help with Security of Institutions	225
Appendix 11: Bomb Threat Checklist	227
Bibliography	231
Index	241
About the Authors	255

Preface

> What is so disturbing today is that the vitriol spewed by today's American terrorists is being fueled by implicit encouragement from political leaders and public figures, including the President. The President's speech on October 22 in Houston, Texas, in which he declared himself a "nationalist," has motivated and energized right-wing extremists. If that rhetoric continues unchecked it will tear the nation asunder.[1]

Our objectives with this book include providing resources to communities and other stakeholders such as academia, law enforcement, and faith groups that are threatened with right-wing extremist activities. We approach the topic from a broad spectrum and with specifics. For example, we provide guides to specific groups and the code language and tactics they use. Case studies provide examples of how individuals, communities, and other stakeholders have dealt with the disruption and violence that these groups pose. In these troubled times, with the renewed rise of hate groups, communities need to be prepared to have their basic values challenged.

Our involvement in this endeavor is both intellectual and personal. As children of U.S. military officers during World War II, we are well aware of the history of the Nazi movement and its growth into a worldwide destabilizing, anti-democratic, and hate-filled force. Our careers encompassed issues of civil rights and prejudice from an early age with an emphasis on preventing discrimination and counteracting hate.

The philosophies embraced by the Nazis existed long before their appearance in the World War II era, and they continue today. Formerly under the radar, groups that adhere to the theories of racial superiority, extreme nationalism, and historical revisionism are now increasingly mainstream. Technology allows them to congregate, recruit, plan, and carry out vile acts. Blogs, podcasts, websites, and social networks enable and empower these individuals and groups to an often overwhelming degree. The results threaten individuals and communities in ways that most do not expect. While preparation is key to confronting the challenge, that preparation is often insufficient or nonexistent.

WHY PREPARE FOR HATE GROUPS COMING TO YOUR TOWN?

The answer may seem self-evident to many, but some may not see their communities as vulnerable. Unfortunately, the threat is real. We've seen mass murders against a Jewish congregation in Pittsburgh; an African American church in Charleston, South Carolina; and people injured and one murdered in Charlottesville, Virginia. Statistics show that the number of hate crimes is growing and the groups targeted are increasingly at risk: LGBT people, African Americans, Asian Americans, Jews, Muslims, and Sikhs. Intimidation is part of the mission of these groups espousing white supremacist and neo-Nazi hate. They shout down people at public forums, mount disruptive rallies at universities, and threaten reporters and news agencies. Social media and websites allow them to continually expand their reach and to recruit and plan.

Neo-Nazis and related hate groups desire a country or a state reserved only for whites who practice their perverted form of Christianity. The racism promoted by these groups is intended to generate fear and hatred of immigrants and people of color. They want to revert to a time of segregated schools and housing. No locale is too big or too small to be a target for their message.

This is not a familiar world unless we have relatives who experienced the Jim Crow period or who survived the Holocaust or other genocidal events. Most of us like to think that such events in the United States are part of history, not relevant to the present: lynchings of African Americans, the pro-Nazi German American Bund prior to World War II, the blacklists during the McCarthy years, persecution of Mormons in the first three-quarters of the nineteenth century, quotas restricting Blacks and Jews in colleges; the list goes on.

Imagine a regime in which all these evil tendencies come together. That's what these hate groups want. Then imagine that your community is seen as a path to such a regime by these groups. Are you prepared to handle their intimidation, threats, and actions?

A RANGE OF APPROACHES

Our goal is to utilize the Big Data of this new environment by organizing the information, tracking trends, reporting on community responses, and recommending strategies that are practical and implementable. By learning what others have done and from scholarly and academic studies, we hope to equip communities to protect themselves and preserve democratic values and the American Dream of social equity and fairness.

The approaches we discuss and recommend in this book range from "soft" ones to extreme approaches based on the degree and extent of threats and reality of violence and harm to people and property. As you participate in this book, we hope that you will

- recognize the hate, prejudice, and bias that lay the foundation for these groups to inflict harm on individuals and communities;
- build coalitions and partnerships that create bridges among diverse groups and strengthen the sense of community among all residents;
- build social cohesion, which consists of belonging, worth, social justice and equity, participation, and legitimacy (these can be measured using the Scanlon-Monash Index);[2]
- provide education about these groups, the philosophies they espouse, and how they communicate;
- monitor incidents of racism, anti-Semitism, and all other forms of bigotry; and
- put in place strategies to deal with hate incidents and crimes in your community.

We know that some communities vary in the knowledge and organization they have in place to counteract the influence and presence of neo-Nazi and white supremacist activists. Given the changing nature of today's environment and technology, we recommend that community leaders across the country explore their communities' readiness for a hate-related incident. Assess whether you are prepared to implement the ideas and recommendations contained in this book and what you need to do to ensure ongoing readiness.

Our strategy is to provide background, context, case studies, and recommendations in each chapter. For those less familiar with the terminology, many of the terms we use are included in the glossary. For those whose efforts are more advanced, in-depth treatments of major topics can be found in the appendices. Additional resources are listed. There are many groups on the extremist right. Their names change and morph but their overall goals and funders stay largely the same. However, in the interest of the broadest community preparation and understanding, we have emphasized behaviors of the groups rather than specific names.

NOTES

1. Blazakis, "American Terrorists."
2. Scanlon-Monash Index.

Chapter One

The Local-Global Context

A LOCAL EXAMPLE: CHATTANOOGA CASE STUDY

On July 16, 2015, the quiet, picturesque city of Chattanooga, Tennessee, experienced a terrorist attack by a young Muslim who had visited the Middle East and returned home radicalized. Muhammad Youssef Abdulazeez's first tragic stop was a drive-by shooting at a military recruiting center. He then drove to a U.S. Army Reserve center where he opened fire until he was killed in a gunfight with law enforcement. As the news unfolded that four marines had been murdered, the community went into shock. One of the three wounded officers, a navy sailor, died two days later, and the Fatal Five became a national news story. Following an investigation, the Federal Bureau of Investigation (FBI) said that the homegrown terrorist was "motivated by foreign terrorist organization propaganda."[1]

As the community struggled to understand how this could happen in a small Southern town, a city-wide ceremony was held for the Fatal Five. Memorials and anniversary commemorations continued for some time. The incident has left its mark on Chattanooga, with increased efforts at community building, interfaith dialogue, and inclusion strategies to offset the worldwide increase in hate groups and violent extremism. Chattanooga's mayor, Andy Berke, is dedicated to pursuing threats of hate and violent extremism and has become a pioneer in community response. He describes his involvement as follows:

> It was important to think of community togetherness and to make sure that no one got radicalized because of the incident. Hate is everywhere. All kinds of different ideologies that permeate the hate eco-system. What they have in common is people who've gotten disaffected from society and are taken ad-

vantage of by groups that promote and encourage violence. The US State Department under [Secretary] John Kerry encouraged me to converse with mayors and leaders of cities across the globe dealing with similar issues through the Strong Cities Network. The initiative provides an international platform for discussing challenges and options. I am now on its Board of Directors. I hosted an event at the German Marshall Fund and have hosted members coming to Chattanooga from the Balkans and Eastern Europe.[2]

At the national level, the U.S. Conference of Mayors is discussing violent extremism. There is agreement that soft power is key to making progress in cities. Combatting hate must come from the people. Following up with the emphasis on local leadership combatting hate, Mayor Berke presented on Chattanooga's local efforts at the conference's annual meeting in January 2019. His vision as stated here and the process of its implementation underway was received positively, with a number of mayors requesting documentation on steps that could be replicated.

> We see hate from national leaders, our schools, our computer screen and phones. We must begin by rejecting the idea that we are powerless against hate. We can change how hate is spread and can create tools to do so. I announced the formation of a Council Against Hate at the State of the City address in April 2018 and proceeded to bring together diverse leaders to serve on the council. Individuals working together can workshop ideas and make them better. Coordination can speed those ideas, continue and replicate them.[3]

The appointed co-chairs from the community, Alison Leibovitz and Wade Hinton, worked with the city's staff to build the structure through surveys, feedback, and brainstorming. In addition, there were briefing sessions by the director of the local FBI office and a regional representative from the Anti-Defamation League, an organization with close ties to the State Department's Strong Cities project. Education is a substantial element of the implementation process. The council provides a list of references on hate and violent extremist groups along with links to internet information.

Despite the emphasis on local leadership, it should be noted that there are fierce objections on the extreme right to initiatives related to international collaboration. This attitude is typified by *The New American* (TNA), a print magazine published by American Opinion Publishing, Inc., a subsidiary of the John Birch Society (JBS), a far-right organization.

> Boiled down to its essence, the SCN is actually a new law-enforcement body whose laws will govern participating cities, including New York, Atlanta, Denver, and Minneapolis, that have already signed on as members. Law-enforcement measures for these cities will dovetail with or emanate from the Institute for Strategic Dialogue and the United Nations, not from the U.S. Constitution and locally elected officials and the laws governing them.[4]

GLOBAL CONTEXT

To understand the current global phenomenon of hate and violent extremism, there must be an understanding of its historical roots.

Historical Background: Eugenics

Racial supremacy has a long history that is often associated with the word "Nazi," which stands for the German phrase "National Socialist." Nazism is a form of fascism developed by Adolf Hitler's National Socialist German Workers Party (Nazi Party) and the state it controlled in Germany and Europe from 1933 to 1945. Nazism echoed the longstanding demonization of the Jewish people as responsible for the death and crucifixion of Jesus and of the so-called Jewish financiers' conspiracy to take over the world, as posed in the apocryphal Russian *Protocols of the Learned Elders of Zion*. The Nazis initiated a program of military conquest and systematic genocide, resulting in the deaths of millions of people. They targeted Jews and other people considered racial enemies or racially inferior, such as gays, people with disabilities, and Roma, who are commonly known as gypsies or Sinta.

One of the principles of the Nazis was the idea that an Aryan race could be improved in terms of health and fitness. These ideas grew from the pseudo-science of eugenics. This is an effort to breed better human beings by encouraging the reproduction of people with "good" genes and discouraging or eliminating (killing, forcibly sterilizing) those with "bad" genes. In the early twentieth century eugenicists in the United States lobbied for social legislation to keep racial and ethnic groups separate; to restrict immigration from Asia, Africa, and southern and eastern Europe; and to sterilize people considered "genetically unfit."

Elements of the American eugenics movement were models for the Nazis, whose radical adaptation of eugenics culminated in the Holocaust. By 1928 in the United States, 376 college courses that enrolled 20,000 students focused on eugenics. An analysis of high school textbooks from 1914 to 1948 shows that the majority presented eugenics as legitimate. Forced sterilization of African American women and women with disabilities was common.

ANTI-SEMITISM AND RACIAL PURITY

Prejudice against Jews is ancient and has appeared at various times shaped by perceptions of religion, ethnicity, and race. Although Jews are a diverse ethnoreligious group, biased critics often project on them a racial identity that has motivated intimidation and violence. The modern origins of the term "anti-Semitism" are traced to the German Wilhelm Marr, who published in 1879 an anti-Jewish pamphlet called "The Victory of Judaism over Germanism," in which the term was first used. Marr also formed the Anti-Semitic League, a proto-Nazi group. The term "anti-Semitism" was a substitute for "judenhass," or "Jew-hatred," and was meant to emphasize the new "scientific" racial (as opposed to religious) anti-Jewish movement in nineteenth-century Germany.

Nazi policies and actions reflected Marr's anti-Semitism and were irrevocably condemned by the Nuremberg International Military Tribunal in 1945–1946 following the defeat of the Nazis and Germans at the end of World War II. The main components of the Nazi machinery of mass murder, such as the leadership corps of the Nazi Party, the Gestapo, the SD, and the SS, were declared criminal organizations. Key figures of the Nazi Party and state apparatus were found guilty of war crimes, massive crimes against peace, and crimes against humanity. A small number of high Nazi officials were hanged or imprisoned for crimes against humanity.

The principles recognized at the Nuremberg Tribunal form a cornerstone of modern international law and led to the drafting of major international legal instruments, including the United Nations Genocide Convention (1948), the Universal Declaration of Human Rights (1948), the Convention on the Abolition of the Statute of Limitations on War Crimes and Crimes against Humanity (1968), the Geneva Convention on the Laws and Customs of War (1949) and its supplementary protocols (1977), and the European Convention on Human Rights (1949). Institutions for the effective implementation and adjudication of these rights were also created, including the UN Human Rights Commission, European Court of Human Rights, Special Criminal Tribunals, and the International Criminal Court.

De-Nazification

De-Nazification was the official policy of the Allies, the victors in World War II, who understood the need for reeducation to counteract Nazism permanently. Shaping that reeducation required an understanding of how Nazism came to dominate an enlightened culture. Designing a reeducation program was a societal challenge as highlighted in letters written home by a U.S. military intelligence officer assigned to interrogate Nazi prisoners of war:

> The stories of German cruelty and oppression are not just stories—they are the real thing . . . much of this was done by what we call ordinary people—not just the party members, but a vast number of common citizens who fell easy prey to the baloney of national socialism. People who were jealous, griped, depraved and plain scared. . . . A large part of the population never belonged to the Nazi Party but 99.9% blamed Hitler only for losing the war and seemed to suffer no pangs of conscience over the origins of the war or the ideology of the Party. . . . Years of mal-education kept them ignorant and proud, selfish and egoistic. What does one do with such people? Ruthless handling of Party

Bigwigs and small terrorizers? Complete re-education of the rest? What a job? But there will be hell to pay again if it isn't done.[5]

Many aspects of Germany were never de-Nazified. The German judiciary, which upheld the genocidal race laws under the Nazis, remained in place. The German railroad system's employees, who transported victims to concentration and extermination camps, remained in place. Nazi rocket scientists were transported to the United States and the Soviet Union to work on those countries' rocket programs. Nazi intelligence officers were employed by the United States and the Soviet Union. An unknown number of German, French, and Italian Nazis fled to South America, where most lived undisturbed. An unknown number of lower-level Nazi functionaries immigrated to the United States and lived quiet lives.

While some Jews remained in Europe, many left for other countries, including the United States and Israel. There was a resurgence of Zionism, the belief originating in the 1880s that Jews should have a national home away from the prejudices of Europe. There have always been Jews in Palestine, but a major influx began from Europe in the 1920s and accelerated after the defeat of Nazi Germany and then again after Jews were permitted to leave the Soviet Union.

Zionism is now, but was not always, associated with Palestine and Israel. Today it is usually associated with Israel, but not all Israel nationalism is Zionism. Zionism is also often associated with anti-Palestinian beliefs and actions, especially by pro-Palestinians. A growing danger in recent years has been the shifting pattern of anti-Semitism. Scholars have identified so-called "secondary anti-Semitism," which shifts blame for anti-Semitism to its victims. For instance, there is an uncomfortably widespread view that Jews are exploiting the memory of the Holocaust for their own purposes, that Israel is treating the Palestinians the same way in which the Nazis treated the Jews, or that Jews are themselves to blame for anti-Semitism (see chapter 12).

INTERNATIONAL CONTEXT: EUROPEAN EXTREMISM

The combination of Aryan philosophy and anti-Zionism, coupled with a renewed insistence on the validity of the conspiracies of *The Protocols of the Elders of Zion*, has resulted in a contemporary version of Nazism. An example of this neo-Nazi extremism is seen in the following description of *The Protocols* currently found on Amazon. Almost all of this is historically incorrect.

> When *The Protocols of the Learned Elders of Zion* were first discovered, Freemasons and Zionist Jews everywhere screamed and complained that these

24 Protocols are a hoax, a forgery, even a blood taint against the Jews. But then came the brutal and barbaric Communist Bolshevik Revolution in Russia and its captive republics, led by covert Masonic Jews—Lenin, Trotsky, Kaganovich, and others. The cruel and sinister crimes of the crypto Jew revolutionaries seemed to have jumped off the pages of *The Protocols*. The Red Terror, with its torturous massacres of innocent people, its monstrous gulag concentration camps, and the setting up of a Jewish dictatorship, also followed the agenda of *The Protocols* as did the persecution everywhere of Christians and churches. The entire world witnessed horrors that were unquestionably a direct result of the heinous prescriptions laid out earlier in *The Protocols*. To this day, almost a century later, the sweep of history has proven the Protocols to be genuine, authentic, and a real-life rendering of the most tragic events that have bedeviled mankind. One nation after another has suffered, and now the Zionist psychopaths have targeted the United States and Western Europe. *The Protocols* continue to ring true and sound the alarm. If we close our eyes and ears and fail to heed this alarm, we will surely find ourselves in great peril. Our very survival depends on our unmasking the agenda set forth in the Protocols of the Zionist and Masonic elite for a Big Brother Police State and a New World Order.[6]

An increase in the number and membership of extremist and xenophobic (hating and fearing strangers) groups has occurred in a number of European countries, such as Hungary, Spain, Austria, Germany, Russia, the United Kingdom, and the Czech Republic. Law enforcement experts have noted increased transfrontier and international coordination of these activities. For example, German skinheads participate in actions in the Czech Republic and racist publications seized from Russian skinheads are printed in Finland.

Europe's largest survey on the subject, done by the European Union Agency for Fundamental Rights, showed a rise in anti-Semitism. About a third of the 16,395 Jews in twelve countries polled in 2018 said that they avoid Jewish events or places out of fear for their safety. A similar number said they have considered emigrating in the past five years because they did not feel safe as Jews. More than 80 percent of respondents said anti-Semitism was "the most pressing problem" facing them. Nearly 40 percent said they had experienced an anti-Semitic incident over the past five years, and of those, 79 percent didn't report it because they said doing so would be a waste of time.[7]

This penetration of extremist movements in European countries, many of which experienced and should understand the consequences of intolerance for cultural diversity, is a source of increasing concern. Emblematic of this trend is the vandalism of Jewish cemeteries, with toppling of headstones and leaving anti-Semitic graffiti. For example, "Jews to the Sand" and "cyclone B," referring to the Zyklon B gas used to kill Jews in Nazi death camps, was written on the gate of a Jewish cemetery in southern Poland.

To effectively address the European upsurge of anti-Semitism and violent extremism, generally defined as ideologically, religious, or politically motivated acts of violence, there needs to be an understanding that Nazism did not spring forth full born after World War I. Fascism first crystallized in Europe in response to the Bolshevik Revolution and the physical and economic devastation of World War I and then spread to other parts of the world. Fascism is an especially virulent form of far-right populism. Fascism glorifies national, racial, and cultural unity and collective rebirth while seeking to purge imagined enemies and attacks both revolutionary movements and liberal pluralism in favor of militarized, totalitarian mass politics. It is also driven by state corporatism and charismatic leadership. Another characteristic of fascism is use of a democratic system, but imposing the group's will on it through street thugs, gangs, violence, and intimidation. Fascism glorifies the will of the individual and the group and the suppression of minorities.

Today's extremism in Europe follows a similar path to the historical version with its emphasis on economic destructuring due to globalism and racial and cultural restructuring due to immigration. Here is a description of the growing phenomenon from Dr. Federico Fioretto, LL.M. MSC, writing from Piacenza, Italy.

> What is extremely sad in the growing support for far right movements in Italy and Europe . . . is the gross ignorance of people and how easily the popular mass is manipulated by false information and impressions. When you see the data of perception against reality, for instance, you learn that while there is a widespread perception of an invasion from Africa, among the 4 million [or so of] immigrants living in Italy 1,400 are Albanians, almost 500[,]000 are from Morocco, 450,000 are Chinese, and there are many Romanians. Illegal landings from the sea dropped by 80% in 2018, yet the discourse is very much still centered on "the invasion from illegal landings." Black Africans are a minority, but they stick out and are an easy target for populist politicians seeking to arouse the mass.[8]

The rising inequality of our societies is the cause of much frustration, depression, stress, and other illnesses. It's very easy for politicians who may be accomplices of those who cause the inequality and unhappiness to blame the situation on migrants and thus increase their consensus. Ignorant people are easily manipulated.

A problem is that neo-fascists don't come from "out of town." In Italy, the neo-fascists are part of the community. There are areas in Rome where "Casa Pound" (that is, the Home of Ezra Pound, a neo-fascist association existing all over Italy) members deliver food and other support to poor Italian families. They are beginning to be present in polls for local administrations.

There had been a vigorous English Nazi movement before World War II and a German American Bund. But it was the growth of anti-communism after World War II in the United States that stirred significant extreme right-wing activity. American Nazism echoed the Nazi opposition to communism in Europe. It also connected with the many strands of racialism in the United States, dating back to the beginnings of American black slavery in the 1600s.

The United States is no exception to the reinterpretation of Nazi ideology. American Nazis have joined together in anti-communism, racialism, anti-Semitism, and anti-immigrant feeling and adopted the ready-made framework of the Nazi fascist state.

RECOMMENDATIONS

Awareness and ongoing education are vital for individuals and communities to deal with Nazi-style extremism. The ability to effectively respond to threats, recruitment, and a growing presence requires an understanding of the history and context of extremist thinking. Articles such as "A Short History of the Nazi Party" are available online.[9]

Details on how history and context have impacted current trends can also be found in the following chapters:

Chapter 2: Hate and Neo-Nazis
Chapter 3: Hate and White Supremacists

Strategies for dealing with hate crimes and violent extremism evolve as these activities become more frequent. We have provided updated information and guidelines for responding in the following chapters:

Chapter 4: The Hate Message Online
Chapter 5: Hate Crime Connection
Chapter 6: Corporate and Legal Context
Chapter 10: Globalization and Economic Disparities

Communities can promote education and events that expand awareness of extremist groups and activities and counteract their impact. Combatting hate messages with moral ones is a powerful element of community planning and action. For more information, see the following chapters:

Chapter 7: Community Organizing
Chapter 8: Recruitment and Radicalization
Chapter 9: What Is Our Moral Obligation?
Chapter 12: The Special Responsibility of Schools

Chapter 13: Interfaith Efforts

NOTES

1. FBI Director James Comey, quoted by CNN, "ISIS Goes Global: 143 Attacks in 29 Countries Have Killed 2,043," February 12, 2018, https://www.cnn.com/2015/12/17/world/mapping-isis-attacks-around-the-world/index.html.
2. Shelley Rose Levine, "Council against Hate," March 15, 2019, https://americandiversityreport.com/category/shelly-rose-trends-in-hate-and-anti-semitism/.
3. Levine, "Council against Hate."
4. McManus, "Beware of the Strong Cities Network."
5. Levine, *The Liberator's Daughter*, 76–77.
6. Marsden, *Protocols of the Zionist and Masonic Elite for a Big Brother Police State and a New World Order.*
7. Liphshiz, "The Latest Poll on Anti-Semitism in Europe Looks Bad. Trust me: It's true."
8. E-mail to authors from Fioretti.
9. Goss, *History of the Nazi Party*; videos are available on YouTube for quick overviews of that history—for example, "The Rise of the Nazis/History" at https://youtu.be/yEk6zGYwyhc. For articles, books, videos, and relevant organizations see the resources, glossary, and appendices.

Chapter Two

Hate and Neo-Nazis

A NEO-NAZI CASE STUDY

In April 1995, the Oklahoma City Bombing by a far right-wing ideologue shocked America with the most dramatic and destructive act of domestic terrorism on native soil. There was a proliferation of neo-Nazi groups that energized the hate groups in the region. In her memoir, *The Liberator's Daughter*, Deborah Levine shares her experiences.

> The Aryan Nation was typical of the more organized groups in the region. The Skinheads were a loosely organized network. Mostly young White males, the Skinheads, were easily identifiable, sporting black leather, piercings, and swastika tattoos. Often recruited by the Aryan Nation, the Skinheads deposited leaflets on the lawns of Jews and African Americans, declaring that neither were actually human, and therefore wouldn't be missed if wiped out. . . . It was a relief to help shine a spotlight on their activities. These loners and small groups could do major damage, including the OK City bombing. Their lack of criminal history and under-the-radar organization allowed them to escape detection until they erupted in deadly violence. . . . It was almost impossible to separate the extremists from the deranged. Oklahoma taught me not to waste time figuring out which category applied to which threat.[1]

THE HATE GROUP PHENOMENON

The term "hate group" is used to describe any organization in society that aggressively demonizes or dehumanizes members of a scapegoated target group in a systematic way. Neo-Nazism has spread in America by using a version of U.S. history to support its theories and targeting. The distance between U.S. history and German history is sometimes not great. For example, a number of scholars have pointed out that the Nazis in Germany adopted and adapted eugenics theories from the United States. People need to know more about U.S. history because of the way it is mal-used by neo-Nazis.

"One of the strategies (though by no means the only strategy) that far-right groups can use to gain support is talking about national history."[2] Right-wing groups often refer to themselves as defenders of their nation (understood as a political community, be it a nation-state like Germany or a larger community like Europe, or even "the West"). For example, those who understand themselves to be engaged in a (literal or metaphorical) battle for the future of their community often look to national myths for examples of others who engaged in similar conflicts in the past and won.

> Referring to national history can be an effective way for extremists to gain wider support despite the radical nature of their goals and behavior. Heroes from national myths often carry tacit—even unquestionable—political legitimacy and moral authority. Far-right extremists who identify with their nation may attempt to claim some of this legitimacy and authority for themselves by retelling the stories of conflict and crisis that feature these national heroes, depicting historical conflicts and crises as parallel to contemporary events, and themselves as the political descendants of the national heroes. These stories can also help outside observers understand far-right actors. They reveal who extremists believe themselves to be, who they understand their enemies to be, and the kinds of behavior they believe are necessary and appropriate to defeat their enemies and achieve their goals.[3]

Some hate groups are grassroots initiatives as in the Italian example cited in the previous chapter. Others have been generously funded by wealthy politically far-right Americans and are emerging as mainstream movements, echoing the developments leading up to the Nazi regime.[4]

It has been said by researcher Paul de Armond that the far-right extremist groups change names, but their essential beliefs and funding sources stay the same. Here are a number of the funders. Note that including them here does not imply that any of their funds are used for violence or any illegal activity.

- William Regnery funds many alt-right groups, per Reveal/Center for Investigative Reporting. "Yes, I'm race conscious," he has stated. "In my ethnostate," he explained, "I would exclude, as a rule of thumb, non-whites, non-Europeans, wherever, however you want to define them. So, that includes blacks. We keep getting back to blacks, but we've got to throw in Han Chinese, have to throw in Amerindians, people who are distinctly different."[5]
- Colcom Foundation, established in the mid-1990s by Cordelia Scaife May, sister of conservative philanthropist Richard Mellon Scaife.

- Donors Capital Fund, to which conservative mega-donors such as the Koch, DeVos, and Bradley families donate.
- David Horowitz Freedom Center, which the SPLC calls "the premier financier of anti-Muslim voices and radical ideologies."
- Robert Mercer.[6]
- Scaife Foundation.[7]
- Ezra Levant.[8]

EXAMPLES OF CONTEMPORARY HATE GROUPS

There are hate groups that have been active for decades with a long history in the United States. Some of the most prominent refer to themselves as "Aryan," a term originating from Sanskrit but adopted by the Nazis to connote purity of white/German.

Aryan Nations

The Aryan Nations group is simultaneously a religious movement and a political one. The two aspects cannot be separated from each other. They are profoundly white racist and anti-Semitic. To achieve its ends, it has resorted to every form of terror, from threats, to intimidation, to armed robbery, to assault, and to murder. There is every indication that it will continue to do so. Its ultimate aims are the destabilization and overthrow of the governments of the United States and Canada and the creation of a white racist state either in the Pacific Northwest or throughout North America. While the influence of Aryan Nations within the much larger Nazi movement continues to rise and fall, and to rise again, the presence of an Aryan Nations outpost constitutes a serious danger to the community in which it becomes established.

Beginning in 1981, racists from throughout the United States and Canada gathered every July at the Aryan Nations compound near Hayden Lake in Idaho for the three-day Aryan World Congress. The group's leader, Richard Butler, lost the compound after he lost a $6.3 million civil judgment in 2000. Two members of a family who had been attacked by Aryan Nations members in 1998 won the judgment in a lawsuit, and Butler was forced to sell the property following bankruptcy.

Aryan Congress

In 1986, the white supremacist Aryan Congress declared the five-state area of Washington, Oregon, Idaho, Wyoming, and Montana to be their "white homeland." Led by Richard Butler, supremacists targeted various ethnic groups, gay men, and lesbians and their supporters for harassment and sometimes murder.

Skinheads

The skinhead movement became popular in the United States, having originated in the late 1960s in England. Initially, skinheads were mostly working-class youth and came from varied social backgrounds. They shaved their heads to avoid their hair being caught in factory machinery and wore steel-toed boots to protect their feet. By the late 1970s, the British National Front, a neo-Nazi group, helped fund and promote skinhead bands and their music for recruiting new members. It was at this time that the skinheads were recognized as a hate group due to the violent hate-filled lyrics in their music.

Migrating to the United States, the idea of skinheads came to the attention of California law enforcement in the late 1980s when their members became foot soldiers to the Aryan Nations, National Alliance, White Aryan Resistance, Knights of the Ku Klux Klan, and other homegrown white supremacist groups. The skinhead groups embraced and espoused pro-Nazi ideology and led the movement to commit racially motivated hate crimes ranging from vandalism to murder. Throughout the 1990s, the California Department of Justice identified sixteen distinct skinhead groups active in California with a membership of about three hundred.

Since 2005, according to law enforcement authorities and the Anti-Defamation League, most sections of the country, including California, have seen a significant resurgence of racist skinhead activity. This renewed growth included a rise in membership and associations of organized racist skinhead groups, as well as a rise in the number of independent or unaffiliated skinheads. This growth also included a rise in the amount of skinhead-related criminal activity. Incidents and hate crimes ranging from vandalism to more serious crimes, like homicides, were on the rise.[9]

ARE HATE GROUPS VIOLENT?

Violence can be defined as conduct that is actionable under criminal law and includes acts of physical aggression that cause injury and death. Alternatively, from the viewpoint of study of the nature of mind and of consciousness and of comparative religion and spirituality, the definition of violence is quite different. Violence can encompass intentions, words, or actions that lead us to experience ourselves as separate from one another.[10]

The current American Nazis nominally disavow aggressive violence but profess that they will defend themselves. Their speech, writings, and websites are full of vitriol, hate, and violent talk. Some have criminal records.

To help assess these threats, the U.S. Department of Homeland Security and the Department of Justice have funded the Extremist Crime Database to collect data on crimes committed by ideologically motivated extremists in the United States. The results of the analyses are published in peer-reviewed journals and on the website for the National Consortium for the Study of Terrorism and Responses to Terrorism.

Read more on the propensity to violence of the neo-Nazis and other hate groups in the following chapter.

RECOMMENDATIONS

- Educate yourself and your organization about the history of Nazism, white supremacy, and far right-wing extremism nationally and locally. By studying the historical development of the Holocaust and other examples of genocide, community members can make the essential connection between history and the moral choices we confront in our own lives.
- Participate in civic education. Learn how to work within the system with full public participation.
- Don't be enticed by conspiracy thinking and theories. Use logic, evidence, facts, and critical thinking.
- Live the American Dream of equity, fairness, opportunity, tolerance, and social justice. Realize that we all have a part to play in civil life in the United States.
- Pursue and follow good community values. "Person by person, family by family, neighborhood by neighborhood, we must take our communities back from the evil and fear that come with so much violence. . . . We have to address simultaneously declining family life and the increasing availability of deadly weapons, the lure of gangs and the slavery of addiction, the absence of real opportunity, budget cuts adversely affecting the poor, and the loss of moral values."[11]
- Set good civic goals, including the following: eliminate unlawful discrimination, harassment, victimization, and any other conduct that is prohibited by law; and advance equality of opportunity and good relations between persons who share a relevant protected characteristic and persons who do not share it.

NOTES

1. Levine, *The Liberator's Daughter*.
2. BBC Radio Four, "What You Can Do to Spot and Stop Unconscious Bias."
3. Council for European Studies, "We Are Patriots."
4. See the following video for explanation of that funding and political rise in the United States: Who Funds the Alt-Right? https://www.facebook.com/becausefacts/videos/194087694860464/UzpfSTExMzQyOTQzMTI6MTAyMTcwNjYwOTI5ODExOTQ.
5. Roston and Anderson, "The Man Behind the Alt-Right."
6. Kotch, "How the Right-Wing Koch and DeVos Families Are Funding Hate Speech on College Campuses Across the U.S."
7. ADL, "Funding Hate."
8. Ling, "Follow the Money."

9. Wikipedia, "Organized Crime in California."

10. Developed from Cheryl L. Conner, a lawyer, economist, educator, and change agent committed to transforming the legal profession and supporting lawyers and organizations in that change, founder of Lawyers with a Holistic Perspective, and co-founder of the New Law Center.

11. U.S. Conference of Catholic Bishops, "Confronting a Culture of Violence."

Chapter Three

Hate and White Supremacists

A handful of Richland residents found racist fliers tucked inside small plastic bags in their front yards Sunday morning. Richland police said Monday that they weren't sure how many residents received the fliers, which were inside bags with small white rocks. And while they said leaving the racist material on lawns isn't a crime, it has brought the white supremacist group mentioned in the fliers to their attention. Diana Rogers and her husband, Richard, spotted a bag in their yard when they left for church. When the family returned, Rogers went to pick it up and was shocked.

"It's like dropping pornography in our front yard," Rogers said. "This is disgusting."

Neatly folded inside the bags were fliers promoting white supremacy, replete with racist messages and slogans against minorities.[1]

While there is considerable convergence of the philosophies of neo-Nazis and white supremacists, these groups are distinct in their political stance. There is enough difference from neo-Nazis to merit a separate chapter on the elements of the white supremacist movement. Some groups have political agendas and may fall in the category of "alt-right," which includes the avowedly violent far right and white supremacist movement as well as the subtler forms of bigotry practiced by so-called Christian Patriots and Christian Identity who may or may not use violence to achieve their goals. These may include nationalism, anti-globalism, being suspicious of centralized federal authority, being reverent of individual liberty, holding conspiracy theories, indulging in paramilitary training, and survivalism. Mainstream conservative movements and the mainstream Christian right are not included.

Chapter 3

POLITICAL PHILOSOPHIES

The Patriot Movements are a good example of the political stance of white supremacist groups:

> The Patriot Movements are right-wing on race but conservative in their embrace of free markets. The conservative focus on patriotism finds expression in movements against supranational political entities, especially the World Court, United Nations, World Bank, and Trilateral Commission. Until the collapse of the Soviet Union, conservative anti-internationalism was grounded in fear of worldwide socialism and communism, but now conservative nationalists promote the superiority of the United States over all other countries. Despite their expressions of nationalism, many conservatives chafe at government authority. They favor individual rights vis-à-vis the state, as evident in campaigns for parental choice in schooling and against regulation of business, professions, and private life.[2]

RELIGIOUS TRENDS

The perversion of Christianity that is common among these extremist groups is typified by Christian Identity or Kingdom Identity. Identity is widespread in the United States and Canada and has a distinct history. As a theology, Identity belief has united diverse sectors of the extreme right, including many groups within the Ku Klux Klan, neo-Nazis, the Posse Comitatus, some groups of Nazi skinheads, and a number of survivalist factions. It should not be imagined, as some commenters do, that Identity religion is simply a convenient cover for psychopathic violence or a method of seeking tax advantages through claiming religious status. On the contrary, Identity believers are often much more devout and committed than many so-called mainstream Christians.

The Central Beliefs of Identity

Christian Identity believes that the biblical God, or Yahweh, created a single race in his own image: the White Race. These are the Chosen People. The message of the Bible, both Old and New Testaments, is a message only for the White People. Only White People have souls or a hope of salvation. The identity of the White People—and hence the name Christian Identity—is that they are the Old Testament Israelites. Some Identity believers follow all of the dietary laws and prohibitions of the early chapters of the Bible, and the majority maintain a fundamentalist belief in the literal interpretation of biblical texts. In their view, Christ was a blue-eyed, blond-haired Israelite, with no Jewish ancestry or any connection to Jews. To claim that Christ had a Jewish genealogy is, from the point of view of Identity, a blasphemy of the first order. The White People eventually became dispersed from Israel and settled in northern Europe, Scandinavia, Britain, and eventually in the United States, Canada, Australia, and New Zealand. These White People are known as Aryans, and where they live are the Aryan Nations.

Before the creation of Adam and Eve, the God Yahweh created a second race. These are sometimes called "Mud People" in Identity literature and are the ancestors of all people of color: Africans, Asians, Aboriginal Australians, African Americans, and so on. These "Mud People" were intended by God to be the servants and slaves of the White People. They have no souls, are not truly human, and are not valued by God.

The third race of people are the Jews. According to Identity, they were not created by God but by Satan. They are not the Old Testament Israelites but have simply falsely assumed that ancestry in order to hide their evil origin and as a cover for their Satanic purposes. The Jews have intermarried with the Mud People and created a variety of mixed racial groups in order to further insinuate themselves into the human community. Lacking souls, or even a conscience, they are able to devote themselves to their true task: the destruction of God's chosen people, the Aryans. The Jews do this through slyly pitting people of color against the Aryans, through taking control of the world banking and financial institutions, through the invention of socialism and communism, by taking control of the media and of the government, and by an endless conspiracy to seize global control through a One World Government.

Identity theology maintains that any intermarriage between Aryans and non-Aryans yields offspring who are spiritually, biologically, and mentally degenerate and who are soul-less. They believe that intermarriage is slowly polluting Aryan gene pools and destroying the Aryan peoples. Any Aryan who has mixed-race children, who marries a Mud Person or a Jew, is a "race traitor." Race traitors, so defined, are frequently the objects of intimidation, assault, or murder. In the white racist state advocated by Aryan Nations and other militant Identity groups, race traitors would be summarily executed by the state. Parenthetically, the term "race traitor" is sometimes used in Identity literature to denote Aryans who are actively opposed to Identity, such as antifascist or anti-racist workers.

Identity also maintains a strong belief in the Second Coming of Christ. Like many fundamentalist Christians, they believe that Christ will return soon and usher in the Millennium—a thousand years of God's Kingdom on earth. However, they also believe that Christ will not return until the Aryan people have done their duty and restored God's original plan, namely, the return of people of color to servant and slave status and the genocide of the Jews.

Identity theology recognizes that the Jews will not kill themselves, nor will people of color voluntarily return to slave status. Therefore many Identity groups are heavily armed and engage in weapons training and survivalism. They are prepared for a racial war—a racial holy war—as a long period of what they call "Tribulations" before Christ's ultimate return. The bombings, murders, and assassinations that Identity organizations have engaged in should be understood within this religious and political context.

CROSSOVER WITH PRISON GANGS

White supremacist gangs include the Aryan Brotherhood (AB) and Nazi Low Riders (NLR), who control much of the white prison population in California. The California prison inmates segregate themselves by race in the institutions. White power skinheads like American Front, Volksfront, Hammerskins, Public Enemy Number One, Sacramaniacs, and Peckerwoods also emerged from hate ideology. White criminal street organizations such as the Family Affiliated Irish Mafia, Contra Costa County Boyz, Fresnecks, Highly Insane Criminals, Humboldt County Gangsters, and Crazy White Boyz are loosely organized and do not all have racist ideologies.

Gangs on the rise include the Aryan Circle and the White Aryan Resistance in Arkansas, the Southern Brotherhood in Alabama, the Nazi Low Riders in California and Nevada, and Soldiers of the Aryan Culture in Utah. One of the largest white prison gangs, World Church of the Creator, founded in Illinois and active in other states, has been difficult to control, authorities say, because of its religious underpinnings, which allow its members to gather for meetings in prison. Once they're in prison, they join with groups. Other groups are active in Utah, including the Fourth Reich, National Alliance, Hammerskins, Krieger Verwandt, Arizona Hammerheads, National Socialist White People's Party, Silent Aryan Warriors, and Krieger Verwandt ("warrior kindred" in German).

There is a crossover and overlap between extreme right-wing groups and white, or Aryan, prison gangs. For example, in November 2018, Florida and federal law enforcement authorities arrested dozens of white supremacist gang members from groups called the "Unforgiven" and "United Aryan Brotherhood" in a Pasco County bust that found illegal firearms, heroin, crack cocaine, methamphetamine, and pipe bombs. The "Unforgiven" gang uses Nazi imagery and is listed as a hate group and prison gang by the Anti-Defamation League. The United Aryan Brotherhood is also listed as a prison gang by the Southern Poverty Law Center (SPLC).[3]

> Groups that function within prisons might also have increased tendency towards violence. There has been frequent discussion about how white-supremacist gangs are particularly problematic for prison administrators as they are frequently involved in violence . . . the SPLC estimates that nearly 20% of the murders that occur within prisons are linked to white supremacist groups. In

addition, some scholars argue that prisons are critical to radicalizing individuals towards violence. Groups that operate in prison have access to individuals with a criminal history, and we hypothesize that this might translate into using violence to further the group's ideology.[4]

Aryan Brotherhood: Prison Gang Case Study

Photos of Aryan Brotherhood (AB) members invariably reveal the same qualities: bull necks, massive forearms, tattoos of fierce Vikings, Nazi lightning bolts, and a distinctive shamrock enclosed in the claws of a swastika with "666" branded on its leaves. Some have knit caps pulled low over their eyes; many sport walrus-like mustaches more befitting Civil War soldiers and Old West outlaws. They have whimsical, cartoon-derived nicknames: "The Hulk," "Bart Simpson," "Blinky," "Speedy," "Tweak." Their eyes are intense and defiant, glaring through the camera. Their slogan says, "blood in, blood out," a maxim meaning "a brother's a brother, until that brother dies." It was coined circa 1967 when they adopted their current name and a virulently racist agenda.

To join the ranks of the AB, one has to murder a Black inmate; to get out, a member must be murdered. Black and Hispanic prison gangs always rely on strength in numbers; the AB make up for their lesser numbers with ruthlessness and brutality, bestowing selective, Mensa-like membership based on each man's physical strength and willingness to kill on sight. (Intelligence matters too: the leaders read Machiavelli, Nietzsche, Tolkien, and Hitler's book, *Mein Kampf*.) Charles Manson was supposedly refused membership because he wasn't violent enough. They earn a reputation for their zero-tolerance policy on "disrespect" from other inmates. They fight gladiator style, which is essentially a street fight magnified tenfold. In a very short time, windpipes can be severed, jugulars torn out, spinal cords pierced, and livers punctured. But the AB make a science of death: their "warriors" study anatomy texts in prison libraries to better understand parts of the human body that can be maimed for maximum effect.

Sometime in the early 1970s, AB leaders signed a truce with the Mexican Mafia ("La Eme") and agreed to unite in war against La Nuestra Familia, La Eme's sworn enemies. Around the same time, the AB discovered capitalism—or capitalist expansion—when their members began to be convicted of federal crimes and sent to federal penitentiaries. By the late 1990s, according to FBI sources and court papers, top AB leaders David Sahakian, Michael McElhiney, Barry Byron Mills, and Tyler Davis Bingham allegedly had established ties in the federal system with jailed Mafia crime bosses Oreste Abbamonte, "Little Nicky" Scarfo, and John Gotti, who turned twice to the AB to carry out murder contracts. The AB borrowed the Mafia's code of omerta (silence). Their "lie or die" oath demanded that potential witnesses perjure themselves by denying any knowledge of the existence of the Brotherhood, a tactic that kept them largely shielded from law enforcement for decades. (Note: Mentioning prison gangs by name is against Federal Bureau of Prisons policy.)

COUNTERING EXTREMISTS: CASE STUDY

A program adopted by the U.S. government as well as some other countries is Countering Violent Extremism (CVE). It includes actions to counter efforts by extremists to recruit, radicalize, and mobilize followers to violence. The three parts of the U.S. approach to CVE efforts include empowering communities and civil society, messaging and counter-messaging, and addressing causes and driving factors. CVE activities are different from traditional counterterrorism efforts—such as collecting intelligence, gathering evidence, making arrests, and responding to incidents—in that they generally focus on preventing an individual from acting out on a motive for committing a crime. CVE actions intend to address the conditions and reduce the factors that most likely contribute to recruitment and radicalization by violent extremists.

CVE efforts, as defined by the White House, do not include gathering intelligence or performing investigations for the purpose of criminal prosecution. CVE efforts aim to address the root causes of violent extremism through community engagement, including the following:

- Building awareness—through briefings on the drivers and indicators of radicalization and recruitment to violence. For example, U.S. attorneys and Department of Homeland Security offices host community outreach meetings in which they provide information on identifying suspicious activity.
- Countering violent extremist narratives—directly addressing and countering violent extremist recruitment messages, such as encouraging alternative messages from community groups online. For example, the U.S. Department of Justice partnered with the International Association of Chiefs of Police to produce awareness briefs on countering online radicalization.
- Emphasizing community-led intervention—supporting community efforts to disrupt the radicalization process before an individual engages in criminal activity. For example, the FBI aims to provide tools and resources to communities to help them identify social workers and mental health professionals who can help support at-risk individuals and prevent them from becoming radicalized.

Note that while the CVE approach remains a helpful model, unfortunately CVE funding has been cut by the Trump administration.[5]

RECOMMENDATIONS

The arrival of neo-Nazi groups presents risks to a community of violence, discord, hate, and the disruption of the democratic process. Here are some ways to identify and combat those risks.

Combat Risk Factors

- Suppress the motivation and legitimacy of the hate groups.
- Encourage authorities to hunt down those pursuing political and other violence.
- Suppress the capability and opportunity of the hate groups.
- Watch out for and report those who might be preparing for violence in material ways such as researching how to kill as many as possible, obtaining guns or other weapons to prepare for a violent attack, and building bombs.
- Suppress the willingness of attackers to accept personal costs.
- Reduce the opportunities for publicity of their violent acts.
- Discourage media from publicizing attackers' identities, life stories, and manifestos. This last recommendation is subject to controversy, discussed later in this book.

Counter-Narrative

It is useful to create a counter-narrative to that of the hate groups. A counter-narrative is a message that offers a positive alternative to extremist propaganda or pushes back by deconstructing, delegitimizing, or demystifying extremist narratives. This could involve the following:

- Focusing on what we are "for" rather than "against"; positive stories about shared values, tolerance, openness, freedom, and democracy.
- Highlighting how extremist activities negatively affect the people they claim to represent.
- Demonstrating the hypocrisy of extremists and how their actions are inconsistent with their own beliefs.
- Picking apart extremist ideologies by undermining their lack of a coherent intellectual framework.
- Emphasizing factual inaccuracies used in extremist propaganda and setting the record straight.
- Mocking or satirizing extremist propaganda to undermine its credibility.

The term "counter-narrative" has come to include a wide range of activities, from preventative public awareness campaigns to targeted interventions that discredit the ideologies and actions of violent extremists. This uses a broad definition of a counter-narrative and is meant for anyone looking to proactively respond to extremist propaganda through messaging.

NOTES

1. Elena Olmstead, "Racist Fliers Dropped in Neighborhood."
2. Blee, "US Holocaust Memorial Museum; Voices on Antisemitism."
3. Davidson-Hiers and Hauserman, "Florida Authorities Make Another Big Arrest Involving White Supremacists and Bombs."
4. Chermak, Freilich, and Suttmoeller, *The Organizational Dynamics of Far-Right Hate Groups in the United States*.
5. Schulberg, "Controversial Trump Aide Katharine Gorka Helped End Funding for Group That Fights White Supremacy."

Chapter Four

The Hate Message Online

Mass Shooters Have Exploited The Internet For Years. New Zealand Took It To A New Level. The Christchurch massacre was built on existing far-right memes that fueled a live-streaming gunman's viral aspirations.[1]

By the time the shooting started, the accused killer appeared to have posted a rambling, irony-laden manifesto to Twitter, Facebook, and 8chan, where a digital death cult of white supremacists and keyboard nihilists cheered him on. Filled with far-right inside jokes and trolling designed to trip up a gullible press, the manifesto was apparently intended to channel attention from the murderous acts toward an online cesspool of propaganda about nonwhite immigration and demographic change.

The killer live-streamed the attack in the style of a first-person shooter video game. "Remember, lads, subscribe to PewDiePie," he also said, invoking an inside joke about YouTube's most popular streamer. Even the terrorist's music playlist as he drove to his first target, which included alt-right faves, was curated for maximum virality.[2]

Hate groups rely on the internet to both spread their message and target those who successfully expose and contradict them. It's vital for communities to be aware of how these groups engage, recruit, and intimidate through their online presence. Understanding their motivation and methodology is vital. Here is an example of an opinion column that prompted targeting by two separate websites known for their promotion of white supremacy and related neo-Nazi theories. The columnist was identified by name with contact information along with labels such as "Jewess" and "Judas to White people."

> Russian President Putin got my attention when he suggested that Jews with Russian citizenship might have interfered in the 2016 US presidential election. "Maybe they're not even Russians," said Putin. "Maybe they're Ukrainians,

Tatars, Jews, just with Russian citizenship—even that needs to be checked." Putin reminded me why my great grandparents made the harrowing journey from Russia and the Ukraine to the United States. My ancestors weren't the only ones. Between 1881 and 1924, over 2.5 million East European Jews sought to escape the relentless persecution and ghettoization. The slice of history was captured in the movie Fiddler on the Roof, but while Hollywood entertained, it didn't fully show the history of anti-Semitism in Russia and Eastern Europe, or its ongoing ripple effect.

Americans are familiar with Hitler's autobiography, Mein Kampf, his anti-Semitic manifesto that ultimately led to the Holocaust. "If it was on German bookshelves, you knew their Nazi affiliation," said my father, a US military intelligence officer assigned to interrogate Nazi prisoners of war. Less well known is that Hitler found fuel for *Mein Kampf* in *The Protocols of the Elders of Zion*, an infamous Russian publication at the turn of the twentieth century. *The Protocols* fabricated a secret Jewish conspiracy for world domination, and although disproved, *The Protocols* are referenced on hundreds of thousands of internet sites to this day.

Putin's words echo those conspiracy theories, but the hate doesn't stop there. A British newspaper reports that authorities will now investigate whether the 1918 killing of Tsar Nicholas II by a firing squad was in reality a "ritual murder." The investigation is prompted by comments by a bishop of the Russian Orthodox Church who is reputed to be Putin's confessor. The term "ritual murder" dates back to the Middle Ages, a theory that Jewish Passover food involved Christian blood. While the Russian Orthodox Church is being cautious about proceeding with this investigation, aware that it could spur a dangerous ultranationalism, the possibility of such an investigation should serve as a warning that anti-Semitic rhetoric is increasingly tolerated.[3]

Some of the symbols of the Nazis are again popular in today's neo-Nazi culture. Others have been modified to fit today's communication, which is primarily online. You may not hear or see the use of "Ubermensch" today, but the philosophy hasn't changed. The German nineteenth-century philosopher Nietzsche was appropriated by the Nazis, especially his concept of the Ubermensch, or Superman. While there is much dispute among professional philosophers as to what he really meant, the Nazis were clear. They latched onto its aspects of strength and individualism. "It returns, what finally comes home to me is my own Self and what of myself has long been in strange lands and scattered among all things and accidents." *Thus Spoke Zarathustra*, The Wanderer. He confessed in *Ecce Homo*: "I am by nature warlike. The attack is among my instincts . . . I attack only causes that are victorious . . . where I stand alone."[4]

The iconic far right-wing publications and their conspiracy theories have fostered the Nazi movement for decades and continue to gain an engaged audience that reads/orders them online.

CONSPIRACY THEORIES

These and more recent conspiracy theories are reaching generations online. Conspiracy theorists spread theories that include the criminality of the Federal Reserve Bank, Jewish influence, who caused 9/11 other than Muslim fundamentalist extremists, that the moon landing was a hoax, quack cures for cancer, that vaccines cause autism, that climate change is fake science, that President Obama is a Muslim who was not born in the United States, and that evolution isn't true science, among others. They generally believe in an extremely limited U.S. Constitution and want to bring back past policies such as the gold standard.

> The international alt-right has, at its core, the explicit rejection of equality and the pursuit of identity and status for white men who feel aggrieved . . . one part is racism and the belief that white people overall are threatened by multiculturalism. But more specifically *white men* are those they consider repressed. The alt-right believes the world should be ordered into strict hierarchies. That includes the belief that strict traditional gender roles are natural. Therefore, they fight against what they think is the emasculating effect of feminism . . . misogyny can function as a pep talk that helps empower men who feel disempowered. See Jack Donovan, who advocates the retreat of men into ethnic tribal "brotherhoods." "Online or offline, the sense of camaraderie fostered in male spaces allows men to validate one another as men."[5]

Cyberspace has allowed communication of extremism and conspiracy theories to reach a young audience that is the target of recruitment. For this audience, critical thinking is not well developed. Critical thinking is a type of reflective thought that requires reasoning, logic, and analysis to make choices and understand problems. Key elements of critical thinking include seeking out opposing viewpoints, using evidence, and engaging in debate. It should be noted that debating the neo-Nazis is unlikely to be helpful.

> Part of the problem with challenging these people's views is that often they are not arrived at logically, so it is hard to reason them out of them. Their worldview is deeply conspiratorial, so straight facts often won't work. Some of them reach their views because of fear or anger, so we need to find a way to speak to them on an emotional level, not merely a rational and factual level. However, by the time people get that far into these movements, it is extremely hard to change their minds. It is better to try to discourage people before they get involved.[6]

> Their common path to extremism begins to take shape when they are introduced to a homologous international youth subculture with a specific ideology (white supremacy), supported and sustained by a specific paramilitary style (shaved or closely cropped hair, white power regalia and an obsession with weaponry) and musical expression of ideology and style (white power rock).[7]

Chapter 4
NAZI SOCIAL NETWORKING

Modern neo-Nazism has new forms of organization. For example, "lone wolves," who nominally act alone, copy the network structures of international terrorism and coordinate their actions by means of anonymous e-mail addresses. In addition, there are now hundreds of Nazi sites on the internet. On these sites one can find not only advertisements for and sales of Nazi memorabilia—flags, swastikas, uniforms, and so forth—and the text of *Mein Kampf* and other works of Nazi doctrine but also details of how to make homemade bombs.

There have been efforts by progressive and anti-Nazi groups to end the ability of neo-Nazi groups to have easy access to funds through petition efforts demanding that financial platforms, including PayPal, cease servicing the far right-wing groups. There have also been efforts to keep sales sites such as Amazon from carrying neo-Nazi and other hate-filled merchandise. Facebook has come under criticism for carrying articles and advertisements from Russian trolls designed to influence U.S. elections and sow discord in the United States. Facebook's effort to police itself may or may not include restricting neo-Nazi groups. Twitter has come under similar criticism. "Between 2012 and 2016, according to a report by George Washington University's Program on Extremism, there was a 600 percent increase in followers of American white-nationalist movements on Twitter."[8]

"Blood Money" is an online tracker from the nonprofit group Color of Change, an online racial justice organization that charts which payment processing companies allow funding to hate groups.[9] More than one hundred funding sources have been removed from white supremacist sites since the beginning of this campaign.

YouTube has been criticized for carrying neo-Nazi music.[10] "The songs glorify violence and frequently talk about the mass killing of Muslims, Jews and other groups in celebratory detail." YouTube is owned by Google. The company's guidelines prohibit "content that promotes violence against or has the primary purpose of inciting hatred against individuals or groups based on certain attributes" including race, ethnic origin, religion, and other categories. "The scale of neo-Nazi music on various online platforms was highlighted by the website Digital Music News shortly after the 'Unite the Right' march in Charlottesville, Virginia, in September 2017. After bloody clashes and the death of a counter-protester, attention focused on extremist content on hosting services and social networks."[11]

Facebook and Instagram allegedly let neo-Nazis run clothing ads on their platforms. Sometimes such ads have been removed by the platforms after there is mainstream media coverage. "The proliferation of white supremacist businesses on Facebook is more evidence of the social media giant's inability to rein in radicalism and hate on its platform." There is controversy over what should and should not be banned under concepts of free speech and avoiding censorship. For example, "Facebook CEO Mark Zuckerberg used Holocaust denial as an example of the kind of speech the company shouldn't take down because it is 'hard to impugn intent and to understand the intent.' After Jewish groups and anti-discrimination groups criticized his statement, he apologized."[12] "Facebook is aware that extremists are using its platform to profit from and promote hateful ideology, and has banned far-right and Islamist extremist groups numerous times. But the company is unable or unwilling to keep these kinds of pages permanently off its platform."[13]

There are questions as to how much these social media websites influence people's beliefs and actions. There is particular concern about how much influence internet content has on young people.[14]

The proliferation of extreme groups on the internet permits people who are inclined to extreme views to easily find like-minded others. We discuss some of these concerns in our discussion of self-radicalization.

There are also questions about whether internet-based content can be kept down because of the diffuse nature of the internet and the existence of the Dark Web, which some experts believe constitutes a large percent of internet use.[15]

ADVOCATE FOR INTERNET ACCOUNTABILITY

Given the rapid change in technology and how people use it, internet companies need to be transparent in their efforts to counteract hate online. Here is a suggested format for these companies to follow and for users to advocate. For information on model corporate policies for internet companies, see chapter 6, "Corporate and Legal Context."

To address hateful activities online, it is important to understand what is occurring, what is working, and what is not. To facilitate this understanding, internet companies should be transparent about the actions that they are taking, why they are doing so, and who is affected. These data should be made available online in easily accessible, comprehensive formats that are both human and machine readable. This will allow researchers, scholars, and others to analyze the data to better understand what is happening, make recommendations, and develop best practices.

The internet company will establish a team of experts on hateful activities with requisite authority who will train and support programmers and assessors working to enforce anti-hateful activities elements of the terms of service, develop training materials and programs, as well as create a means of tracking the effectiveness of any actions taken to respond to hateful activities.

Larger internet companies that operate internationally should locate their assessment operations such that cultural, social, and political history and context are consistent with large user populations. For example, outsourcing assessment to contractors in other countries where there is little knowledge of the United States' cultural, social, and political history and context almost ensures errors in the enforcement of these terms of service.

Internet companies should engage researchers to track the effectiveness of company efforts to respond to hateful activities performed on or facilitated by their services and then use that research to improve company efforts to remove hateful activities. A recent study by researchers at the Georgia Institute of Technology tracking the outcome of banning hate-filled subreddits can be used as a model to track what happens when an internet company does act to address hateful activities.[16]

COUNTER WITH SOCIAL MARKETING

Social marketing is the application of commercial marketing concepts and tools to programs designed to influence the voluntary behavior of target audiences where the primary objective is to improve the welfare of the audiences and/or the society of which they are a part. Community-based social marketing is pragmatic and involves the following activities:

- Identifying the barriers to a behavior.
- Developing and piloting a program to overcome these barriers.
- Implementing the program across a community.
- Evaluating the effectiveness of the program.

What Can Social Marketing Achieve?

- Raise awareness.
- Increase knowledge.
- Influence attitudes.
- Show benefits of behavior change.
- Reinforce knowledge, attitudes, and behavior.
- Demonstrate skills.
- Prompt an immediate action.
- Increase demand for services.
- Refute myths and misconceptions.
- Influence norms.
- Raise the volume of the social equity/justice voice.

Some far right-wing groups have used forms of marketing for their own ends. For example, Kathleen Blee has noted, "The Ku Klux Klan was able to develop on the basis of mass marketing, because it was appealing to the values that many people already held in that society."[17]

TRADITIONAL NAZI SYMBOLS

Some websites and blogs capitalize on Nazi symbols. Some are historically associated with the Nazi movement and Hitler, including those listed here.

Swastika: The swastika is the best known symbol of the Nazi regime and appears on its flag. Originally a Hindu icon indicating good fortune, the swastika became the emblem of the Aryan race on the Nazi flag. It symbolized nationalistic pride as well as racial supremacy.

Imperial eagle: The eagle was originally a symbol used by ancient Rome and later by medieval Germany, Austria, and Poland. Hitler made the eagle a national emblem that would appear with the swastika. Today the symbol remains popular and is often used for tattoos.

Topenkopf: The "Topenkopf" was the skull and crossbones symbol that was adopted by the Nazi SS. It later became the symbol of the SS branch that guarded the death camps. It is now a popular symbol of contemporary Nazi groups.

EMERGING NAZI SYMBOLS

Alphanumeric Code

Many contemporary symbols are based on numbers and not easily recognizable. The Anti-Defamation League lists many of these symbols on its website. An example is "21-2-12." Members of the Unforgiven, a Florida-based racist prison gang, use the numeric symbol 21-2-12 as a slogan. Substituting letters for numbers, 21 stands for U ("Unity"), 2 stands for B ("Brotherhood"), and 12 stands for L ("Loyalty").[18]

Humor and Memes

"The alt-right's use of offensive humor and its trolling-driven approach, based in animosity to so-called political correctness, can make it difficult to determine true motivations."[19]

"The overall goal is to destabilize people so you can then fill them with your own views," says Keegan Hankes, a senior research analyst with the Southern Poverty Law Center. "If you make racism or anti-Semitism funny, you can subvert the cultural taboo. Make people laugh at the Holocaust—

you've opened a space in which history and fact become worthless, period."[20]

Memes are photoshopped graphics online and are often intended to be humorous and engaging, like the cartoon of Pepe the Frog. Some of the popular alt-right memes are outlined in the article "Get to Know the Memes of the Alt-Right and Never Miss a Dog-Whistle Again," which notes "after the ADL added Pepe to its official list of hate symbols, there is no reason to believe that anyone using the character today is unaware of the Nazi sentiments attached to it and should therefore be regarded as complicit in spreading said sentiments with his or her usage of the cartoon."[21]

Hate symbols are also promulgated in the low-tech way of graffiti on structures. These can be erased or painted over, but the lessons should not be forgotten. The symbols are not free speech but vandalism and property destruction. They can make targeted victims feel less secure and more threatened. Vandalism is common, such as breaking windows, discharging fire extinguishers, breaking tables, and smearing items.

WHITE POWER MUSIC

"Music is the most powerful recruitment tool in the world. . . . Can music kill people? Yeah, it can."[22]

Music of neo-Nazi and white supremacist groups was at one time associated primarily with the heavy metal genre.

> Back in the 1980s, these white supremacists created their own genre of music—White Power—which has since become an essential ingredient of neo-Nazi skinhead propaganda. Originated in Britain, these pounding rhythms soon spread across the continent and to the US (and beyond). Unsurprisingly, it has much the same racist undertones in whichever country or region it is made. This so-called Oi! scene presents an attitude of anger and aggression, rage and hatred, stressing the need for white survival, racial pride, and "Aryan" supremacy. It also celebrates white violence against ethnic/religious minorities and Jews. Three decades on, this hate-fueled music genre remains a thriving transnational entity and, to the concern of many, appears more popular than ever.[23]

Today there are many genres of white supremacist music. They are designed to appeal to a broad audience. Not only is this music a recruitment tool, but music websites are money-making internet tools where books, jewelry, and insignias are sold. The internet has provided many options for music videos, including YouTube, which despite its efforts to curtail these groups remains a popular platform. The range of styles is substantial and appears on private websites that appeal to different demographics. White power music is music that promotes white nationalism. It encompasses various music styles, including rock, country, experimental music, and folk. Ethnomusicologist Benjamin R. Teitelbaum argues that white power music "can be defined by lyrics that demonize variously conceived non-whites and advocate racial pride and solidarity. Most often, however, insiders conceptualized white power music as the combination of those themes with pounding rhythms and a charging punk or metal-based accompaniment."[24] Genres include Nazi punk, Rock Against Communism, and National Socialist black metal.[25]

RECOMMENDATIONS

Actions Parents Can Take

Questions you should ask yourself as a parent or legal guardian include the following:

- Does my child have several accounts on social media (Facebook, Twitter, Instagram, Snapchat, Tumblr, etc.) and does he/she use different identities in a specific network?
- Is there any indication that my child communicates online through indirect methods such as video or online games?
- Does my child use nontraditional search engines (other than Google, Yahoo, etc.) to navigate the Invisible Web (Dark Web)?
- Are my guns locked up securely?
- If my child starts to behave bizarrely or engage in violent or cruel behavior, who will I call for help?
- Can I recognize if my child is adopting neo-Nazi symbols and music?

While researchers have found that parents and peers can influence the development of biases in children, new studies focus on adolescents and the role that empathy and cross-group friendships play in bias formation. One simple solution to being surrounded by prejudice is cross-group friendships, which lead to more empathy and concern and a more welcoming attitude toward immigrants.

Online Strategies

The Opportunity Agenda, an advocacy group, has developed the following points for countering far right-wing propaganda, based on the idea that it is based on lies and myths.

- Decide who your audience is. You probably have more than one. There is the "friendly" audience, whom you want to build into an effective coali-

tion, and the "unfriendly" audience, whom you want to dissuade from violent actions. There is also the neutral audience, who are persuadable.
- Once you've decided on your audience you need a "story" to tell them. A story is a message with a purpose. Your message should speak *with* your audience, not *at* them. Creating a message that says "extremism is bad" or "this extremist group is bad" without offering a positive alternative or an explanation is not the best option. The most effective messages don't sound like they're lecturing—they offer something to think about and reflect on. There are a number of ways to achieve this:

    - Deconstruct, discredit, and demystify an extremist message with facts. Inculcate a belief in and use of facts, evidence, logic, and critical thinking.
    - Make an emotional appeal to the audience to consider the adverse impacts of extremism and violence.
    - Undermine extremist propaganda through satire and humor.
    - Choose a specific aspect of an extremist narrative to counter or undermine.
    - Offer a positive alternative message or narrative.

- Think about what your audience will gain from your message. Do you want to encourage critical thinking and boost people's understanding of the intent behind extremist content? Are you looking to challenge prejudicial behavior or attitudes towards other races or religions? Or are you trying to highlight the hypocrisy of an extremist group or ideology? Thinking about the answers to these questions will give you a more comprehensive understanding of how to craft your message and the best medium or "packaging" to deliver it to your audience.[26]

If You Are Targeted

Contact the local FBI, law enforcement, and Anti-Defamation League (ADL) and ask them to investigate the level of threat to your person. You can report the incident to the ADL online at https://www.adl.org/reportincident.

NOTES

1. Blumenthal, Schulberg, and O'Brien, "Mass Shooters Have Exploited the Internet for Years. New Zealand Took It to a New Level."
2. Blumenthal, Schulberg, and O'Brien, "Mass Shooters Have Exploited the Internet for Years. New Zealand Took It to a New Level."
3. Levine, "Pandora's Box of Hate."
4. Nietzsche, *Ecce Homo*.
5. Hermansson, "My Time Undercover with the Alt-Right."
6. Hermansson, "My Time Undercover with the Alt-Right."

7. Hamm, "Apocalyptic Violence," 323–39.
8. Reitman, "All-American Nazis."
9. https://www.bloodmoney.org/.
10. See, for example, BBC, "YouTube's Neo-Nazi Music Problem."
11. BBC, "YouTube's Neo-Nazi Music Problem."
12. Singer, "Mark Zuckerberg Argues that Holocaust Denial Is a Freedom of Speech Issue."
13. Robins-Early, "Facebook and Instagram Let Neo-Nazis Run Clothing Brands on Their Platforms."
14. See, for example, Hurley, "Social Media and Teens."
15. Reilly, "Dark Web 101."
16. Fernandez, "Curbing Hate Online."
17. Blee, "US Holocaust Memorial Museum; Voices on Antisemitism."
18. Hate on Display™, "Hate Symbols Database."
19. Hawley, *Making Sense of the Alt-Right.*
20. Reitman, "All-American Nazis."
21. Vice, "Get to Know the Memes of the Alt-Right and Never Miss a Dog-Whistle Again."
22. Gore, "Former Neo-Nazi Shares Stories of Hatred at Cal State–Chico."
23. May, "Hearing Hate."
24. Teitelbaum, "Saga's Sorrow."
25. Wikipedia, "White Power Music."
26. "Counter-Narrative Toolkit."

Chapter Five

Hate Crime Connection

No one at the yoga studio in Tallahassee, Florida, expected Scott Paul Beierle to open fire, killing two people and wounding five others by gunfire before killing himself. Even though Beierle had posted videos online vilifying women in interracial relationships, there was no personal connection to the victims and no warning. No one at services at Pittsburgh's Tree of Life Synagogue anticipated that white supremacist Robert Bowers would murder eleven of them and injure seven more, including four police officers. Even though Bowers was a known anti-Semite and blamed Jews for arranging the immigration of nonwhites into the United States, there was no personal connection and no warning. It's unlikely that MeShon Cooper, an African American woman in Shawnee, Kansas, suspected that she would be stabbed to death by Ronald Lee Kidwell, a tattooed white supremacist. Kidwell had a history of assaults, targeting victims based on race, but he was known to pretend friendliness before ambushing them.

There are good reasons why the victims of these hate crimes had no warning, or even suspicion, of the attacks on their lives. Hate crimes are message crimes, according to Dr. Jack McDevitt, a criminologist at Northeastern University in Boston. They are different from other crimes in that the offender is sending a message to members of a certain group that they are unwelcome in a particular neighborhood, community, school, or workplace.

The study *The Organizational Dynamics of Far-Right Hate Groups in the United States: Comparing Violent to Non-Violent Organizations* made the following correlations of far right-wing groups to violence:

- As groups increased in the number of years in existence or in the number of their members, the likelihood of them being involved in violence increased.

- Groups that published ideological literature, such as newsletters or pamphlets, were significantly less likely to be involved in violence.
- Groups being linked to others did not increase the propensity for violence. However, groups that had a specific conflict with another far-right hate group were significantly more likely to be involved in extreme violence.
- Groups that had charismatic leaders or advocated for or used leaderless resistance tactics were significantly more likely to be involved in violence.
- Geographic region was consistently related to a group's propensity to be involved in violence. Groups in the West and Northeast were significantly more likely to be involved in violence.
- It is hypothesized that groups that recruit most aggressively and successfully will be more likely to be involved in violent crimes. Importantly, groups that target specific types of members may be more likely to be involved in violence. Groups that recruit at protests and/or concerts and specifically target youths are likely to be attracting members that are more prone to participate in violence.
- It could be that groups with more funding sources have increased capabilities that result in a more efficient and cohesive organization. In turn, these groups may be more violent.[1]

PROPENSITY TO VIOLENCE

Types of Right-Wing Violence

There are at least five kinds of violence in white supremacy:

1. "Go out and beat up people on the street" violence—an example of skinhead violence.
2. Strategic violence is meant to send a message to a big audience so that the message is dispersed and the victims are beyond the people who are actually injured.
3. Performative violence binds together its practitioners in a common identity, as when white power skinheads engage in bloody clashes with other skinhead groups.
4. Bullying and threats on social media and by telephone.
5. Individual mass murder.

Motivation for Violent Hate Crimes

There are four major risk factors. The first is a potential shooter being *motivated* toward unrest or violence. This is the most common risk. Believing, for example, that other ethnic or religious groups are a threat to one's personal safety or the future of the country can be motivating, even if that belief is misguided.

The second is the potential shooter's belief that violence is legitimate. While there are norms in the United States against political violence, there are those who may deem it acceptable to do whatever is necessary to defeat one's adversaries as a preemptive "defense" against those who pose real or imagined threats.

The third is capability and opportunity. Capability can include access to firearms and explosives, but it doesn't have to, as demonstrated by the motor vehicle attacks that have become far too common. Opportunities to attack large numbers of victims are everywhere, from shopping malls, to places of worship, to political gatherings, to public streets, and, as shown by the recent bombing attacks, selected political and media leaders.

The fourth is willingness to accept the personal costs to be violent. When attackers take up arms or assemble bombs, they are probably aware that their actions will likely result in arrest at the very least and quite possibly death. Most people are not willing to do this. However, if there is widespread social unrest in an area, willingness to participate can spread like a virus among members of a community.[2]

WHAT IS A HATE CRIME?

The FBI definition is a legal term that describes criminal acts motivated by prejudice.

> For the purpose of Uniform Crime Reporting, a hate crime is defined as: "A criminal offense committed against the person or property which is motivated, in whole or in part, by the offenders bias against race, religion, sexual orientation group, or ethnicity/national origin. Hate crimes are not separate, distinct crimes, but any traditional criminal offense that is motivated by the offender's racial, religious, ethnic, or sexual orientation bias."[3]

"Ethnoviolence" is a broader term that describes acts of intimidation whether or not they are illegal. Congress amended the Hate Crimes Statistics Act in 1994 to add disabilities as a category for which hate crimes data are to be collected. Because the FBI only began collecting statistics on disability bias in 1997, results are not yet available. However, we know from social science research that the pervasive stigma that people apply to both mental and physical disability is expressed in many forms of discriminatory behaviors and practices, including increased risk for sexual and physical abuse. The Judge David L. Bazelon Center for Mental Health Law, a national organization representing low-income adults and children with mental disabilities, states that such hate crimes are motivated by the perception that people with disabilities are not equal, deserving, contributing members of society and therefore it is okay to attack them.

Anti-gay hate crimes are those in which victims are chosen solely or primarily because of their actual or presumed sexual/affectional orientation or preference, gender identity, and/or status. Hate crimes are also committed based on race, religion, ethnicity, and national origin. Hate crimes may include property crimes or physical violence resulting in injury. They are unique because they send messages to entire groups —as well as to their families and supporters—that they are unwelcome and unsafe in particular communities. Most anti-gay hate crimes are committed by otherwise law-abiding young people who see little wrong with their actions and who sometimes believe that they have societal permission to engage in such violence. Hate-motivated violence has heretofore been understood as attacks that denigrate a class of people for their beliefs or immutable characteristics. It is committed because of characteristics such as race, color, creed, ethnicity, national origin, or sexual orientation.

Hate crimes as a whole have been on the rise. According to the FBI, the number of hate crimes reported slightly rose from 7,462 in 2002 to 7,489 in 2003. It has continued to rise. Racial bias represented the largest percentage of bias-motivated crimes with 51.3 percent, followed by religious bias (17.9 percent), sexual orientation (16.5 percent), ethnicity (13.7 percent), and disability (0.4 percent). California reported the highest number of hate crimes, followed by New York, New Jersey, Michigan, and Massachusetts. In its report for 2017, the FBI found that the numbers are increasing. The number of hate crime incidents reported to the FBI increased about 17 percent in 2017 compared with the previous year, according to the Uniform Crime Reporting (UCR) Program's annual Hate Crime Statistics report. The most common bias categories in single-bias incidents were race/ethnicity/ancestry (59.6 percent), religion (20.6 percent), and sexual orientation (15.8 percent). In addition to the 7,106 single-bias incidents reported last year, there were also 69 multiple-bias hate crimes reported.

Forty-eight states have laws that specify hate crimes as crimes that are committed on the basis of race, ethnicity, gender, religion, disability, or sexual orientation, or crimes with an overlay of biased statements. According to the *Atlanta Journal-Constitution*, the Georgia State Supreme Court overturned Georgia's hate crime law in October 2018. The law, which allowed for enhanced prison sentences if a person or their property were victimized "because of bias and prejudice," was controversial because it did not specify to which groups of victims it applied.

Hate Crime Indicators

In determining whether or not a hate crime has been committed, law enforcement officials consider the following bias indicators: perceptions of the victim(s) and witnesses about the crime; the perpetrator's comments, gestures, or written statements that reflect bias, including graffiti or other symbols; any differences between perpetrator and victim, whether actual or perceived by the perpetrator; similar incidents in the same location or neighborhood to determine whether a pattern exists; whether the victim was engaged in activities promoting his or her group or community (that is, by clothing or conduct); whether the incident coincided with a holiday or day of particular significance; involvement of organized hate groups or their members; and the absence of any particular motive, such as economic gain.

In *Wisconsin vs. Mitchell*, the U.S. Supreme Court upheld penalty enhancement hate crime laws, saying they do not violate the right to freedom of speech. These are laws that add to the punishment if hate was an additional factor. The Supreme Court ruled that when hate speech is used as evidence to establish the elements or to prove motive or intent of a hate crime, it does not conflict with a person's First Amendment (freedom of expression) rights. Currently, state and local law enforcement officials play the primary role in the prosecution of hate-motivated violence.

Federal hate crime laws have significant barriers that prevent the federal government from assisting state and local law enforcement in punishing and deterring hate-motivated violence. At present, federal prosecutors can only intervene and make use of federal hate crime law if the crime takes place on federal land or if the hate crime victims are engaged in certain federally protected activities. Federal lands include the District of Columbia and national parks and protected activities include serving on a jury, attending a public school, applying for employment, or voting. In very limited circumstances, federal prosecutions can be brought if the attorney general or a designee certifies in writing that an individual federal prosecution would be in the public interest and necessary to secure substantial justice or if local officials are either unable or unwilling to handle the case effectively. Because the requirements for federal prosecution are so narrow, in most instances, it is unfortunately the general responsibility of underfunded and understaffed state and local law enforcement agencies to investigate and prosecute hate crimes. Federal hate crime laws do not cover bias-motivated attacks that occur because of the victim's gender, sexual orientation, or disability.

Information gathered under the Hate Crimes Statistics Act is an invaluable tool to police. It also holds them, and our elected officials, accountable for increases in hate crimes within their jurisdictions. The act defines a hate crime as a crime against a person or property motivated by bias toward race, religion, ethnicity/national origin, disability, or sexual orientation. The FBI's authority to investigate hate crimes motivated by a disability bias is generally limited to incidents interfering with the victim's housing rights.

It can be helpful to look to Canada from the United States to see what they have done. Their approach may differ, but their goals are very similar. Sometimes their approaches are more creative. In Canada, the issue of hate crimes has been defined somewhat differently than in the United States. The various laws that refer to "hatred" do not define it. Rather, Canada's Supreme Court has explained the meaning of the term in various cases that have come before the court. For example, in *R vs. Keegstra*, decided in 1990, Chief Justice Dickson for the majority explained the meaning of "hatred" in the context of the Canadian Criminal Code:

> Hatred is predicated on destruction, and hatred against identifiable groups therefore thrives on insensitivity, bigotry and destruction of both the target group and of the values of our society. Hatred in this sense is a most extreme emotion that belies reason; an emotion that, if exercised against members of an identifiable group, implies that those individuals are to be despised, scorned, denied respect and made subject to ill-treatment on the basis of group affiliation.[4]

More recently, in 2013, Justice Rothstein, speaking for the unanimous court, explained the meaning of "hatred" in similar terms, in relation to the *Saskatchewan Human Rights Code*:

> In my view, "detestation" and "vilification" aptly describe the harmful effect that the Code seeks to eliminate. Representations that expose a target group to detestation tend to inspire enmity and extreme ill-will against them, which goes beyond mere disdain or dislike. Representations vilifying a person or group will seek to abuse, denigrate or delegitimize them, to render them lawless, dangerous, unworthy or unacceptable in the eyes of the audience. Expression exposing vulnerable groups to detestation and vilification goes far beyond merely discrediting, humiliating or offending the victims.[5]

The issues of vilification and detestation are important for our situation in the United States, where political discourse has become polarized. Efforts toward understanding, empathy, and communication will need to take these factors into consideration. In the United States, the concept of hate crimes tends to be ill defined and does not sufficiently take these concepts into consideration.

President George W. Bush said that all violent crime constitutes hate crime. That belief ignores the common feature of bias-motivated lynching, draggings, beatings, and firebombings: they are committed because of characteristics such as race, color, creed, ethnicity, national origin, or sexual orientation.

Hate Crime and Malicious Harassment: Case Study

A person is guilty of malicious harassment in the state of Washington if he or she maliciously and intentionally commits one of the following acts because of his or her perception of the victim's race, color, religion, ancestry, national origin, gender, sexual orientation, or mental, physical, or sensory handicap:

a. Causes physical injury to the victim or another person;
b. Causes physical damage to or destruction of the property of the victim or another person;
c. Threatens a specific person or group of persons and places that person, or members of the specific group of persons, in a reasonable fear of harm to person or property. The fear must be a fear that a reasonable person would have under all the circumstances. For the purposes of this section, a "reasonable person" is a reasonable person who is a member of the victim's race, color, religion, ancestry, national origin, gender, sexual orientation, or mental, physical, or sensory handicap. Words alone do not constitute malicious harassment unless the context or circumstances surrounding the words indicate the words are a threat. Threatening words do not constitute malicious harassment if it is apparent to the victim that the person does not have the ability to carry out the threat.

Social science attempts to explain the reasons for these crimes in a substantial body of literature, which has been expanding over the last several years. Economic competition by minorities is proposed by some scholars as an aggravating factor in some attacks, which may be a partial explanation of the vandalism and arson directed toward Korean-owned businesses during the 1992 post–Rodney King verdict rioting in Los Angeles. There were numerous examples of anti-Arab behavior during the Persian Gulf War.[6] Howard J. Ehrlich further notes "that three basic threats evoke a violent response: violations of territory or property, violations of the sacred, and violations of status . . . the victim's behavior or potential behavior is defined by the actor as leaving no choice but to respond with violence."[7]

Current feelings against minorities are described by Dr. Brian Ogawa in his *Color of Justice: Culturally Sensitive Treatment of Minority Crime Victims*. "White supremacy groups are attempting to forcibly move our nation toward a form of apartheid whereby white males will rule no matter how racially diverse we become. In the paranoia that they are an endangered species, they seek to permanently establish racial separatism by any means necessary."[8]

> Of all crimes, hate crimes are most likely to create or exacerbate tensions, which can trigger larger community-wide racial conflict, civil disturbances,

and even riots. Hate crimes put cities and towns at-risk of serious social and economic consequences. The immediate costs of racial conflicts and civil disturbances are police, fire, and medical personnel overtime, injury or death, business and residential property loss, and damage to vehicles and equipment. Long-term recovery is hindered by a decline in property values, which results in lower tax revenues, scarcity of funds for rebuilding, and increased insurance rates. Businesses and residents abandon these neighborhoods, leaving empty buildings to attract crime, and the quality of schools decline due to the loss of tax revenue. A municipality may have no choice but to cut services or raise taxes or leave the area in its post-riot condition until market forces of supply and demand rebuild the area.[9]

Youth and Hate Crimes

Nearly 20 percent of all known perpetrators of hate crimes are teenagers or juveniles. According to the 2016 Uniform Crime Reporting Program, of the 4,100 individuals for which offender age data was reported in 2016, 3,436 hate crime offenders were adults and 664 hate crime offenders were juveniles. Most hate crimes are committed by single or small groups of young males unaffiliated with organized hate groups. With the rise of social media, however, the concept of "affiliated" has become more fluid. Data from victims' reports in a study of jurisdictions in New York City and in Baltimore County, Maryland, suggest that offenders in bias crimes are even more likely than offenders in nonbias crimes to be young and male. Nationally, the majority of bias-motivated offenders are young men in their late teens and early twenties.

According to Janet Reitman, writing in *Rolling Stone*, "'Ordinary' boys from ordinary towns in relatively ordinary economic circumstances had suddenly aligned themselves with white supremacy. They had come to believe, through an intricate online world, that everything they'd ever learned was a lie. In the language of the internet, they'd been 'red pilled,' Matrix style."[10] This means they felt they were suddenly exposed to the truth.

In classifying types of hate crimes based on the offenders' motivations, Levin and McDevitt defined three distinct categories. The first, "thrill-seekers," the largest group, most often consists of youths and represents individuals who commit such crimes because of boredom, to have fun, and to feel strong. The second category, "reactionists," are interested in protecting their resources from intruders. "Mission offenders," the last category, is composed of those who believe they are appealing to a higher authority by eradicating an inferior group.[11]

> What perpetrators fear is diversity, and it is this discomfort, rather than heightened feelings of resentment due to economic pressures, that sets these individuals apart . . . juvenile hate crime results from the intersection of two epidemics facing youth: violence and prejudice.[12]

Actions by Youth to Counteract Extremists

In 2018, in response to anti-Semitic and hate incidents at Albany High School in the San Francisco, California, Bay Area, students organized an effort called SPEAK. It is a program designed to encourage young people to identify and fight bigotry. The facilitators are high school students who present workshops on social justice and empathy to third, fourth, and fifth graders in the local public school district. The high school students designed a curriculum that focuses on combating prejudice and discrimination. "SPEAK's curriculum calls for teen facilitators to explain what prejudice is and that everyone has prejudices. It helps the children identify prejudice—their own and others'—and to work against it. The coordinators share examples of prejudice they or loved ones have experienced. They also talk with the students about how to try to stop prejudice in their communities."[13]

REPORTING OF HATE CRIMES

One of the largest problems faced by law enforcement across the country is a lack of reports of hate crimes and incidents. Criteria differ from state to state and the number of reporting agencies continually shifts, making it almost impossible to determine an accurate trend to determine where to invest the most resources or where to reinforce successful efforts to reduce crimes. The main reasons for the deficiency are that victims of hate crimes or suspected hate crimes often do not come forward and that some police departments do not report hate crimes.

Ambiguity about the meaning of hate crimes has made it difficult to collect reliable data. American crime statistics come from the UCR program of the FBI, which compiles statistical reports from state and local law enforcement agencies. Requests for hate crime data began in 1990, a time when many states still had not passed hate crime statutes. Participation in the UCR program has increased in the past decade, but state involvement remains highly variable.[14]

The Special Responsibility of Law Enforcement

As Peter Moskos has pointed out in his book, *Cop in the Hood*, the police are actually in the social control business. We call upon them when things get out of hand or we don't know what else to do. Because one of the main ways that neo-Nazis manifest is to disrupt social controls, very commonly law enforcement has a major role to play in dealing with them. A heavy responsibility thus comes to rest on law enforcement, including decisions to act and not to act, to act in excess or not enough. Devon Bell, a California undersheriff, has made these astute recommendations:

> To affirm legitimacy, government must act appropriately and, more significantly, establish a pattern of this appropriateness. It is imperative that government officials be transparent and communicative. Those who violate the public trust must be held accountable by those within the system. Failure to act lends credence to the narrative that the government is comprised of criminals and is therefore illegitimate. Restoring the confidence in government by the majority of Americans will work to marginalize the in-group of the SCM. Unfortunately, the reciprocal is also true. As government legitimacy wavers, the message of the SCM may resonate with more and more people until it reaches the status that it desires; their extremist views become more mainstream and they are viewed on par with Thomas Jefferson, John Adams, and Patrick Henry. The SCM threat is directly tied to the perception that the government lacks legitimacy. Grievances with government are as old as society itself; however, when the question shifts from the government's actions to the legitimacy of the government's existence, it is time for government officials to embrace ethics, transparency, and communications that support their constituents and, therefore, the government's very existence.[15]

Civic officials should ensure that law enforcement authorities recognize that they have an important role in preventing targeted harassment and violence and that they do not need to be solely reactive.

Law enforcement can use a "focused deterrence" approach that targets groups that engage in violence. Such a strategy concentrates on chronic offenders and sends the message that violence will be quickly met with enhanced sanctions. It also involves offering opportunities and resources to these individuals, such as vocational training, housing, and substance abuse treatment to help end their criminal behavior.[16]

Extreme Response by Law Enforcement

There were over eighty-two school mass shootings in 2018, by far the highest annual number on record, according to the Naval Postgraduate School's Center for Homeland Defense and Security, which maintains a database of them.

Police departments today often follow "active shooter" protocols. In very brief form, these involve first responders rushing into the scene of a violent confrontation in order to kill or capture the shooter and reduce civilian casualties. However, many failures can occur. A recent example of such failures is the mass shooting at Marjory Stoneman Douglas High School in Parkland, Florida, in early 2018. A state commission found many problems with the response of school and law enforcement officials. Errors included the following:

- Mental health counselors knew the shooter was seriously mentally and behaviorally troubled but did not have a complete picture of how dangerous he had become.

- Warnings about the shooter were missed, especially those he posted on social media.
- Lack of interoperable electronic communications devices is a common problem in disasters of all kinds.
- Active shooter protocols were ignored.
- Facility security procedures and devices failed.
- The school was a "soft target," a place where people gather but that has few barriers to entry and little protection.
- Facility monitoring was ignored.
- Many students had nowhere to hide; there were no "safe spaces."
- Warning devices such as fire alarms sent students in the wrong direction.
- Law enforcement, including the FBI, failed to act on tips about the shooter's impending violence.

An innovation in recent years in response to active shooter situations has been "panic buttons": cell phone apps that can instantly send 911-type alerts during a shooting and hopefully reduce the number of injuries and fatalities.

> The mobile application, which every school employee will be able to access, sends alerts to emergency personnel in much the way 911 systems work, but it includes several added features. The app distributes information about a fire, medical, police or active shooter emergency to other cell phones connected to the same school safety network. So if an active shooter incident is reported by a teacher or staff member, their fellow employees will receive the same information being given to the police. Secondly, the app gives automatic access to additional information even if the person triggering the call can't—the address of the school, a floor plan of the building, the best points of access, the number of students and teachers in the building; and the layout of the entire school campus. It also will provide contact information for key school personnel.[17]

ENCOURAGE HUMAN RIGHTS AND PUNISHMENTS FOR VIOLATIONS

One theory holds that a coarsening of human rights, such as the United States's lack of implementation of the Geneva Conventions, leads to tacitly giving permission for cruel acts. The Geneva Conventions were agreed to by many countries and establish international humanitarian standards. The criminal nature of the Nazi policies and actions was overwhelmingly substantiated and irrevocably condemned by the Nuremberg International Military Tribunal in 1945–1946. Key figures of the Nazi Party and state apparatus were found guilty of massive crimes against peace, war crimes, and crimes against humanity. The main components of the Nazi machinery of mass murder, such as the leadership corps of the Nazi Party, Gestapo, SD, and SS, were declared criminal organizations.

The rulings of the Nuremberg Tribunal remain of great historical importance. The principles recognized at the Nuremberg Tribunal form a cornerstone of modern international law and led to the drafting of major international legal instruments such as the UN Genocide Convention (1948), the Universal Declaration of Human Rights (1948), the Convention on the Abolition of the Statute of Limitations on War Crimes and Crimes against Humanity (1968), the Geneva Convention on the Laws and Customs of War (1949) and its supplementary protocols (1977), and the European Convention on Human Rights (1949), as well as to the creation of institutions for the effective implementation and adjudication of these rights, such as the United Nations Human Rights Commission, the European Court of Human Rights, the Special Criminal Tribunals, and the International Criminal Court.

WHAT IS THE ROLE OF GOVERNMENT AGENCIES?

The U.S. Department of Homeland Security and the FBI have jurisdiction over domestic terrorism and many hate crimes within the United States. States and local law enforcement authorities have jurisdiction over violations of state and local laws. They engage in intelligence gathering, law enforcement, interdiction of attempted and planned terrorist acts, protection of transportation, and other efforts. They possess a great deal of information that is usually not shared with anyone other than law enforcement agencies. They may surveil, watch, and record alleged terror groups. Community groups engaged in anti-Nazi activities may want information and cooperation from these agencies. Alternatively, these agencies may want information from the community groups. It can be a difficult ethical problem to figure out whether or not to cooperate. The FBI, for example, may want cooperation from Muslim groups in the United States. However, members of these groups may feel victimized by the FBI. Unfortunately, the FBI has a long history of such equivocal relationships. For example, during the Civil Rights Movement, the FBI infiltrated the Ku Klux Klan but did very little or nothing to stop violent acts by it.

OFFICIAL SYSTEMS

An example of the difficulty in compiling accurate statistics can be found in Washington State. Compiling information for the state's input to the FBI's annual hate crimes report has been assigned by the state legislature to the Washington Association of Sheriffs and Police Chiefs. Unfortunately, the input from the various cities and towns of the state varies widely. Theories as to why include lack of interest by some sheriffs and police departments, lack of training, and lack of sensitivity.

Another obstacle to gaining an accurate count of hate crimes is the reluctance of many victims to report such attacks. In fact, they are much less likely than other crime victims to report crimes to the police, despite — or perhaps because of — the fact that they can frequently identify the perpetrators. This reluctance often derives from the trauma the victim experiences, as well as a fear of retaliation.

In a study of gay men and lesbians by Dr. Gregory M. Herek, a psychologist at the University of California, Davis, and his colleagues, Drs. Jeanine Cogan and Roy Gillis, about one-third of the hate crime victims reported the incident to law enforcement authorities, compared with two-thirds of gay and lesbian victims of nonbias crimes. Dr. Dunbar, who studies hate crime in Los Angeles County, has found that victims of severe hate acts (such as aggravated and sexual assaults) are the least likely of all hate crime victims to notify law enforcement agencies, often out of fear of future contact with the perpetrators. It also appears that some people do not report hate crimes because of fear that the criminal justice system is biased against the group to which the victim belongs and, consequently, that law enforcement authorities will not be responsive. The National Council of La Raza holds that Hispanics often do not report hate crimes because of mistrust of the police. Mistrust of the police is also very common in African American communities.

Victim Assistance Services

> Victim assistance is one of the most important aspects of any hate crime and bias motivated incident response policy. Support should be made available to all victims of an incident whether they were directly or indirectly involved. Victims of hate occurrences need to be assessed both physically and emotionally. As hateful activity can tarnish an entire community, the victim's family and surrounding neighborhood should also be included in the healing process. In first approaching a hate crime or bias motivated incident, it is important to understand that although an occurrence may appear to be minor, the long term emotional impact upon the victim and the campus community may be immense.[18]

Another reason for the underreporting of hate crimes is the difficulty of identifying an incident as having been provoked by bias. A municipality or county should assure that its law enforcement agencies adopt the model policy supported by the International Association of Chiefs of Police for investigating and reporting hate crimes. This model policy uses the standard reporting form and uniform definition of a hate crime developed by the FBI.

The FBI offers training for law enforcement officers and administrators on developing data collection procedures. The Community Relations Service of the Department of Justice and the FBI recommend a two-tier procedure for accurately collecting and reporting hate crime case information. It includes:

(1) the officer on the scene of an alleged bias crime making an initial determination that bias motivation is "suspected"; and (2) a second officer or unit with more expertise in bias matters making the final determination of whether a hate crime has actually occurred. For more information, see the FBI's Training Guide for Hate Crime Data Collection and Hate Crime Data Collection Guidelines. Note that some minority groups may not be happy to cooperate with the FBI because of its anti-terrorism efforts focused on certain groups on the basis of religion and ethnicity.

RECOMMENDATIONS

1. There are controversies about domestic intelligence gathering by national security agencies. Anticipate that some people will object to this domestic spying.
2. Anticipate the equivocal feelings and relationships with local law enforcement agencies, particularly among African Americans, who have often been harmed by police.
3. If your organization knows of neo-Nazi activity in your area, share this information with the police.
4. Encourage victims to come forward and make formal reports.
5. Establish relationships with local law enforcement before a crisis hits. Crisis managers always say that it is too late to wait until after a crisis occurs to establish relationships.
6. If you know of neo-Nazi group members employed by law enforcement authorities, report those people to the highest officials.
7. Ask for briefings and trainings by law enforcement authorities for protection of your organizations and structures.
8. Work with local law enforcement authorities to ensure that they get the best, most current training available on far right-wing extremism.
9. Make sure that any far right-wing advocates who are serving as law enforcement officers are weeded out and fired. There have been instances of police officers adopting neo-Nazi style tattoos and t-shirts. This sends the wrong message to the community.
10. Encourage community-oriented policing.
11. Make sure that your local police department provides correct data in reporting hate crimes.
12. Become familiar with your state's definition of hate crimes.
13. Insist that instances of hate crimes be charged as such. Some prosecutors are reluctant to charge using hate crime enhancement laws.

NOTES

1. Chermak, Freilich, Suttmoeller, The Organizational Dynamics of Far-Right Hate Groups in the United States.
2. Hollywood, "Suppressing Motivation, Legitimacy Can Help Avoid Political Violence."
3. Federal Bureau of Investigation, "Uniform Crime Reporting Program's Hate Crime Frequently Asked Questions."
4. *R vs. Keegstra*, Canada Supreme Court, 1990, 3 SCR 697, at p. 714.
5. *Saskatchewan (Human Rights Commission) v. Whatcott*, 2013, SCC 11.
6. Kellina M. Craig-Henderson, cited in Perry, "The Psychological Harms of Hate."
7. Herek and Berrill, *Hate Crimes*, 108–9.
8. Ogawa, *Color of Justice*, 140.
9. U.S. Department of Justice, "Community Relations Service."
10. Reitman, "All-American Nazis."
11. Levin and McDevitt, *Hate Crimes*.
12. Steinberg, Brooks, and Remtulla, "Youth Hate Crimes."
13. Chabin, "Facing Anti-Semitism at Her California School, This Jewish Teen Takes Matters into Her Own Hands."
14. Grattet, "Hate Crimes."
15. Bell, "The Sovereign Citizen Movement."
16. Homeland Security, "Enhancing School Safety Using a Threat Assessment Model"; Valasik and Reid, "White Nationalist Groups Are Really Street Gangs, and Law Enforcement Needs to Treat Them that Way."
17. Charles, "A Growing Response to School Shootings."
18. U.S. Department of Justice, "Community Relations Service."

Chapter Six

Corporate and Legal Context

In 2018, the journalism effort ProPublica in partnership with the Latino-oriented TV network Univision reported that there have been dozens of hate events at Walmart stores, not perpetrated by employees but by customers. This is understandable, given the size of Walmart. Walmart has almost 5,400 stores in the United States, employing about 1.4 million people. In some small towns, the local Walmart is the de facto town square, where many human interactions take place. About 90 percent of the U.S. population lives within ten miles of a Walmart.

> "Both inside stores and in parking lots, the majority of those who reported incidents say they were harassed or threatened by customers due to their race, religion or ethnicity, or because they were speaking a language other than English. Most chronicle hateful speech directed at strangers." Michelle Christian, an Assistant Professor in the Department of Sociology at the University of Tennessee, who has studied the impact of Walmart on communities, said Walmart's strategy of putting stores in underserved areas means it attracts customers with a wide range of backgrounds, which can result in clashes.[1]

CORPORATE RESPONSIBILITY

The corporation is embedded in society and relies upon special legal privileges, such as limited liability, and the law treating a corporation as a person, but without the punishments that a person can experience after breaking the law. Many corporations today contribute to partisan politicians and political campaigns, so it would be inconsistent to take a "neutral" attitude toward today's ideological and extremist disputes.

Yet corporations and other businesses have a duty to society as well as to their owners and stockholders. The World Business Council for Sustainable

Development states, "Corporate social responsibility is the continuing commitment by business to behave ethically and contribute to economic development while improving the quality of life of the workforce and their families as well as of the local community and society at large."[2]

Elements of social responsibility include investment in community outreach, employee relations, creation and maintenance of employment, environmental stewardship, and financial performance. It can also include developing and implementing ethical and sustainable business or manufacturing processes, championing diversity and inclusion, nondiscrimination, enhancing corporate reputation and employer brand through philanthropic endeavors, and investing in alternative and renewable energy.

What Can Companies and Stores Do to Tamp Down Hate?

- First, as we discuss in the section of this book on bystander efforts, store employees and management should not stand idly by while customers are treated in a hateful way.
- Second, they can refuse to sell hate-oriented products.
- Third, they can decline to serve people who express hate.
- Fourth, they can train employees to notice and respond to hate incidents.
- Fifth, when a customer targets an employee with hate speech, management can back that employee up. Ensuring a safe and welcoming environment fits into many companies' growing focus on diversity and corporate social responsibility.
- Sixth, companies can acknowledge that they have substantial involvement in what happens in their parking lots.
- Seventh, companies can be clear with customers that spewing hate on the store's premises is not tolerated and that it will take action if someone doesn't respect that. "One of our core beliefs is respect for all individuals. We do not tolerate discrimination of any kind," Randy Hargrove, Walmart's senior director of national media relations, told Univision. "We have no tolerance for inappropriate language or disrespectful actions like those highlighted in this story."[3]

Corporate Policies: Case Study

A written policy that addresses hateful activities in the workplace is essential for counteracting them. Here is a sample process and outline pertaining to internet companies that can be applied broadly across the corporate sector.

Model corporate policy: The internet company will integrate addressing hateful activities into the corporate structure in three ways:

- Assign a board committee with responsibility for assessing management efforts to stop hateful activities on their services.
- Assign a senior manager, with adequate resources and authority, who is a member of the executive team, to oversee addressing hateful activities company wide and name that person publicly.
- Create a committee of outside advisers with expertise in identifying and tracking hateful activities who will have responsibility for producing an annual report on effectiveness of the steps taken by the company.

Model corporate policy/term of service: The internet company will provide to the general public, via easy online access, regularly—meaning at least quarterly throughout the year—and rapidly updated, summary information that describes:

1. The corporate strategy and policies intended to stop groups, state actors, and individuals engaged in hateful activities from using their services.
2. The number of hateful activities identified by the company on its services by protected categories—race, color, religion, national origin, ethnicity, immigration status, gender, gender identity, sexual orientation, or disability.
3. The number of hateful activities identified by the company on its services by type of hateful activity, whether incitement to or engagement in that activity, and whether it was violence, intimidation, harassment, threats, or defamation.
4. The number of hateful activities identified by the company on its services broken down by whether this identification was the result of user flagging or some other company action.
5. The total number of potentially hateful activities flagged by users, whether the company agreed with the flagging or not.
6. The number of potentially hateful activities flagged by users that were found by the company to have been hateful activities under its policies by protected category.
7. The type of flagger, including whether the flagger was an individual, organization, and/or trusted flagger.
8. The number of times that content was removed as a result of government action or request, broken down by the government entity, actor, or representative making the request, and broken down by whether a legal process was followed and if so, which one.
9. How many people have been denied services for hateful activities-oriented violations of terms of service, disaggregated by the quality of denial—whether it was a termination of services in full, denial of services in part, or removal of a specific piece of content.

10. Type of victim targeted—group, individual, organization, among others.
11. How many users appealed denials of service and the success rates of appeals.

Such information shall be published in an aggregate and/or de-identified format consistent with best practices for protecting personally identifiable information of users and shall be made available in human- and machine-readable formats.[4]

LEGAL CONSIDERATIONS

We have discussed elsewhere in this book how the Southern Poverty Law Center sued a chapter of the Ku Klux Klan a number of years ago and bankrupted it. We have also noted that cities threatened with neo-Nazi demonstrations can use legal means to restrict permits and open carry of guns. Another tactic is the use of state and federal hate crimes and malicious harassment laws. While much of what neo-Nazis say is protected speech in the United States under the First Amendment, not all speech is protected and immune from limitations and punishment. Limits on free speech include defamation, libel, slander, false advertising, incitement to violence, "shouting fire in a crowded theater," hate speech, using speech to harass, and speaking against the interests of one's employer. Government employees enjoy relatively little freedom of speech. Similarly, while the Second Amendment provides very substantial protections to owning and bearing guns in the United States, such rights are subject to reasonable regulation. Making threats with arms can create an opening for such regulation.

In 2018, another example of a free speech lawsuit was settled, in which an African American student at American University suffered threats, harassment, and verbal and social media abuse by a neo-Nazi. The student sued in *Dumpson v. Ade*. She was represented by the Lawyers' Committee for Civil Rights. In the settlement agreement, among other terms, the defendant agreed to the following:

- Issue a sincere apology to the plaintiff (the student) with a full understanding of the harm he has inflicted.
- Cooperate with the plaintiff by acknowledging defendant's activity in this matter and providing information about his involvement with white supremacy.
- Undergo anti-hate training and counseling for at least one year.
- Complete academic coursework on race and gender issues.

- Do two hundred hours of community service related to racial justice or serving a minority community.
- Renounce and publicly advocate against white supremacy, hate, and other forms of bigotry.
- Refrain from ever engaging in hateful activities against the plaintiff or anyone else.
- The Lawyers' Committee will monitor the defendant's efforts and compliance with the agreement.

Other legal avenues include using RICO (Racketeer Influenced and Corrupt Organizations) laws to police neo-Nazi groups, and the possibility of using civil asset forfeiture against malefactors. In Andrew McCabe's book published in 2019, *The Threat: How the FBI Protects America in the Age of Terror and Trump*, he notes the big change that occurred in the FBI when they shifted over from investigating and prosecuting individuals to taking action against organized crime enterprises. McCabe was head of the FBI's counterterrorism unit for many years. Hate groups that threaten or commit violence can be treated as criminal enterprises.

> RICO law refers to the prosecution and defense of individuals who engage in organized crime. In 1970, Congress passed the Racketeer Influenced and Corrupt Organizations (RICO) Act in an effort to combat Mafia groups. Since that time, the law has been expanded and used to go after a variety of organizations, from corrupt police departments to motorcycle gangs. RICO law should not be thought of as a way to punish the commission of an isolated criminal act. Rather, the law establishes severe consequences for those who engage in a pattern of wrongdoing as a member of a criminal enterprise.
>
> Title 18, Section 1961 of the United States Code sets forth a long list of racketeering activities, the repeated commission of which can form the basis of a RICO Act claim. These underlying federal and state offenses exist independently of the act, and include the crimes of homicide, kidnapping, extortion, and witness tampering. Racketeering activities also include property crimes such as robbery and arson. A number of financial crimes are also listed, such as money laundering, counterfeiting, securities violations, as well as mail and wire fraud. . . . As a tool for dismantling criminal enterprises, following a conviction the government is automatically given a forfeiture of all of the defendant's interest in the organization. So not only do defendants lose all their money and property that can be traced back to the criminal conduct, but the organization itself can be severely crippled. And the government need not wait until after a guilty verdict, when the property expected to become subject to forfeiture may be difficult to locate. The rules of procedure in a RICO prosecution allow the government to freeze the defendant's assets before the case even goes to trial.[5]

It is potentially useful that civil claims are permitted under RICO law also. "For civil claims brought by private parties who have been victimized by a criminal organization, the burden of proof is less onerous than in criminal court. A preponderance of the evidence standard applies. This means the jury must find that it is at least slightly more likely than not that the racketeering activities happened as alleged. Despite the lower burden of proof, civil RICO lawsuits are difficult and expensive for individuals to pursue. Those who win are rewarded, however. Successful plaintiffs can recover 'treble damages,' or in other words, three times the amount of money they lost due to the defendant's actions."[6]

> The Supreme Court considered the issue, and determined that an enterprise can be any group with members who are associated in a relationship in order to achieve a common purpose.

> Law enforcement's ability to seize money and property without evidence of a criminal act is known as civil asset forfeiture. . . . Civil asset-forfeiture is unusual since it is the seized property itself, rather than the person or persons in whose possession the property was found, that is prosecuted. Because of this, the seized assets are presumed guilty and must be proven innocent.[7]

Prosecution of neo-Nazis and other extremist right-wing groups is not easy. For example, the federal prosecution of the right-wing terrorists who took over a federal land area in Malheur, Oregon, in 2016 failed completely. There is much debate as to why this was so. Was it due to the incompetence of the federal prosecutors? That they charged with crimes too hard to prove and did not include lesser offenses that would have been easier to prove? That the local jury was itself far right wing and the prosecution did not attempt a change of venue to a more neutral location?

Yet another legal approach involves anti-mask laws. These laws were an effort to "unmask the Klan." While the Supreme Court has not addressed the constitutionality of anti-mask laws, several Court decisions have found that such laws are also constitutionally sound so long as the prosecution can prove that the mask wearer knew or reasonably should have known that the conduct would provoke a reasonable apprehension of intimidation, threats, or violence. In a key 1990 case, the Georgia Supreme Court upheld that state's anti-mask law against challenges premised on the freedom of speech, freedom of association, vagueness, and overbreadth.[8] These anti-mask laws are important again because some of the neo-Nazi groups have taken to wearing masks during demonstrations.

Following the tragic events in Charlottesville, Virginia, in 2017, Mary McCord, a senior litigator at the Institute for Constitutional Advocacy and Protection and a visiting professor at the Georgetown University Law Center, and Michael Signer, a lawyer, city councilor, and former mayor of Charlottesville, wrote the following in the *Washington Post*:

Most states have constitutional language, criminal statutes or both barring unauthorized paramilitary activity. Every state except New York and Georgia has a constitutional provision, akin to Virginia's, requiring that "in all cases the military should be under strict subordination to, and governed by, the civil power." In other words, private armies are proscribed in 48 states. . . . In addition to constitutional provisions, 28 states have criminal statutes that prohibit individuals from forming rogue military units and parading or drilling publicly with firearms, while 25 states have criminal statutes that bar two or more people from engaging in "paramilitary" activity, including using firearms or other "techniques" capable of causing injury or death in a civil disorder. A dozen states have statutes that prohibit falsely assuming the functions of law enforcement or wearing without authorization military uniforms or close imitations.

Virginia's anti-paramilitary laws were used to bring a lawsuit in Charlottesville, led by Georgetown's Institute for Constitutional Advocacy and Protection on behalf of the city and several businesses and associations there. They also note, "Other jurisdictions can also dust off constitutional provisions and state laws to restrict weapons and paramilitary activity at events—whether through the permitting process or public announcements—where anticipated attendance by extremists poses serious threats to public safety."[9]

There are still some states that do not have hate crimes laws. In those states, those working against neo-Nazis and extremist right-wing groups should work through their state legislatures to pass hate crime laws with a broad list of protected classes. The ADL has stated, "Laws shape attitudes. Bigotry cannot be outlawed, but hate crime laws demonstrate an important commitment to confront and deter criminal activity motivated by prejudice."[10] Sample hate crimes laws are available online. An excellent discussion and list appears here: https://www.adl.org/sites/default/files/documents/assets/pdf/combating-hate/Hate-Crimes-Law-The-ADL-Approach.pdf.

Creative and vigorous legal tactics should be considered and used against neo-Nazis and other extremist right-wing groups. Even where such prosecutions fail, the malefactors are forced to hire expensive legal defense and come under the scrutiny of law enforcement officials. One of the consistent takeaways of this book is how the full range of tactics and remedies should be considered in efforts to repel, suppress, and eliminate hate and violent efforts against social equity, fairness, and justice.

RECOMMENDATIONS

While many of the recommendations in this book are oriented toward individuals and community groups, businesses such as corporations, as members of the community, have a duty to counteract neo-Nazis and extremist right-wing groups. Useful actions include implementing corporate social responsibility programs. These include taking responsibility for untoward actions that happen on the business's premises, including parking lots.

- Establish written policies that define behavior and language standards for employees.
- Do not encourage employees to be inactive bystanders.
- Reward employees who exemplify positive standards of behavior.
- Do not assist or serve as a catalyst for hate activities.
- Do not serve those who promulgate hate.
- Protect customers and employees from abuse.
- Provide training for implicit bias so that employees can improve awareness and sensitivity to demeaning attitudes, speech, and behavior.
- Provide training to employees on what to do if they witness or are the victim of hate on the job.

We have also laid out the responsibility of the legal profession, and how legal tools can be used to counteract neo-Nazis and extremist right-wing haters. We do not claim to have listed all possible legal tactics. Of course, our recommendations do not constitute legal advice. Before undertaking any legal course of action, competent and experienced legal counsel should be obtained. We recommend that the legal system be used creatively to bankrupt, interfere with, punish, and eliminate extremist right-wing groups. Such actions include the following:

- Suing them civilly.
- Prosecuting them under criminal law.
- Restricting their ability to bear arms to demonstrations, to march, and to gather through regulations.
- Suing their members individually for wrong committed under law.
- Passing and enforcing hate crimes laws.
- Enforcing anti-masking laws.
- Exposing neo-Nazi and extremist right-wing perpetrators to their employers.
- Enforcing anti-paramilitary laws.
- Using RICO and civil asset forfeiture against them.
- Consulting with highly skilled and creative attorneys when considering pursuing these means.

NOTES

1. Derived in part from Weiss, "Dozens of Hate-Fueled Attacks Reported at Walmart Stores Nationwide."

2. Lord Holme and Richard Watts, "Making Good Business Sense," quoted in Soundarya, "Corporate Social Responsibility."
3. Derived in part from Weiss, "Dozens of Hate-Fueled Attacks Reported at Walmart Stores Nationwide."
4. Fernandez, "Curbing Hate Online."
5. HG.org Legal Resources, "RICO Law."
6. HG.org Legal Resources, "RICO Law."
7. Leamer and Street, "A Chance to Fix Civil Asset Forfeiture."
8. ADL, "Hate Crime Laws—The ADL Approach."
9. McCord and Signer, "This Legal Tactic Can Keep Neo-Nazi Protests out of Your City."
10. ADL, "Hate Crime Laws—The ADL Approach."

Chapter Seven

Community Organizing

The film *Not in Our Town* is about the positive experience and actions of the residents of Billings, Montana, when Nazis came to town in 1995. Based on this experience, the formation of a community-based anti-racist and anti-fascist organization is essential. Peaceful marches and picketing send a strong message to racists that the community will not tolerate an organized racist presence among them. An attempt should be made to effectively shut down any public manifestation of organized racism.

BUILDING COMMUNITY

Networks of civic engagement are built on social capital, which is those stocks of social trust, norms, and networks that people can draw upon to solve common problems. Networks such as neighborhood associations, sports clubs, and cooperatives are an essential form of social capital, and the denser these networks, the more likely that members of a community will cooperate for mutual benefit. Even in the face of persistent problems of collective action (tragedy of the commons, prisoner's dilemma, etc.), they can provide the following:

- Foster sturdy norms of generalized reciprocity by creating expectations that favors given now will be returned later;
- Facilitate coordination and communication, and thus create channels through which information about the trustworthiness of other individuals and groups can flow, and be tested and verified;
- Embody past success at collaboration, which can serve as a cultural template for future collaboration on other kinds of problems; and

- Increase the potential risks to those who act opportunistically that they will not share in the benefits of current and future transactions.

In racially fragmented communities social capital may be low. Two key aspects of social capital are participation in social activities or groups and trust. Using data from the General Social Survey (GSS), Alesina and Ferrara provide evidence that in American cities individuals of different races are less willing to participate in social activities in racially mixed communities.[1] There are two nonmutually exclusive explanations. One is that members of different racially identified groups have different preferences on what a group should do and how it should be run, and the second is that there is a cost in sharing a group with different races simply because of an unfortunately common aversion to "racial mixing." Researchers have shown that in American cities individuals living in more racially fragmented communities have a lower propensity to trust other people, while they do not exhibit lower levels of trust toward institutions.

Researchers also show that income inequality reduces participation and social capital, but the effect of racial conflict seems stronger. Experimental evidence on trust and participation is also consistent with these results: even in experimental settings and among a relatively homogeneous group of individuals (in terms of education), trust does not travel well across racial lines. According to Mike Miller of the Organize Training Center, community organizing

> does two central things to seek to rectify the problem of power imbalance—it builds a permanent base of people power so that dominant financial and institutional power can be challenged and held accountable to values of greater social, environmental, and economic justice; and it transforms individuals and communities, making them mutually respectful co-creators of public life rather than passive objects of decisions made by others.
>
> Community organizing is the process of building power through involving a constituency in identifying problems they share and the solutions to those problems that they desire; identifying the people and structures that can make those solutions possible; enlisting those targets in the effort through negotiation and using confrontation and pressure when needed; and building an institution that is democratically controlled by that constituency that can develop the capacity to take on further problems and that embodies the will and the power of that constituency.[2]

Distinguishing characteristics of community organizing that make it a tremendous social capital builder include the following:

- Community Networks—Development of a voluntary and community sector network which caters to specific ethnic minority groups and creates a range of relationships, activities, and focal points within a neighbourhood.

- Increasing race awareness and understanding—All members in partnership structures should have awareness and understanding of race equality issues that supersedes an in-principle commitment.
- Understanding ethnic minority community needs—Many efforts have suffered through poor design, poor promotion, and poor implementation. A lot can be gained from engaging target communities in the design of creative and sensitive consultation formats (such as family days) as well as identifying who to consult with (not all supposed community leaders are able to reflect the diversity of opinion within a community), where to consult and when. Proper analysis of findings is equally important.
- Targeting—For services to help communities of color they need to be relevant to the needs and targeted directly to those communities.
- Community Capacity Building—Capacity building in its widest sense can include information, training, seminars, consultancy, placements and can be targeted toward organizations, communities, or individuals.
- Monitoring—Tracking the performance of policies and programs is central to overall program management. A clear strategy for what will be monitored, by whom, in what way and with what frequency should be formally stated and formally communicated.
- Engagement in service delivery—Projects led by communities of color are more likely to be sensitive to and responsive to the needs of the communities they serve. Further, they are generally perceived within the communities as committed to improving available services and not just to delivering a fee-paying contract.[3]

PREPARATION GAPS

> Most people engage in wishful thinking, deluding themselves into believing that by ignoring bullies, they'll eventually moderate their own behavior. In reality, just the opposite takes place.[4]

As discussed earlier, communities where neo-Nazi activities have occurred include Billings, Montana, which is discussed in the film *Not in Our Town*, which launched the organization of that name. Others include Olympia, Washington, discussed elsewhere in this book; and Berkeley, California; Portland, Oregon; and Charlottesville, Virginia, where violence occurred. Some community organizing was underway before the incidents, and much more after. Groups involved in the events that became violent include the neo-Nazis, police, hardcore counter-demonstrators, peaceful demonstrators, media, and bystanders. Each played a role. Particularly criticized for their actions were the neo-Nazis and the violent counter-demonstrators. Criticized for inaction were the police, who were ill prepared and overwhelmed. An example of an after-action report that included criticism of police is the one prepared after the Charlottesville tragedy. It is discussed in "Final Report: Independent Review of the 2017 Protest Events in Charlottesville, Virginia," prepared by consultants Hunton and Williams, a law firm, in 2017. The report is extensive. At least one death occurred due to the actions of a neo-Nazi, and there were many injuries.

EXPOSURE, EDUCATION, AND ORGANIZING

> Racism and extremism are best addressed firstly by being open in naming them when they occur. Extremist groups are best confronted by exposing their beliefs and tactics, especially to the young people who they often seek to recruit.[5]

To expose white nationalist activity for what it is, you've got to lift the veil of denial that says this activity only goes on in northern Idaho or in the Deep South. Exposure, education, and organizational approaches once such activity is acknowledged include the following:

- Satyagraha (nonviolent resistance)
- Violent resistance
- Violent counter-demonstrations
- Peaceful counter-demonstrations
- Cutting off access to social media and web platforms
- Boycotts of firms that support neo-Nazis
- Financial pressure (financial resources are required to maintain internal security, mount operations, maintain communications and safe houses, provide training, produce documents, conduct intelligence, and obtain weapons; similarly, resource mobilization theorists from the social movement literature argue that for groups and movements to succeed they must have sufficient resources such as money)

It should be noted that the authors are not advocating violent approaches or any approaches that involve breaking the law. However, it should be acknowledged that some major pro-social initiatives during the Civil Rights Movement, which was unusually successful, did involve breaking laws, such as marching and demonstrating without a permit and breaking Jim Crow laws. This is relevant to today's situation, where some groups such as Antifa directly confront neo-Nazis and are sometimes accused of breaking the law. Anyone who decides to break the law must be aware of the consequences, think carefully, and be willing to encounter law enforcement authorities. The Civil Rights Movement demonstrators were taught about the virtues and dangers of nonviolent resistance and that they might be beaten and arrested.

Any group that decides to use such tactics to confront neo-Nazis should seriously consider adopting similar awareness, training, and commitment.

Note: Public meetings by racist speakers should be boycotted and alternative rallies and positive activities held on the same day. This has been tried on some college campuses, including turning backs on the speakers. In one town, the shops closed on the day of the neo-Nazi march.

STEPWISE PROGRESSION OF RESPONSES

Recognize what is happening. It is a myth that disasters occur with no warning. Often there have been warning signs, but they were not noticed, were ignored, or were evaluated improperly.

In the case of neo-Nazi groups trying to move into a community, community values include openness, tolerance, acceptance, social equity, fairness, nondiscrimination, public participation, inclusion, diversity, and nonviolent solutions to community problems. These are all components of the American Dream. It is not always easy to articulate these values and put them into practice. Values clarification can help with this process. Values are the principles a group of people use to evaluate alternatives or consequences of decisions and actions. A value is a concept that describes the beliefs of an individual or culture and is identity based. Values are how people understand what they are and what they will and will not tolerate. Values define their sense of honor and respect. They are often unchangeable. According to George W. Kaufman in *The Lawyer's Guide to Balancing Life & Work*, values are "human qualities we practice or admire."[6]

Larry Krieger refers to values as "the generalized content of important, overarching goals that a person endorses."[7] The Austrian neurologist, Holocaust survivor, and *Man's Search for Meaning* author Viktor Frankl said that people are "pushed by drives and pulled by values."[8]

A true value must meet these seven criteria:

1. Chosen freely: you have ultimately chosen it yourself.
2. Chosen from among alternatives: without two or more alternatives there is no choice and no true value.
3. Chosen after consideration of consequences: after reflection on positive and negative consequences.
4. Prized and cherished: the key is the enthusiasm associated with the value.
5. Publicly affirmed: you are willing to acknowledge it and if confronted by another person you would not deny it.
6. Acted upon: unless acted upon it is not a value, but rather a good idea or belief.

7. Part of a definite pattern of action: a single act alone does not constitute a value.[9]

Reach out to broader constituencies, particularly those that are targeted for recruitment by the extreme right. Expand internal institutional memory to keep the information brought in through research and analysis and distribute it throughout the organization, developing the organizational respect required to internalize it enough to keep the information flowing beyond any single person's involvement.[10]

RISK ASSESSMENT AND ANALYSIS

Risk assessment helps us focus on the risks that require the most effort. The definition of risk is the probability of failure times the consequences. The uncertainty of event occurrence is subjective and indicates the existence of "whether or not," "when," "circumstance," and "severity." In the subject covered by this book, that means knowing a lot about neo-Nazis, extreme right-wing groups, and domestic terrorists. If the knowledge does not reside within the local government, expertise must be sought elsewhere. Risk assessment practice attempts to answer the following questions.

What Can Go Wrong? The Precautionary Principle

"According to the precautionary principle, typically invoked in environmental epidemiology, if there is uncertainty as to the likelihood of a catastrophic event, the costs and consequences of doing nothing are greater than those of prevention."[11]

- How likely is it that demonstrators will carry weapons? What type?
- How likely is the demonstration? What are the historical data? What have the demonstrating groups done in the past? Consult with other places if necessary to find out.
- What are the possible consequences? This is determined by considering the description of an outcome of an incident before assessing how likely an occurrence would be within this timescale. These assessments have been carried out by a small team of professionals from the police, fire and rescue service, environment agencies, local authorities, primary care trusts, and the Civil Contingencies Unit based on its experience and knowledge.

The objectives of risk assessment are to help develop the most efficient and effective path toward protection of the public good, life preservation, property preservation, tranquility, and a positive image.

- Exercises in risk assessment include "what if": The purpose of the what if analysis is to identify specific hazards or hazardous situations that could result in undesirable consequences.
- Develop a checklist, a specific list of items used to identify hazards and hazardous situations by comparing the current or projected situations with accepted standards.
- Screen out unacceptable risks.

What are the vulnerabilities? What do our law enforcement resources consist of? Are they trained in crowd control, separating disputing groups, mass arrests, and first response to emergency situations? Inventory and marshal available resources.

For example, in Charlottesville, Virginia, due to very poor planning, civilian vehicles were permitted in the demonstration area. This resulted in the death of a female counter-protester when a neo-Nazi drove a car at high speed into a crowd.

Because it is impossible to completely predict and prevent all negative incidents, the approach of balancing risk reduction and planning for all eventualities is complementary. It might be said, "Hope for the best and plan for the worst."

Local Government Responses

There are many lessons to be learned from the failure of local authorities in Charlottesville, Virginia. Many recommendations were made in the after-action report. Different sets of errors were made by University of California at Berkeley (Cal) authorities in response to far right-wing provocations there. Cal was sued by the Young America's Foundation and the UC Berkeley College Republicans, accusing Cal of bias in creating roadblocks to speaking events by far right-wing provocateurs. The U.S. Department of Justice filed a statement of interest in the lawsuit, backing the conservatives. The crux of their argument revolved around two campus policies that they claim violated students' First and Fourteenth Amendment rights: an unspoken high-profile speaker policy and an on-the-books "Major Events Policy." Cal agreed to settle with the plaintiffs for $70,000 and a few changes to policy, including rescinding the high-profile speaker policy, some aspects of the security fee policy, and reducing obstacles to conservative speakers. Under these terms, Cal will no longer be allowed to place a 3:00 p.m. curfew on conservative events or relegate conservative speakers to remote or inconvenient lecture halls on campus while giving other speakers access to preferred parts of campus. Of course, we don't know how much cost Cal would have incurred had the events gone on as the speakers planned and outsiders and students responded.

The point is that a local government taking action to prevent or ameliorate what it foresees as a dangerous event can result in legal liability. Local governments should obtain skilled and experienced legal counsel before setting out on such a course. Nevertheless, it might be a useful tactic to invoke legal protections, especially to avoid the downside risk of violent confrontation, injuries, deaths, destruction of property, and generation of bad publicity. In Charlottesville and some other places, local authorities accepted state law on carrying guns in public. They believed that they would be subject to unbearable legal liability if they tried to prohibit carrying guns during the neo-Nazi demonstrations. But no constitutional provision is a suicide pact. If local authorities had conducted an adequate risk assessment (see elsewhere in this book for why and how to conduct one), they would have arrived at the conclusion that a very substantial risk of violence existed and could have legally justified a temporary rule against carrying guns.

BUILD COALITIONS OF TARGETED GROUPS

Develop coalitions of groups who were victims of the Nazis during the Holocaust: Jews, LGBT people, people with disabilities, people of color, socialists, communists, Seventh Day Adventists, Pentecostals, and so on. Oppose the rise of fascism as a group. Advocate for likely targets in America today such as Native Americans. There is already a great deal of rhetoric against Native Americans by "property rights" advocates. Some members of marginalized groups who are themselves victims of discrimination may nonetheless make anti-Semitic arguments. Fight anti-Semitism.

LIGHTNING ROD EVENTS

Be alert to initiatives that draw the attention and presence of neo-Nazi groups. These actions include taking down or relocating Confederate statues and disconnecting government support from Confederate monuments, burial grounds, and flags. These sites have become popular gathering places and protest arenas for supremacist groups. The merging of their agenda with a revisionist view of slavery and the Civil War has led to a fierce identification with these Confederate sites and symbols. While the rationale might be excellent, these situations and locations can attract violent protest.

NEGOTIATION AND POLITICAL DIPLOMACY

This model tries to alter people's beliefs in hope that they'll modify their behavior. But the behavior's the problem—the pathology and effects of violence and intimidation must be stopped. Some experts say it may require violence to do it. While as progressives we abhor violence, this is what stopped and ended the Nazis in World War II.

Researcher Paul de Armond has stated, "Liberal groups quite frequently try to get into a negotiating situation with people who have no interest in negotiating with them . . . essentially diplomacy or political negotiation, and [it] is quite frequently inappropriate. What's to negotiate with a Holocaust denier or a gay basher?"

"Opposition research," he says, "doesn't even occur to liberal organizations. They know nothing but their own ideological stance and these fantasy pictures that they bill to the opposition. They start reacting to that fantasy and the opposition just runs right over them."[12]

THE PUBLIC HEALTH MODEL

The public health model can be applied to responses to neo-Nazi activities. Violence has sometimes been called a public health problem. Health is defined as a positive concept that emphasizes social and personal resources, as well as physical capabilities. It includes prevention of problems, collection and use of data, evaluation of social and behavior factors, risk identification and assessment, analyzing and assessing causes and vectors, diagnosis, intervention, prescription, advocacy, empowerment, provision of information, mobilizing community partnerships, respecting cultural differences, collaborating with stakeholders, assigning responsibilities, receiving feedback from the community, incorporating diversity, breaking the chain of causality, treatment, cure, and evaluation.

> Initial interventions must be locally led, scientifically sound, technically feasible and cost effective. These will often be the first steps towards a longer-term solution and so developing local commitment is essential.[13]

> The first principle of public health practice is . . . the identification of the root cause or causes of all health problems, from the diseased individual to the effects on that individual of family, social, community, national, global, environment and other factors. The second principle is . . . the utilisation of the resources of the community, the nation and the world to effect a lasting and, often, a cheaper solution to health problems.[14]

Take Anticipatory Action

> An effective public health system is one that actively participates in collaborative decision making with various organizations and institutions about housing, transportation, crime, employment, agriculture and other vital realms of social life that affect the health of communities. This means that improving health transcends the traditional functions performed by public health author-

ities . . . an effective system extends to engaging a broader constituency of diverse fields to take anticipatory action to develop healthy communities, instead of responding to problems as they arise.[15]

In the public health model, actions taken should be transparent, clear, and accountable, with mechanisms for public and stakeholder consultation and debate to develop policy and to make policy choices. Communities at greatest risk and burden should be provided the most assistance. Local observation can be useful in determining this. On a larger scale, reports such as those on hate crimes by the FBI and the Southern Poverty Law Center can be useful. These are discussed elsewhere in this book.

Look at the causative mechanism, how the behavior is transmitted, and what sort of interventions can either prevent or modify it. Frances E. Aboud noted in *Children and Prejudice* that children first show signs of prejudice at a very early age. Children's prejudice levels are often quite high around the age of five and will usually decrease, or show greater flexibility, as the child grows older. Some studies suggest, however, that the prejudice displayed in early childhood returns as children reach the preteen years and beyond, particularly if prejudice is more noticeable in their immediate social environment. For example, there is reason to believe that children's attitudes toward ethnicity are significantly related to the ethnic attitudes of their mothers, with more prejudiced mothers having more prejudiced children.

Early studies have also found evidence that parents high in authoritarianism, which is characterized by greater rigidity, coldness, and intolerance for difference, have more prejudiced children. Although the exact causes of children's prejudice development are not currently known, recent research with adults suggests that children's expressions of prejudice usually shift to take on a more socially acceptable form as they move to adulthood.[16]

Changes and local initiatives should be sustainable. Sustainability is a way of creating and using a resource so that it is not depleted or permanently damaged or can be renewed without creating damage. It is a set of practices by people or groups designed to promote the long-term sharing of resources with future generations. Sustainable development is development that meets the needs of the present without compromising the ability of future generations to meet their own needs. In part, this can be done by focusing on policy, organizational practice, and norms. It includes social equity—factors and criteria addressing, but not limited to, diverse populations, low-income people, traditionally discriminated against people, people with disabilities, indigenous populations, and weighing benefits and burdens on local populations. Actions taken should be durable, resilient, and robust.

RECOMMENDATIONS

The following methods are helpful in achieving the goal of a community program when there is an incursion of neo-Nazis into the community and the decision is made to resist their entrance.

- Identify the desired outcome and goals.
- To be effective, the goals must be embraced by an ever-widening group in the community. The organizers should identify the individuals it needs to continue to influence policymakers; it must also identify long-term sources of financial support that can be brought to bear during the campaign.
- Leaders should command respect and be able to speak about the issues that are most important to the community.
- Speak to self-interest and the interests of the community. "We all want to live in a peaceful town where everyone gets along and we can work things out peacefully."
- Identify and gather potential allies and stakeholders.
- Develop a common vision.

The goal is to have a resilient community that can resist appeals to prejudice and hate. Prejudice is like a force of nature, one that lies dormant in any society or large group and can easily surface given the right incentives. Prejudice can also evolve alongside more positive forces like cooperation, and they may even help sustain each other. "When those with prejudicial behaviors start grouping together and discriminating, it promotes others to form similarly prejudicial groups," says Roger Whitaker, a professor of collective intelligence. "Cooperation can still exist in this context, but it becomes focused within groups, rather than between them, effectively resulting in islands of cooperation."[17]

> Because it is a strategy that can be learned by identifying and copying the behavior of another agent, the adoption of prejudicial attitudes is not a decision that requires very sophisticated cognitive abilities. Some factors that can help limit the effects of prejudice, include the diversity of interactions between simulated agents, diverse types of agents and being able to learn from a wider range of population members. In other words, societies in which in-group diversity is present and that value global learning from interactions with out-group populations are the best equipped to stem the proliferation of prejudice.[18]

- Identify the target audience.
- Craft a "Big Tent" to include as many people from all walks of life as possible.

- Develop a community consensus, such as "We're better than this." "We don't need or want Nazis in our community." "We can all get along here." "Not in our town."
- Form a committee to monitor and track organized racists. Groups to involve include the following:

  - Advocacy groups
  - Ethnic/racial interest groups
  - LGBT groups
  - Faith-based groups
  - Chambers of Commerce
  - Organized labor
  - Service organizations
  - Law enforcement
  - Educational groups

- Determine the target audience's present behaviors.
- Are there any policies, practices, or regulations that need to be changed? For example, is the threat sufficient that public safety demands that open carry gun rules should be restricted? What weaknesses in the community may have helped invite the neo-Nazis in? Who has been left out of the discussion? Are marginalized communities involved?
- Determine what motivates and disincentivizes the target audience.
- Take polls and surveys.
- Conduct focus groups.
- Develop a strategy.

Any strategy should answer the following questions:

- What are our specific short- and long-term goals?
- What resources are currently available for accomplishing them?
- Who will help and who will hinder our efforts?
- What people or institutions have the power to give us the results for which we are looking?
- What actions can we take to achieve these results?

- Decide how you will confront, ignore, boycott, minimize, or arrest the neo-Nazis.
- Craft the appeal using this information.
- Implement the strategy.
- Develop an outreach/media/implementation campaign.
- Use social marketing techniques.
- Establish good media relations.

- Be aware of the opposition. Keep an eye out for your opponents, respect their opinions, and try to explain yours. Understand the process of inclusion.
- Measure results.

Be Sustainable

It will not be possible to sustain the anti-Nazi efforts without broad-based community ownership. Inclusiveness is not just a goal but also a process requirement.

- Never make empty threats.
- Plan to build on the reaction from the other side.
- Negotiate with them when appropriate. Everybody needs something. However, you do not need to make concessions to hate. No amount of hate or violence is acceptable.
- Follow the rules of community organizing featured here.

THE TEN RULES OF COMMUNITY ORGANIZING

1. Nobody's going to come to the meeting unless they've got a reason to come.
2. Nobody's going to come to a meeting unless they know about it.
3. If an organization doesn't grow, it will die.
4. Anyone can be a leader.
5. The most important victory is the group itself.
6. Sometimes winning is losing.
7. Sometimes winning is winning.
8. If you're not fighting for what you want, you don't want it enough.
9. Celebrate!
10. Have fun![19]

Explore Funding and In-Kind Support for Community Projects

Use websites with large databases to find available funding from government sources, civil society foundations, charitable organizations, academic or research funding.

- Grants.gov
- Foundation Center
- Pivot
- The Chronicle of Philanthropy New Grants
- Research Professional

- Council on Foundations
- The Grantsmanship Center: GrantSelect and GrantForward
- Open Society Foundations, from the arm of the organization that makes 501(c)4 grants for advocacy

In addition to these granting organizations, you can ask professional tech, content, or campaigning experts or companies whether they might be willing to help you with pro bono or in-kind support. Further, private sector organizations are increasingly getting involved in countering extremism. Many of the leading tech and social media companies are involved with fighting back against extremists using their products or networks. For example, Google offers its Ad Grants program to provide monthly in-kind advertising support to charities.

Consider crowdfunding options with websites such as:

- Kickstarter
- Indiegogo
- Patreon
- Crowdrise
- Razoo

Use the following steps for social marketing:

- Determine the goals of the program.
- Know what the desired behavior is. Is it keeping neo-Nazis out of the community? Converting them away from far right-wing views? Eliminating violence? Protecting vulnerable communities?
- Research the scope of the problem.
- Review the research literature.
- Identify where the desired behavior should be displayed (place).
- Know how to identify and measure the desired behavior, directly or through proxy measures.
- Weigh the importance of each barrier and the expected benefit from overcoming it against the expected investment.
- Identify the target demographic group.
- Segment the audience or clientele.
- Gather data on that group.
- Find partners, sponsors, champions, and funders.
- Identify the barriers to a behavior among the demographic group.
- Minimize key barriers.
- Identify people's receptivity to the desired action.
- If it is necessary to increase their receptivity, how will you do this?

- Identify precursor activities to the action that is desired to be stopped or lessened. What is the critical path to success? Can the chain be broken? Where?
- Form partnerships to enhance credibility and facilitate access to target groups.
- Find out how the demographic group gets its information, what influences its beliefs, belief systems, what causes it to act or not act, who it listens to, how it communicates (information channel preferences), and so forth.
- Involve the target audience in the design process,
- Determine the real "market opportunities" for influencing change.
- Figure out incentives to bring out or increase the behavior and/or disincentives to lower or stop it.
- Link the desired actions to these motivators.

When communicating about something that is intangible, make it more tangible. If the person does not have much experience with it, relate it to something with which he or she has more experience.

1. Provide "markers" of participation. Raise the positive visibility of participation. Don't keep good news a secret.
2. Choose a theory of change. A theory of change is the articulation of the underlying beliefs and assumptions that guide a service delivery strategy and are critical for producing change and improvement. Theories of change represent beliefs about what is needed by the target population and what strategies will enable them to meet those needs. They establish a context for considering the connection between a system's mission, strategies, and actual outcomes, while creating links among who is being served, the strategies or activities that are being implemented, and the desired outcomes.

NOTES

1. Alesina and Ferrara, "Participation in Heterogeneous Communities."
2. Beckwith and Lopez, "Community Organizing."
3. Ruhl and Will, "RAXEN Focal Point for THE UK; National Analytical Study on Racist Violence and Crime."
4. Paul de Armond, quoted in Taber, *Salvaging Democracy*.
5. Blee, "Our Misconceived Picture of Racists."
6. Kaufman, *The Lawyer's Guide to Balancing Life & Work*.
7. Quoted in Roskie, "Values as Part of the Clinical Experience."
8. Frankl, *Man's Search for Meaning*.
9. Adapted from *Values Clarification* by Sidney Simon.
10. Burghart, cited in Taber, *Salvaging Democracy*, 34.
11. Stanton et al., "The Precautionary Principle."
12. Paul de Armond, quoted in Taber, "Research as Organizing Tool."
13. Bellagio, "Bellagio Principles."

14. Sofoluwe, *Principles and Practice of Public Health in Africa*.
15. DeMilto, "Turning Point."
16. Steele, Choi, and Ambady, "Stereotyping, Prejudice, and Discrimination."
17. Braswell, "Could Robots Develop Prejudice on Their Own."
18. Braswell, "Could Robots Develop Prejudice on Their Own."
19. Beckwith and Lopez, "Community Organizing."

Chapter Eight

Recruitment and Radicalization

WHO IS RECRUITED AND RADICALIZED?

Extremist groups, regardless of their ideology, have long sought to incite youth by exploiting existing cultural and moral grievances and capitalizing on the natural desire for adventure shared by many young people. Radicalization can often be triggered by victimization and perceived injustices toward the individual or a group or a cause with which the individual identifies. This process of radicalization of a vulnerable individual causes an ideological change that, through progressive evolution combined with group effect, can legitimate the use of violence. Isolation, a sense of failure, and a lack of social integration skills increase the vulnerability of the individual. The search for a sense of belonging to a group or a "noble" cause bigger than oneself obliterates the past and builds a new identity.

There are also people who self-radicalize. Radicalization is a process by which an individual or group comes to adopt increasingly extreme political, social, or religious ideals and actions that reject or undermine the status quo or contemporary ideas and expressions of the nation or larger society. In these days of the availability of near-infinite information over the internet, a person can sit alone in his or her room and acquire the most dangerous information. He or she then can get access to materials and supplies that are commercially available or use the internet itself to make threats. Paranoia can also be networked through digital technologies, political performances, and social media to radicalize white men. There is unfortunately a general reluctance among government officials to identify some white men as self-radicalized terrorists or use a domestic terrorist profile.

Conspiracy theories help fuel this radicalization. This is yet another reason to encourage use of fact, evidence, and logic. Unfortunately, trust in the media and government is at an all-time low. The neo-Nazi response effort therefore can reasonably include trust-building exercises to restore this faith. To accomplish this, government and the media must be and do good. This is a tall order and speaks to the need for general civil engagement. As in so many other fields of social endeavor, neo-Nazi response efforts must interconnect with other social infrastructure efforts in order to have the best chance of being effective.

> Social infrastructure includes a wide range of services and facilities that meet community needs for education, health, social support, recreation, cultural expression, social interaction and community development. Social infrastructure (including schools, community centers, libraries, community health centers and recreation facilities) are essential features of holistically planned communities and contribute to overall community well-being. Also considered to be social infrastructure are some of the basic services that are essential for the proper functioning of a community.[1]

The Nazis are targeting white teenage boys, ages fourteen to nineteen, as well as members of the military. They sometimes encourage their members to get military training so that they will learn how to use explosives and weapons. This is discussed in detail in A. C. Thompson and Jake Hanrahan's article "Ranks of Notorious Hate Group Include Active-Duty Military."[2]

The army and marines have taken strong positions against the presence of such radicals. The commanders of the U.S. Army, Air Force, Navy, and Marine Corps have issued strong statements condemning intolerance and racism after protests in Charlottesville, Virginia, turned deadly. The Department of Defense bans actively advocating supremacist, extremist, or criminal gang causes. Doing so can result in dismissal from military service.

The military has acknowledged it has a problem, most notably after army veteran Timothy McVeigh blew up a federal office building in Oklahoma City, Oklahoma, in 1995, killing 168 people. The Department of Defense went on a campaign to oust militants. Some criminal gangs and white nationalist groups in the United States encourage adherents to join the military, particularly the army and marine corps, according to Southern Poverty Law Center studies. Some nationalist groups advocate a "race war" against African Americans, Jews, and other minorities, and they want members with weapons and tactical experience.[3]

ADDRESS THE NEEDS OF BOYS

In the past two decades in the United States, it has become apparent that there is a "boy problem." Boys are experiencing particular difficulties, some of which can make them open to recruitment by extreme right-wing organizations. Some of the problems stem from big changes in the U.S. economy, which make it much more difficult for boys to follow in their father's blue-collar professions. More education, with more science, technology, and mathematics, is required to succeed. Judith Kleinfeld, a psychologist and professor at the University of Alaska in Fairbanks, has written on this subject. Through interviews with boys, she noticed that "so many of them just seemed lost."[4]

Kleinfeld found in her research that the lack of engagement is occurring throughout the United States, particularly among people of color and lower- to middle-income families. Boys are trailing girls academically and attending college less frequently. According to National Center for Education Statistics data, for every 100 women who earn bachelor's degrees, only 73 men earn them. She is working with the Boys Project (www.boyproject.net), a national coalition of researchers, educators, journalists, education policy experts, healthcare professionals, and parents she formed in 2006 to help boys reach their potential. Mentoring programs are one way to combat negative stereotypes and boost school performance, the Boys Project is finding.[5]

The Toolkit on Juvenile Justice in a Counter-Terrorism Context notes, "Children can be more vulnerable to recruitment by terrorist groups and to radicalization to violence than adults. To prevent children from being recruited and radicalized to violence effectively requires an understanding of the local context, conditions and environment that can lead to radicalization such as circumstances of poverty, displacement, migration, discrimination, a sense of marginalization, seeking protection from extremist groups and inadequate access to health care and education services."[6]

Youth Correctional Programs

One theory is that the Nazis troll for members among incarcerated and adjudicated white boys. See the section in this book on extremist group organizing in prisons. Mark S. Hamm states that youth have been radicalized in correctional facilities.[7]

High School Programs among White Teenage Boys

"The thing about the younger generation . . . is they don't know where to focus their alienation or their anger."[8] One approach is to familiarize students in history classes with decisions and moral dilemmas in everyday life, so they can better understand parallels to their own experiences.

Chapter 8
EXITING/LEAVING/CONVERSION/DERADICALIZATION

One theory of adolescents' participation in far-right movements is a connection to masculine rites of passage and development rather than to a serious commitment to racist and militant ideologies. Scholars distinguish between deradicalization and disengagement, concluding that deradicalization regarding ideological conviction is not necessary for disengagement from terrorism. "Successful disengagement or de-radicalization involves both the exit from the extremist milieu and the re-engagement of the non-extremist environment. There are organizations and people trying to help individuals exit white supremacist milieus and groups. Oftentimes, programs and public observations may ignore or downplay the equal importance of finding a new identity and life in the non-radical society."[9]

This resonates with discussions elsewhere in this book about the need for empathy and understanding for members of far-right groups to ease their return to nonhateful positions. There are "push" and "pull" factors. Barelle found that "disillusionment with the behavior of group leaders was the most commonly cited reason for leaving, followed closely by disillusionment with the behavior of group members and then physical/psychological burnout. Closely related but separately referenced was the detrimental impact of using violence. Once disillusioned by in-group behavior, burnt-out, repelled by violence or frustrated with the lack of impact from the radical method, other activities and roles became relevant and attractive. Examples include paid employment, returning to a career, having a relationship or family and/or pursuing other interests."[10]

To help in the conversion of neo-Nazis, recognize the concept of the stigmatized person. Kathleen Blee refers to

> Erving Goffman's description of a stigmatized person as one who is "reduced in our minds from a whole and usual person to a tainted discounted one" capturing the stigma that attaches to those involved in the modern racist movement in the United States. . . . Media depictions of racist activists typically portray them in caricature as poorly educated, ignorant, pathological, irrational, gullible, and marginal persons who try to compensate for their social and psychological failings by scapegoating other groups. This representation of racists as exhibiting . . . "hatred, boorish irrationality, and violence or violent intent," is widely accepted, notwithstanding studies that find that most racist activists have rather average backgrounds, personalities, and ways of thinking before joining racist groups. Moreover, negative characterizations of racists tend to become explanatory. The personality problems and social isolation of racist activists are accepted as the reason for their distorted ideas, although evidence suggests that such characteristics are likely to be the outcome of being in racist groups, rather than a cause. Unlike many other stigmatized groups, racist activists are stigmatized on the basis of a set of beliefs and practices they have chosen to adopt. In this sense, the stigma of racism is

voluntary and under the control of the person who is stigmatized, rather than assigned on the basis of an ascribed characteristic like disability.[11]

Blee also provides a valuable description of the process of leaving these groups:

> Leaving a racist group is a process . . . that requires people to rebuild their identity, rebuild their social network, often rebuild their economic livelihood. For all those things, people need a great deal of support. If people are going to successfully leave racist groups, they need people they can turn to for advice, people who have been through the same process, people who can help them build a new set of friends and a new set of supporters outside of that racist world. . . . People are not in the group one day and out of the group another day. Leaving a racist group is like leaving any kind of a world that people are in. . . . People can start to leave, go back, pull out again, go back and forth for a long time . . . people have to exit on many levels . . . in the sense of breaking their ties with people, changing who they're hanging around with. They exit in terms of leaving the lifestyle, maybe the criminal actions or the violent actions they were associated with. And they exit in terms of changing their ideas.[12]

Daniel Koehler, director of the German Institute on Radicalization and De-Radicalization Studies, argues that deradicalization can only happen when an individual has a "cognitive opening" and an environment that supports personal reflection. In this kind of environment, a program could then initiate deradicalization by applying and engaging what psychologists and researchers term the "significance quest theory" (SQT) as one component of the deradicalization process. The SQT postulates that all individuals are motivated by a desire to have significance in their lives—essentially, to matter. When applied to violent extremism, the theory suggests there are three elements that can translate this basic human need into motivation for violence: a need for personal significance, an ideological narrative (often political or religious) that presents violence as an acceptable method, and a social network that supports this path.

Some Islamic State recruits, for example, have cited political motivation or spiritual duty. Similarly, neo-Nazi and Ku Klux Klan propaganda often promises members a fulfilling role in protecting women, children, and country. Psychologists including David Webber, of Virginia Commonwealth University, and Arie Kruglanski, of the University of Maryland, argue that successful deradicalization efforts might specifically address an individual's significant "deficits." That means analyzing their needs, narrative, and network, and redirecting those desires toward more positive goals such as meaningful jobs or community roles through therapy, education, and networking. When done well, this kind of approach sees former extremists as complex, multifaceted people.[13]

There are parallels and differences between foreign Islamic fundamentalist violent groups and domestic neo-Nazi groups. The former have been studied a great deal, and of late the latter have also. Until recently, however, there was a reluctance in the media and among law enforcement and governmental officials to call the domestic violence perpetrators "terrorists." In this book, we do not often use that word but recognize the similarities with foreign terrorists. If the motive is to instill fear in the victims and in the general population, that is the definition of terrorism.

> Those convicted of racially aggravated crimes tend to come from (predominantly white) areas of deprivation where there is local tolerance of violence and racism.[14]

Psychological theories of the origin of hate crimes perpetrators include the following.

Perpetrators typically come from areas of high social deprivation and marginalization (though by no means all do), which may not directly motivate racist violence but is a significant predisposing factor.[15] Deprivation is likely to operate in conjunction with other influences such as background cultures of racism, media representations of ethnic minorities, and sociopsychological factors. The theory suggests that threats to the social bond come either from excessive closeness or "engulfment" or from isolation and separation, in which the parties mutually misunderstand or reject each other. The result in either case, according to some recent research, is alienation and estrangement, accompanied by "unacknowledged shame," which in turn leads to humiliated fury and violence and aggression.[16] With racist violence, shame/rage is directed against scapegoats who are perceived as more privileged both economically and culturally than the putative "white" community.

Former extremists or "formers" who have "been there, done that" can provide a good way to reach radicalized individuals or people viewing extremist content. Although formers might be viewed with some suspicion or anger by those still in extremist groups, they are able to speak to the futility and flaws of violence and extremism. They can describe the grim day-to-day reality of extremist networks and are often best positioned to delegitimize violence-promoting narratives based on their firsthand experiences. There are many examples of organizations that feature such testimonies including the Against Violent Extremism Network, the Global Survivors Network, the Network of Associations of Victims of Terrorism, and the Forgiveness Project.

> Successful approaches to work with perpetrators of targeted harassment included: acknowledgement of a problem by the perpetrators themselves; the availability of targeted resources; finding capacity in other agencies who were able to make the required interventions; not adopting a "one size fits all"

approach but instead treating perpetrators as individuals with unique needs and reasons for their behaviour; and enforcing the importance of intervention and enforcement with young perpetrators.[17]

Hate Is Exhausting

Jvonne Hubbard, former KKK member, describes the transformation process:

> I believe it all came down to listening to that inner voice we all have—the one that makes us feel uncomfortable or even exhausted when we act out of hate. I'm not sure that I believe love is stronger than hate, but hate is just exhausting. Paying attention to how I felt when I acted, and what my inner voice was telling me, helped me move in the other direction. You have to be willing to walk away from everything you've ever known for the greater good of your own health and well-being. A life of hate, violence, and trauma accomplishes nothing but the wasting of precious time. The truth is, we are all exactly the same in value to this impartial universe, where we are merely beings made of flesh that will turn back to dust after this brief experience. That is everyone's fate, no matter their skin color. Let that sink in, and then tell me you have any valid reasons to hate.[18]

RECOMMENDATIONS

> Cultivate a clear culture of well-being [in communities]. Community leaders have an opportunity to lead the charge for well-being improvement by promoting social and community activities that reinforce a culture of well-being. Businesses, government, education, healthcare, faith, and the arts can all play a substantial role in improving well-being.[19]

Healthy, vibrant social institutions will help resist the infection of neo-Nazism. Robert D. Putnam, in *Bowling Alone*, described the decline of community and joint activities in American towns. He noted how we have become increasingly disconnected from family, friends, neighbors, and our democratic structures. He warns that our stock of social capital —the fabric of our connections with each other—has plummeted, impoverishing our lives and communities. He pushes for civic reinvention. The book spawned a number of efforts, including a website, BetterTogether.org, an initiative of the Saguaro Seminar on Civic Engagement at Harvard University's Kennedy School of Government.[20] Thomas H. Sander and Robert D. Putnam have noted that "both *Bowling Alone* and a 2001 Harvard report known as Better Together argued that America could be civically restored in two ways: by encouraging adults to socialize more, join more groups, or volunteer more; and by teaching the young, whose habits are more malleable, to be increasingly socially connected."[21]

Community Suggestions from Europe's Improving Security By Democratic Participation

These suggestions can be applied locally in the United States:

- Raise awareness of the various forms of radicalization that exist within the European Union and the drivers that lead to radicalization.
- Equip front-line staff and practitioners to identify and respond to all forms of radicalization.
- Enhance engagement with civil society to strengthen the resilience of individuals and communities against all forms of radicalization.
- "Tomorrow's successful communities will probably be those that invest in infrastructure, knowledge, and relationships resilient to shock—whether economic, environmental, societal, or cyber. A prepared, integrated, and orderly society is likely to be cohesive and resilient in the face of unexpected change and have a high tolerance for coping with adversity."[22]
- Create safe spaces to address grievances perceived by communities.
- Create support mechanisms to allow practitioners to improve engagement at the grass roots level.
- Allow practitioners to build their knowledge on how to counter the phenomenon of radicalization by promoting critical thinking.
- Devise and introduce a range of training resources to create a flexible joint strategy to tackle violent extremism capable of introduction into all Member States.
- Achieve meaningful engagement with key stakeholders in participating Member States to share good practices in anti-radicalization and counter-radicalization.
- Sustain effective engagement with key stakeholders to increase resilience in communities and reduce the threat of international and domestic terrorism.
- Use targeted prevention, also called secondary prevention or selective prevention:
- "Prevention is most effective with early detection of already existing symptoms, problems and behavioral deviations in individual humans and groups. It aims at persons and groups with a high-risk potential, to prevent (further) misdevelopment and to support those affected in the design of more constructive ways of life."[23]

Be aware of characteristics that increase vulnerability to recruitment and radicalization:

- Needing to belong/affiliation needs
- Wanting to feel empowered
- Being an outcast

- Perceived economic disadvantage
- Feeling that one is a member of the downtrodden
- Feeling threatened by foreigners/xenophobic threats
- Gang affiliation

Note that white gang members in California tend to dress similarly, almost emulating California Hispanic gang member dress. "White gang members will wear sleeveless t-shirts, long shorts, and pocket chains. White power tattoos incorporate significant numbers, phrases, and symbols that identify with Nazi beliefs such as swastikas and lightning bolts. White pride groups can be identified with their 'laces and braces' (shoe laces and suspenders)."[24]

Symbols of belonging are expressed through style. For racist skinheads, the markers of racist style include behaviors (Nazi salutes), appearance (shaved heads), body art (swastika tattoos), musical tastes (white-power hardcore), and language (racial slurs). By such display, racist activists convey their authenticity.

NOTES

1. NSW Government, "Healthy Urban Development Checklist."
2. Thompson and Hanrahan, "Ranks of Notorious Hate Group Include Active-Duty Military."
3. Dawson, "US Military Commanders Reject Extremists in the Ranks."
4. Chamberlin, "Lost Boys."
5. Chamberlin, "Lost Boys."
6. The International Institute for Justice and the Rule of Law, October 2017.
7. Hamm, "Terrorist Recruitment in American Correctional Institutions."
8. Burghart, cited in Taber, *Salvaging Democracy*, 34.
9. Koehler, *Understanding Deradicalization*, 80.
10. Barrelle, "Pro-Integration."
11. Blee, "The Stigma of Racist Activism."
12. Quoted in Lenz, "Life After Hate."
13. Souris and Singh, "Want to Deradicalize Terrorists? Treat Them Like Everyone Else."
14. Ruhl and Will, "RAXEN Focal Point for THE UK; National Analytical Study on Racist Violence and Crime."
15. Ruhl and Will, "RAXEN Focal Point for THE UK; National Analytical Study on Racist Violence and Crime," 10.
16. Ruhl and Will, "RAXEN Focal Point for THE UK; National Analytical Study on Racist Violence and Crime," 10.
17. Chakraborti et al., "Research Report 74."
18. Dilawar, "'Hate Is Just Exhausting.'"
19. Gallup-Healthways, "State of American Well-Being."
20. Putnam, *Bowling Alone*.
21. Sander, "Still Bowling Alone? The Post-9/11 Split."
22. Director of National Intelligence, "The Near Future."
23. European Commission, "The Contribution of Youth Work to Preventing Marginalisation and Violent Radicalisation."
24. Wikipedia, "Organized Crime in California."

Chapter Nine

What Is Our Moral Obligation?

> When we experience people as wholly different from us, other, it is possible to feel a wide range of negative emotions toward them, such as disgust, revulsion, contempt, rage, hatred, or terror. These feelings not only contribute to our experiencing them as other, but justify categorizing them as other. The category then justifies continued expression of these feelings. Over time, the person becomes dehumanized. Dehumanization, the process by which people are viewed as less than human, a process that individuals, groups and nations all do, obstructs caring about the other.[1]

CREATE MORAL BARRIERS

A moral barrier is a bulwark against immoral behavior. While what is moral is greatly in dispute, there are generally community standards. We believe that violence and hate are not moral. We are writing of putting moral standards into action. This is moral agency. It involves both the power to refrain from behaving inhumanely and the proactive power to behave humanely. It is the opposite of moral disengagement. Moral disengagement may center on restructuring inhumane conduct into appearing to be benign or worthy conduct by moral justification, sanitizing language, refusing to take blame or responsibility, disavowal of personal agency in the harm one causes by refusing responsibility, disregarding or minimizing the injurious effects of one's actions, and attribution of blame to, and dehumanization of, those who are victimized. Civilized life requires, in addition to humane personal standards, safeguards built into social systems that uphold compassionate behavior and renounce cruelty. People suffer from the wrongs done to them regardless of how perpetrators justify their inhumane actions.

Individuals need to adopt standards of right and wrong that serve as guides and deterrents for wrong conduct. In the face of situations that might encourage behaving in inhumane ways, people can choose to behave otherwise by exerting self-influence. People do not usually engage in harmful conduct until they have justified the morality of their actions to themselves. Cultural hatreds create low thresholds for the disengagement of moral self-sanctions. While we emphasize the importance of enlisting organizations in anti-Nazi efforts, the individual must take responsibility. Where responsibility is distributed too broadly, no one really feels responsible.

The sins and destructive effects of Nazis must be made visible. It is easier to harm others when their suffering is not visible and when destructive actions are physically remote and remote in time from their injurious effects. The practical effects have been shown in a few instances where neo-Nazis became directly aware of the physical results of their actions. Seeing the suffering of others helped reach their remaining moral centers. The same kind of thing has happened in restorative justice programs, in which the perpetrator meets with the victim's relatives and hears about the effects of his or her actions in human terms.

Moral and ethical approaches include the following:

- Beneficence: Potential benefits to individuals and to society should be maximized and potential harms minimized. Beneficence involves both the protection of individual welfare and the promotion of the common welfare.
- Nonmalevolence: Harmful acts should be avoided.
- Justice: Emphasize a mixture of criteria so that public utility is maximized, with a just distribution of benefits, determined by the utility to all affected. An egalitarian theory of justice holds that each person should share equally in the distribution of the potential benefits of resources. Other theories of justice hold that society has an obligation to correct inequalities in the distribution of resources, and that those who are least well off should benefit most from resources.
- Respect for autonomy: Focus on the right of self-determination.

Community Values

Community values are principles typically contained in ethical codes and practice, such as beneficence, autonomy, and justice. Treat people with dignity. Respect the humanity of other people. Humans have worth. Implement the Social Contract. Dignity is a standard for good governance and includes reason, security, human rights, accountability, transparency, justice, opportunity, innovation, and inclusiveness. Respect vulnerable persons and their personhood. Respect justice. Minimize harm. Maximize benefit. Include the affected in considerations: "Nothing about us without us." Insist on accountability. Individuals have intrinsic value. Human dignity relies on the assumption that every human being has intrinsic worth. From a religious perspective, the core ideas of human dignity are found in the Hebrew Bible: God created mankind in his own image and likeness and imposed on each person the duty to love his neighbor as himself. Such concepts are repeated in the Christian New Testament.

While there are sociopaths and psychopaths who feel no remorse, for most people who see and hear the suffering they cause, distress and self-censure can serve as self-restraints. It shows that victims are real people with feelings, hopes, and desires to reinforce morality. The individual can then triumph as a moral agent over compelling situational forces. We need to find leaders who are willing to speak out, and then have those leaders speak in a rhetoric that resonates with the particular constituency.[2]

> Researchers have concluded that hate crimes are not necessarily random, uncontrollable, or inevitable. . . . There is overwhelming evidence that society can intervene to reduce or prevent many forms of violence, especially among young people, including the hate-induced violence that threatens and intimidates entire categories of people.[3]

When appropriate, a victim-offender restitution program or offender counseling program can be an effective sanction for juveniles. Educational counseling programs for young perpetrators of hate crime can help dispel stereotypes, prejudice, fears, and other motivators of hate crime. Counseling may include sessions with members of marginalized groups and visits to local correctional facilities. However, it should be noted that repeated studies show that "Scared Straight" programs do not work. "Restorative justice," the concept of healing both the victim and the offender while regaining the trust of the community, may be appropriate. The offenders are held accountable and are required to repair both the physical and emotional damage caused by their actions.

WITNESSING

James Hatley defines the term "witness" in the following manner: "By witness is meant a mode of responding to the other's plight that . . . becomes an ethical involvement."[4] Witnessing especially relates as a response to Nazism because work on the subject began to be developed in the late 1950s by people taking testimonies from Holocaust survivors. As those who witnessed the Holocaust grow old and pass away, there is danger that historical memory will be lost. A number of institutions, such as the Holocaust Museum in Washington, DC, are dedicated to preventing the loss of these powerful witness testimonies.

These are some characteristics of witnessing:

- Intentional versus unintentional (whether one sets out to become a witness or happens upon an incident)
- Witnessing but disempowered (being a witness does not necessarily empower one to do anything or be believed)
- Witnessing with power (when unaware of the implications of his or her actions—that's the unaware but empowered position)
- Unaware of being a witness (therefore is disempowered and can't take effective action)
- "Toxic witnessing" (all kinds of "us/them" or "black/white" thinking, fearfulness, and helplessness comes when we are witnessing on the problematic side of the witnessing coin;[5] the impact of that is to create further distance and separation)
- Passive witnessing (the "innocent bystander")

Compassionate Witnessing

Founded on an ability to recognize and express a common bond with another person, compassionate witnessing helps us recognize our shared humanity, restore our sense of common humanity when it falters, and block our dehumanizing others.

Witnessing Oneself as Victim, Witness, or Perpetrator

> The ability to reflect on one's experience is a key capacity that fosters resilience. It allows one to witness the self and to witness others. It allows one to be aware. Without this ability we are much more likely to repeat the past. If the past is replete with violence, violence will permeate our future.[6]

Impact of Witnessing

> There is tremendous cultural variation about what people respond to and it makes an enormous difference whether you witness alone or in community, whether or not there's an effective outlet for what you've seen, and also whether the witnessing has witnesses. The traumatic impact of witnessing differs, depending on these circumstances.[7]

Mourning

> Our job as caring individuals is to acknowledge losses, to support mourning and grief, to humanize the enemy, and to witness individual and collective pain with as much heartfelt compassion as we can muster. In the immediate aftermath of societal traumas, this work is much more complex than it is decades after traumatic violence, but it is better to start, better to try than to not try.... Many experts point to acknowledging and mourning losses as essential to the interruption of cycles of violence.[8]

This is not easy to do, either for individuals or societies. In the aftermath of societal violence, people are left with intense emotions of fear and rage, hatred and humiliation. People must find ways of managing these charged emotional states at the same time as they tend to the task of survival. Without support, both from people who have suffered the same losses and from those who have witnessed the losses, it is common for people to suppress or deny the depth of their pain and loss, as a short-term solution to the complexity of the realities they now face.[9]

> People who fail adequately to mourn their losses and to work through the pain of their suffering are more likely to repeat their past. This is as true for societies and nations as it is for individuals, who after all are the citizens of nation states.[10]

Marshall Rosenberg, the father of Non-Violent Communication (NVC), said, "NVC shows us a big difference between mourning and apology. Apology is basically part of our violent language. It implies wrongness—that you should be blamed, that you should be penitent, that you're a terrible person for what you did. And when you agree that you are a horrible person and when you have become sufficiently penitent, you can be forgiven. Sorry is part of that game, you see. If you hate yourself enough, you can be forgiven. Now, in contrast, what is really healing for people is not that game where we agree that we're terrible, but rather going inside yourself and seeing what need of yours was not met by the behavior. And when you are in touch with that, you feel a different kind of suffering. You feel a natural suffering, a kind of suffering that leads to learning and healing, not to hatred of oneself, not to guilt."[11] While NVC might be helpful in dealing with neo-Nazis directly, it is a difficult therapy to learn. However, it exemplifies one of many possible psychological approaches to dealing with neo-Nazis.

Restorative Justice

Other approaches include restorative justice, which is a philosophy and practice of the delivery of justice that seeks to address the harm to victims, the community, and offenders arising from crime. Examples of restorative justice measures include: (1) restitution using a variety of approaches (including community reparations boards; Vermont has a network of fourteen such boards); (2) community service; (3) a range of correctional practices focused on restoring the offender to the community, such as the Genesee, New York, "community sponsors" effort; (4) postadjudication victim-offender reconciliation programs; and (5) victim impact statement mechanisms.

Restorative justice brings together victims, offenders, families, community members, law enforcement officials, and others into a voluntary process that can help both victims and offenders. Participants talk about the harm an offender has done and what amends would help. Offenders may realize how they have hurt individuals, families, and communities. When the process works, it can make offenders less likely to repeat. It also can serve community development by bringing people together to strengthen the community fabric.

Restorative justice processes have various forms and names: victim offender mediation, restitution, community service, group conferencing, and sentencing or peacemaking circles. Restorative justice asks us to connect with each other through deep dialogue and authentic presence and to work toward forgiveness, reconciliation, and transformation. Restorative justice is about healing relationships. The issue at stake is not punishment of perpetrators for deeds done in the past but restoration as a basis for reconciliation. Reconciliation is necessary for the restoration of social harmony of the community in general and of social relationships between conflict parties in particular. The aim is not to punish, an action that would be viewed as harming the group a second time. Reestablishing harmony implies reintegrating the deviant members.

RECOMMENDATIONS

Practice Nonviolent Communication

NVC holds that conflict results from miscommunication about human needs. If people can express their unmet needs and recognize the unmet needs of others, they can deflect criticism as expressions of those unmet needs rather than as personal attacks and reduce the likelihood that an exchange will escalate into an argument.

Note how we feel in relation to what we are observing. This is self-empathy, especially awareness of our unmet needs and taking care of one's self before helping others.

- Engage in empathic listening: focus on the content and delivery and respond with a description of the speaker's feelings.
- Show *honest expression*, which comprises four interrelated components. The process begins with a nonjudgmental *observation* expressed in descriptive language and often tied to an objective measure ("You've been working late and you don't get home until after I've gone to bed"). Next comes a statement of *feelings* ("I feel sad that I don't see you") followed by an expression of *needs* or description of how to establish a connection ("It's important to me for us to spend time together"). The final step is a specific *request*.
- Find the needs, values, desires, and so on, that are creating our feelings.
- State the concrete actions we request in order to enrich our lives.

- When faced with conflict, we often think our only choices are to stifle ourselves and give in to keep the peace or to demand what we want, though this may lead to a painful struggle. Neither one of these alternatives is very satisfying. Nonviolent communication offers an alternative. It provides a way of expressing ourselves with full authenticity in a way that helps others to hear us and a way of hearing what others wish we could understand. It also supports self-awareness.
- When we communicate in this way, conflict is less likely to drive us apart. Instead transforming conflict can actually help us feel closer and release locked-up vitality. We find that even in aspects of our lives where there is little obvious conflict, things can start going more smoothly, and we can enjoy life more fully.

- Nonviolent communication involves shifts in the way we are in the world to address not only explicit violence but also the subtle roots of violence that pervade most cultures.

Use Values-Based Messaging

Values are our most fundamental principles, the ideas so essential to our personal and national identities that violating them seems unthinkable. They are a powerful communications tool, a way of making human connections that can cut through stereotypes and partisan suspicion. Leading with facts and figures can reinforce an idea but doesn't do much to persuade, particularly in this age of "fake news." Leading with values activates emotions and opens an audience's hearts and ears to the message.

- Be explicit about the problem and how it threatens shared values, creates a sense of urgency, and connects individual stories.
- Offer a solution to the audience and give them a sense of hope and motivation. The best solutions are connected directly to the problem offered and make clear where the responsibility for change lies.
- Assign an action to give the audience a concrete next step that they can picture themselves doing, and create a feeling of agency.
- Center on the truth, stating it up front.
- If the lie is dominating headlines, refer to the story but not the myth.
- Examine the intention behind the myth being spread.
- Remember that an affirmative position is more powerful than a defensive position.
- Identify personal stories from the community that will have the greatest influence.
- Offer a vision of the world as you believe it should and can be.

- Take an intersectional approach. Intersectionality is the overlap of various ways of identifying oneself. We are all members of various groups. We are not all one thing.
- Creative strategies are an essential component of achieving lasting social change, but many advocacy organizations in the social justice movement either do not fully recognize their potential or do not know how to blend them with more traditional approaches. For example, when neo-Nazis invaded Billings, Montana, in 1993, local community members invented the poster slogan "Not in Our Town," which became the name of a movie and an advocacy organization. Because the incident happened around the time of Hanukkah, the local newspaper printed an image of a menorah, and town residents cut it out and taped it in their windows to show their solidarity with local Jews.
- Emphasize opportunity—America can and should be a place where everyone enjoys full opportunity.
- Emphasize mobility—Where we start out in society should not determine where we end up.
- Emphasize equality—All people are created equal in rights, dignity, and the potential to achieve great things.
- Embrace American democracy as a system that depends on the ability of all of us to participate, debate, and own the public dialog.
- Emphasize that all people are redeemable and capable of loving and receiving love.
- Demonstrate that community is a cherished value because we are all in it together as Americans and human beings, not competitors.
- Provide access for all people to ways to provide for their own needs and those of their families.

Suggestions for talking with children and teens about hate and intolerance include:

- Acknowledge that hate groups exist and that their messages are threatening.
- Keep children and teens away from the scene of hate demonstrations or events. Find alternative and safe places to discuss the issues and voice opinions.
- Let children and teens know that there are professionals who are trained to handle the situation and reassure them they are safe.
- Recognize that children, especially those older than age nine, often are more aware of what's happening in the news than parents realize.
- Take time to talk about your personal reactions in age-appropriate language. It is helpful for children and teens to understand their parents' perception of the situation.

- Encourage children and teens to talk about their feelings and help them find ways to express themselves in nonviolent ways.
- Involve children and teens in deciding how to respond. When they are uncomfortable or outraged by a situation, it is comforting for them to voice their opinion.
- Encourage respect for diversity by teaching understanding and talking in a positive way about differences.
- Seek out multicultural activities, books, or websites that encourage family participation.
- Make children and teens aware of your disapproval if you hear them use insensitive language.
- Remember that you are a role model and you can teach your child tolerance and acceptance.[12]

NOTES

1. Weingarten, "Compassionate Witnessing and the Transformation of Societal Violence."
2. Burghart, cited in Taber, *Salvaging Democracy*, 34.
3. American Psychological Association, "Hate Crimes Today."
4. Hatley, *Suffering Witness*.
5. Weingarten, "Restorative Justice Seminar Series, Seminar 2."
6. Weingarten, "Compassionate Witnessing and the Transformation of Societal Violence."
7. Weingarten, "Compassionate Witnessing and the Transformation of Societal Violence."
8. Weingarten, "Compassionate Witnessing and the Transformation of Societal Violence."
9. Weingarten, "Compassionate Witnessing and the Transformation of Societal Violence."
10. Weingarten, "Compassionate Witnessing and the Transformation of Societal Violence."
11. Rosenberg, "Speak Peace in a World of Conflict."
12. Kim Allen and Jean Kirch-Holliday, Center on Adolescent Sexuality, Pregnancy and Parenting (CASPP), Human Development and Family Studies, College of Human Environmental Sciences, University of Missouri Extension.

Chapter Ten

Globalization and Economic Disparities

I attended Tonganoxie High School in rural Kansas in the early '70s, then found my way to the University of Kansas, which was close to my hometown. Financing my college tuition was a real struggle, but I'd soon learn that things could be much worse: In my third semester, my father died. I probably would have quit school if a friend's father hadn't paid for my following semester. School was financed thereafter by a combination of part-time jobs, small scholarships and a monthly VA check (my father was a WWII veteran). I graduated with a Bachelor of Science in Business Administration.

We had trouble paying the bills each month. Tuition ($350 per semester) was an insurmountable sum for my family in the 1970s. Adjusting for inflation, the fee would be equal to $1,200 today, but University of Kansas students now pay $5,000 per semester, or nearly 15 times what I did. And many government aid programs have since been cut, a variable that has contributed to the perfect storm of student debt. After graduation, I was about $5,000 in the red—a lot of money for me, but pocket change when compared with the $37,172 in college debt the average grad carries today. Add all those grads and you're looking at a $1.3 trillion crisis affecting 44.2 million students, according to a study by Make Lemonade, as reported in *Forbes*.[1]

GLOBALIZATION AND DISPARITIES

The economic status origins of hate extremism are difficult issues, with strong differences among scholars. Materials from the United Kingdom emphasize that far right-wing extremism is partly driven by fear of losing economic status. Hate messages are intended to appeal to this category of people, making an easy connection between economic fears and hate. In a global sense, building a thriving economy for all is a solution. However, the issue of globalization is so complicated that nostalgia for an elusive version of the past is a common solution to the disparities and fear that globalization has created. For example, a renewed desire for segregation is seen among some white Southerners, and envy of alleged Jewish prosperity along with a variety of conspiracy theories is increasingly visible across the United States.

ECONOMIC EFFECTS OF MARGINALIZATION

Marginalization is a process whereby people or groups of people are pushed to the margins of a given society due to poverty, disability, lack of education, also by racism or discrimination due to origin, ethnicity, religion, sexual orientation.[2]

Population groups within a society or community whose interests are not represented by the core polity of the society are marginalized. Marginalized groups are identified according to socioeconomic or cultural characteristics, such as a person's income or wealth, ethnicity or race, gender, geographical location, religion, citizenship status, internal displacement, or physical or mental condition. They are pushed to the margins of the dominant society based on their characteristics that make them different, at least as perceived, from members of the dominant society. An example of a marginalized group is the homeless.

Being marginalized means receiving less respect and fewer services. It can also mean lower income and poorer living conditions. The high incidences of poverty and deprivation among some marginalized social groups are due to their continuing lack of access to income-earning capital assets (such as homeownership, agricultural land, and nonland assets), heavy dependence on wage employment, high unemployment, and low education. Limited education, lack of language fluency, regional mismatches, and discrimination can create and continue marginalized status. Some marginalized groups, such as LGBT people, do not necessarily share the low-income characteristic. The definition can be very broad, and can include the homeless, street children, immigrants, undocumented people, ex-offenders, refugees, migrant farm workers, and commercial sex workers.

IMPACT OF DEMOGRAPHIC CHANGES

The United States is becoming much more Hispanic and Asian American in numbers and percentages. The percentage of those born abroad is rising, and there are many who do not speak English as a first language. Some non-Hispanic whites fear their "country being taken away from them." President Trump has fueled that fear through slogans like "Make America Great

Again" and "America First." Various studies also indicate that racism was one of the motivators for those voting for him and other far right-wing Republicans.[3]

> In a study of individual incident reports to the Bias Crime Unit of the New York Police Department over an 8 year period, sociologists found that racially motivated crime stemmed not from economic frustration but instead from an exclusionary impulse on the part of residents defending what they perceived to be their territory in the face of large scale demographic change. Where a racial group has long been the predominant community in an area, racially motivated crime becomes more severe with in-migration of other racial groups. While economic grievances may be infused in the rhetoric of bias crime perpetrators, the sociological data discounts the actual role of macroeconomic conditions in instigating racially motivated crimes. For instance, no relationship has been found between the fluctuation in the rates of unemployment and rates of racially motivated crime . . . it is where a racially homogenous group wishes to preserve their residential homogeneity that racially motivated crime will be deployed as a "turf defense . . . when institutionalized racism limits the socioeconomic mobility of Black youths in under-resourced public schools and erects network barriers to promising employment opportunity, it is not so surprising that youthful social frustration might be misdirected to desperately trying to maintain racial dominance over the limited physical space accorded to Blacks."[4]

One form of economic change that can set the stage for racist hate crimes occurs when people of color first move into an ethnically homogeneous area. According to Dr. Donald P. Green, a political scientist at Yale University, the resulting violent reaction seems to be based on a visceral aversion to social change. The offenders frequently justify the use of force to preserve what they see as their disappearing, traditional way of life. The more rapid the change, holds Dr. Green, the more likely violence will occur.

The 1980s, for example, witnessed the rapid disappearance of homogeneous white enclaves within large cities, with an attendant surge in urban hate crimes. A classic example is the Canarsie neighborhood in Brooklyn, which was primarily white until large numbers of nonwhites arrived. The influx led to a rash of hate crimes. Hate crimes may occur when unemployed or underemployed workers vent anger on available scapegoats from the minority groups.

Conversely, says Dr. Green, integrated neighborhoods, sometimes characterized as cauldrons of racial hostility, tend to have lower rates of hate crime than neighborhoods on the verge of integration. The message is that integration and diversity work.

However, "Economic factors are not reliable predictors of terrorist activity. Although in some estimations, US states with lower economic output overall experience more attacks, right-wing terrorism does not seem to be driven by joblessness, income inequalities, poverty and the decline of agricultural and manufacturing employment. This reinforces the non-material root causes of terrorism. However, it also removes more straight-forward policy interventions to fight terrorist activity, such as poverty alleviation, job retraining and wealth redistribution."[5]

GROWING WAGE AND WEALTH INEQUALITY

Income includes the revenue streams from wages, salaries, interest on a savings account, dividends from shares of stock, rent, and profits from selling something for more than you paid for it. Income inequality refers to the extent to which income is distributed in an uneven manner among a population. In the United States, income inequality, or the gap between the rich and everyone else, has been growing by every major statistical measure for about thirty years. Income disparities have become so pronounced that America's top 10 percent of wage earners now average more than nine times as much income as the next 90 percent. Americans in the top 1 percent are even higher. They average over forty times more income than the bottom 90 percent. But that gap pales in comparison to the divide between the nation's top 0.1 percent and everyone else. Americans at this level are taking in over 198 times the income of the bottom 90 percent.[6]

DECLINING PHYSICAL AND SOCIAL MOBILITY

The current challenges to achieving the American Dream are described by Professor Raj Chetty in the Opportunity Atlas.

> The defining feature of the American Dream is upward mobility—the aspiration that all children have a chance at economic success, no matter their background. However, our research shows that children's chances of earning more than their parents have been declining. 90% of children born in 1940 grew up to earn more than their parents. Today, only half of all children earn more than their parents did.[7]

The Brookings Institution has stated:

1. The chances of making it, Horatio Alger-style, from a childhood in poverty to an adulthood in affluence (i.e., moving from the bottom to the top income quintile) are lower in the US than in other nations.
2. There is a very strong relationship between the incomes of parents and the incomes their children will have as adults. Inequality, in other words, is strongly inherited.

3. Rates of relative intergenerational mobility in the U.S. appear to have been flat for decades.
4. Place matters for mobility. There are significant differences in upward mobility rates across different places, down to the county and city level. Cities in the Deep South and Midwest tend to have more sluggish mobility than other regions. In this sense, the American Dream persists, but is unevenly distributed.
5. There is a gender gap in terms of the impact of place. Boys who grow up in low-opportunity places feel the effects much more strongly than girls.
6. The chances of going to college soon after high school are very strongly related to household income. In theory, college education is the great equalizer; in practice it is the great stratifier.[8]

There are very high structural barriers to social mobility in the United States.[9] Issues of class, which Americans don't like to discuss, may be key.

> Conflict between rich and poor now eclipses racial strain and friction between immigrants and the native-born as the greatest source of tension in American society. . . . About two-thirds of Americans now believe there are "strong conflicts" between rich and poor in the United States, a survey by the Pew Research Center found.[10]

Metropolitan areas that attract a diverse population are more economically viable.[11] However, Americans are physically moving less from place to place. Geographical mobility has declined. "About 3 percent of the working-age population—defined as people from ages 25 to 59—moved to a different state in a given year during the 1980s. . . . Starting in the 1990s, this rate declined steadily, falling below 1.5 percent by 2010. . . . However, many policymakers have worried that lower mobility is associated with a more rigid economy where workers cannot move to locations with good jobs. Lower mobility might cause the labor market to be slow in adjusting to shocks, making downturns longer and recoveries slower."[12]

INCREASING SOCIAL TENSIONS

These economic trends increase social tension. The U.S. Director of National Intelligence has stated, "The next five years will test US resilience. As in Europe, tough economic times have brought out societal and class divisions. Stagnant wages and rising income inequality are fueling doubts about global economic integration and the 'American Dream' of upward mobility. The share of American men age 25–54 not seeking work is at the highest level since the Great Depression. . . . Despite signs of economic improvement, challenges will be significant, with public trust in leaders and institutions sagging, politics highly polarized, and government revenue constrained by modest growth and rising entitlement outlays. Moreover, advances in robotics and artificial intelligence are likely to further disrupt labor markets."[13]

Russian ads purchased on Facebook in 2016 were designed to prey on racial, religious, and other social tensions in the United States. "At times, these Kremlin-sourced ads even played on both sides of an issue—advancing and opposing causes including Black Lives Matter and gun control, for example—in a bid to stir potential political unrest."[14]

A plurality of Americans think racism in the United States is getting worse, according to the NBC News and Survey Monkey poll. Reports suggest that individuals' views on race are shaped by where they live, the ethnic and racial makeup of their social circles, and other issues connected to exposure. Americans rarely discuss race issues.

"It's hard to imagine being able to work toward a solution to a problem that large percentages of people won't even discuss."[15]

RECOMMENDATIONS

- Improve economic opportunity for all by realizing personal potential.
- Prepare to tackle long-term issues, to deal with the larger structural questions of economic disadvantage, income inequality, job loss, racism, anti-Semitism, and other forms of bigotry.
- One theory is that the Nazis prey on white people who are economically disadvantaged. Ensure that target groups have economic opportunity so they do not develop feelings of helplessness.
- Increase the cost of far right-wing hate activities and actions. For example, towns can charge for demonstration permits, porta-potties, police protection, road closures, cleanup, and parking. Introduce a cost for bad behavior.
- Make arrests of far right-wing hate group members and force them to hire lawyers to defend themselves. Use RICO, conspiracy, defamation, libel, slander, incitement, and asset forfeiture laws.
- When investigating hate crimes, follow the money and prosecute those who have provided money and guns to the perpetrators.
- Introduce alternative ways for young men who feel economically disadvantaged to feel part of a positive group.
- Increase the amount of low- and no-cost education available and apprenticeships, paid internships, and job training.
- Bring manufacturing jobs back to the United States.
- Introduce universal health care and improved mental health services.

- Use infrastructure repair and improvement to spur growth. There is much that needs doing, like rebuilding the antiquated electrical distribution system, installing much more solar power, replacing the corroded water pipe system, and installing insulation/low flow toilets/double pane windows.
- End the war on drugs.
- Ensure that women receive equal pay for comparable work.
- Pay people for currently unpaid work, such as child care.
- Give small businesses better access to low-interest loans. Reduce the cost of starting a small business.
- Provide free child care, preschool, and all-day kindergarten.
- Increase the minimum wage. Consider adopting a "living wage" to address the real cost of housing.
- Increase funding for after school programs.
- Set a limit on corporate executives' salaries and benefits.
- Increase the stock of affordable housing.
- Permit and encourage local hiring preferences for government contracts.
- Provide low-cost high-speed broadband throughout the United States.
- Build alternative career pathways for disconnected youth.
- Provide more middle skills jobs (jobs that don't require a full college education).
- Reduce concentrated poverty.
- Use contact theory to improve intergroup relations (the idea that working, going to school, and living near people with different characteristics increases understanding).
- Support low- to middle-income households through the means discussed here plus paid family leave.
- Expand the Earned Income Tax Credit, which provides low-income working people with a federal tax refund.
- Minimize the unintended negative consequences of technology and import penetration.
- Increase educational attainment by using incentives to stay in and finish school.
- Address and fix climate change, global warming, and rising ocean levels.
- Address and fix rural economic problems.
- Reduce the negative economic efforts of incarceration, for example by "banning the box." Banning the box means stopping inquiries about a person's previous convictions.
- Help small manufacturers join global supply chains.
- Help families with young children "move to opportunity."

NOTES

1. Leat, "Commentary."

2. European Commission, "The Contribution of Youth Work to Preventing Marginalisation and Violent Radicalisation."
3. For example, see Wood, "Racism Motivated Trump Voters More Than Authoritarianism."
4. Hernández, "Black-on-Mexican Violence in Staten Island, NY."
5. Piazza, "The Determinants of Domestic Right-Wing Terrorism in the USA," 52–80.
6. Saez, "Income Inequality."
7. Opportunity Insights, "The Opportunity Atlas."
8. Reeves and Krause, "Raj Chetty in 14 Charts."
9. Reeves and Krause, "Raj Chetty in 14 Charts."
10. Tavernise, "Survey Finds Rising Perception of Class Tension."
11. Florida, *The Rise of the Creative Class.*
12. Karahan and Li, "What Caused the Decline in Interstate Migration in the United States?"
13. National Socialist Movement, "Twenty-Five Points."
14. Romm, "Russia-Purchased Ads on Facebook during the 2016 Election Were Aimed at Stoking Social Tensions."
15. Scott, "Most Americans Say Race Relations Are a Major Problem, but Few Discuss it with Friends and Family."

Chapter Eleven

Bias, Prejudice, and Hate

PSYCHOLOGICAL APPROACHES: OUR "DARK SIDE"

The famous Swiss psychiatrist C. G. Jung discussed a "dark side" of our personality—dark both because it tends to consist predominantly of the primitive, negative, socially, or religiously depreciated human emotions and impulses like sexual lust, power strivings, selfishness, greed, envy, anger, or rage, and due to its unenlightened nature, obscured from consciousness. The psychologist Stephen A. Diamond has noted, "Whatever we deem evil, inferior or unacceptable and deny in ourselves becomes part of the shadow.... Especially concerned with those pathological mental states historically known as 'demonic possession,' Jung's psychological construct of the shadow corresponds to yet differs fundamentally from the idea of the Devil or Satan in theology.... Such projection of the shadow is engaged in not only by individuals but groups, cults, religions, and entire countries, and commonly occurs during wars and other contentious conflicts in which the outsider, enemy or adversary is made a scapegoat, dehumanized, and demonized."[1]

Understanding that having a "dark side" is a common aspect of individual psychology can help us understand and show empathy for those who have views greatly different from our own. And knowing that this dark or shadow side is an aspect of psychology can help in treating, dealing with, and remediating its effects. Knowing this increases insight and self-knowledge and can help us feel empathy for others.

Psychiatric Approaches

Within the psychiatric community, there is disagreement about whether extreme racism can be considered symptomatic of psychopathology. Some have proposed that extreme racism is a serious mental illness and have considered whether DSM should include a diagnosis of delusional disorder—racist type. Others have cautioned against turning a group's extreme views into psychopathology for fear that the view that a hate crime perpetrator may be "not guilty by reason of insanity" will undermine the idea of culpability.[2]

How Different Are Alt-Right People from Us?

Most of us think we are good-minded people and far different from neo-Nazis. But Park McDougald, writing in *New York* magazine about the book *Kill All Normies*, notes, "In it, the alt-right emerges as something not quite as alien as many would like to think. Rather, it is a bastardized version of the cultural currents that most of the book's likely readers—myself included—participate in and valorize."[3]

RACISM, HATRED, AND PREJUDICE

In today's divisive environment, tolerance has become an increasingly difficult and complex state of mind to accomplish. It's defined as acceptance and open-mindedness to different practices, attitudes, and cultures; it does not necessarily mean agreement with the differences. William Ury notes, "Tolerance is not just agreeing with one another or remaining indifferent in the face of injustice, but rather showing respect for the essential humanity in every person."[4]

Radicalization is the process by which individuals are introduced to an overtly ideological message and belief system that encourages movement from moderate, mainstream beliefs toward extreme views. Radical thinking is not a crime in itself. Sympathizing with radical thinking does not necessarily lead to violence or terrorist action. However, radical thinking becomes a threat to national security and local peace when it leads an individual or group to espouse or engage in violence as a means of achieving political, ideological, or religious goals. Radicalization to violence is not a new phenomenon and is not limited to a single group, social class, religion, culture, ethnicity, age group, or worldview. Vulnerable individuals and groups searching for guidance and seeking a sense of belonging are more at risk of radicalization regardless of their background and level of education. There is not one single profile.

Hatred is a compelling mindset, aroused by the experience of frustration and, in its most stark and uncompromising manner, by events that are felt to threaten life. If sustained and unresolved, hate may engender revenge in the form of a criminal act. Such crimes, known as hate crimes or bias crimes, create fear, mistrust, and hostility among members of society. Hate crime violence in America is rooted in the persistence and pervasiveness of racism, prejudice, and bigotry, which are learned behaviors.

The sense of a racial threat can result in this racism. Racism is strong prejudiced feelings against one race or all races other than the one to which one belongs. For example, white citizens may adopt more racist attitudes, and support more racially biased policies, as their perceived dominance becomes "threatened" by the growth of African American or other minority populations or people of color in or near white-dominated communities. In his 1995 theory of the racist mind, Ezekiel argues that white racists often fear for their own survival and that belonging to white supremacist groups gives them comfort and reassurance.[5]

Prejudice

Prejudice literally means to "prejudge" and involves preconceived ideas, usually negative, about a group or its members based on ignorance, stereotyping, or other filters of bigotry. Prejudice is not just a statement of opinion or belief but an attitude that includes feelings such as contempt, dislike, or loathing. There is a distinction between *prejudice* (an attitude) and *discrimination* (a behavior). Prejudice can be unconscious or conscious, and any set of prejudiced ideas may be transformed into an ideological viewpoint. While prejudicial attitudes often, although not always, end in discrimination, no law can prevent prejudiced attitudes. However, the law can prohibit discriminatory practices and behaviors flowing from prejudice.

Statutory definitions of hate crime differ from state to state, but essentially hate crime refers to criminal conduct motivated by prejudice. Prejudice, however, is a complicated, broad, and cloudy concept. We all have prejudices for and against individuals, groups, foods, countries, weather, and so forth. Sometimes these prejudices are rooted in experience, sometimes in fantasy, and sometimes they are passed down to us by family, friends, school, religion, and culture. Some prejudices (for example, anti-fascist) are considered good, some (for example, preference for tall people over short people) relatively innocuous, but other prejudices provoke strong social and political censure (for example, racism, anti-Semitism, misogyny). Even in this latter group, there is a great deal of confusion about what constitutes an acceptable opinion or preference (for example, "I prefer to attend a historically Black college," or "I oppose Zionism and a Jewish state," or "I don't like men as much as women") and what constitutes unacceptable, abhorrent prejudice.

Though sociologists and social psychologists have long wrestled with the concept of prejudice, they are unable to agree on a single definition. One point of consensus is that there are many kinds of prejudice. An individual can be prejudiced in favor of something (for example, his religion) or prejudiced against something (for example, someone else's religion).

Some social psychologists have theorized that prejudice may be an innate human trait. According to one theory, because of various social pressures, humans have a need to classify and categorize people we encounter in order to manage our interactions with them. We have a need to simplify our interactions with others into efficient patterns. This essential simplification leads naturally to stereotyping as a means to desired efficiency. The resultant stereotyping has as an unfortunate side effect, the bigotry and prejudice that so frequently make social relations with others difficult.

Prejudice has also been explained as a "learned behavior." Abraham Kaplan, a professor of philosophy, offers the following illustration: A young child returning from his first day of school is asked, "Are there any colored children in your class?" to which the child replies, "No, just black and white." Without instruction, the child has no concept of the prejudice that gives meaning to the disparaging term "colored." (But one might wonder how the child developed the constructs of "black" and "white" rather than there just being children with different shades of skin, hair, eyes, etc.)

In his classic book *The Nature of Prejudice*, the Harvard psychologist Gordon Allport distinguished between hate-prejudice and love-prejudice. With hate-prejudice, the hater "desires the extinction of the object of hate." Allport characterizes hate as an enduring organization of aggressive impulses toward a person or toward a class of persons. Because it is composed of habitual bitter feeling and accusatory thought, it constitutes a stubborn structure in the mental-emotional life of the individual. By its very nature, hatred is extropunitive, which means the hater is sure that the fault is in the object of his or her hate. So long as he or she believes this, he or she she will not feel guilty for his or her uncharitable state of mind.

Certain groups and individuals (for example, Nazis, Ku Klux Klan) hold prejudices that amount to an ideology, a set of more or less elaborate assumptions, beliefs, and opinions that are espoused as a basis for policy or action.

The Challenge of Bias

Implicit, or unconscious, bias exists within the individual without intention to do harm but can lead to manifestations of prejudice and hate against those who are perceived to be different and/or a threat. These actions can be taken as an individual or as a group with a sense of doing the right thing, however violent the actions may be.

Bias Theory and Practice

A common saying among educators working to promote children's appreciation of diversity is that there is no gene for racism. Thus, they believe that even though children may initially develop and act on intolerant attitudes, they can be educated to value human differences. At an early age, children notice differences among the people around them, often in relation to their own characteristics.[6] They soon become aware that certain human differences are connected with power and privilege, while others cause people to be treated less respectfully.[7] In addition, they are more apt to be taught that intolerance is an acceptable reaction to diversity than how to deal creatively and nonviolently with conflict, anger, and other unpleasant emotions. As a result, young children may develop "pre-prejudice": misconceptions, discomfort, fear, and rejection of differences that can blossom into full-fledged prejudice if they are not helped to overcome their initial negative feelings.[8] Moreover, given "the relative imperviousness of adult prejudice to the effects of conflicting evidence and experience," it appears that predispositions acquired at early developmental levels may lay a potent foundation for later racism.[9]

Bias incidents range from hate crimes such as assault, murder, or institutional vandalism in which bias is the motivation to the public display of messages or symbols deemed offensive to particular groups, to rallies or gatherings that may draw protests or provoke violent opposition.[10]

> A bias-related incident is any incident in which an action taken by a person or group is perceived to be malicious or discriminatory toward another person or group based on bias or prejudice relating to such characteristics as race, color, religion, national origin, ancestry, age, mental or physical disability, sexual orientation, gender, or gender identity or any situation in which inter-group tensions exist based on such group characteristics. Bias-related incidents may be violations of criminal law, such as hate crime, or violations of civil law, such as unlawful discrimination in employment, housing, education or public accommodations. Many bias-related incidents are not violations of any law, yet they can create dangerous levels of tension between individuals and groups—tension that can escalate into violence and civil unrest. This is true of the activities of organized hate groups, and other public expressions of bias or hatred. Ethnic or racial jokes or name-calling in a school, workplace or community are bias-related incidents that, if not addressed, create a climate in which people do not feel valued and respected and in which severe forms of inter-group tension can develop.[11]

Addressing the issue of bias is complex but necessary to counteract prejudice that leads to negative perceptions and actions toward those who are different. A three-part strategy is outlined as follows.

If we want to address unconscious bias effectively, we need to first be aware of how the senses, emotions, and brain interact to create unconscious bias. Second, we must go beyond awareness of our biases to sensitivity to their impact. Last we need to develop a system that internalizes decision making with ongoing reinforcement of that competence.

The complexity of the process of bringing unconscious bias to long-term wise decision making should rule out quick responses. A one-time lecture with PowerPoint slides should be considered as an introductory lesson only. If that lecture is accompanied by an interactive group facilitation, the process will have gotten underway but is by no means complete. Scientists tell us that it takes daily practice of three weeks for new habits to establish themselves in our minds.

Let us understand the magnitude of moving from unconscious bias to competence and wisdom. It's not a matter of simply being aware of diversity. Research has shown that forcing people into awareness of cultural differences can often add stress to relationships and defensiveness to communication. Further, labeling people as racist and sexist seldom enhances their desire to be inclusive and respectful. This was dramatically demonstrated in the case of a Google engineer who rejected the training as "shaming" and insisted that women are biologically unsuited to technical computer work. Rather than bludgeoning people, there needs to be a more sophisticated, nuanced, and humane approach.

Broadening minds requires the development of new neurological pathways with additional connections to produce awareness and sensitivity that can produce a changed mindset.[12]

STUDENT-LED INITIATIVE: CASE STUDY

The program "Speak" was created in response to the appearance of swastikas and racist pictures and was created by students at Albany High School in March 2017. The pain and anger caused by the racism prompted a group of determined students to take action and develop an influential social justice group.

According to the group's website (https://www.ahsstudentsspeak.org), a cultural change within Albany schools needed to be made, and the only people who could truly make that happen were young people. Students needed to hold peers accountable for hateful remarks. Students needed to invest in an inclusive and safe community for everyone.

By the end of the school year the group had written a pilot lesson and presented it to several elementary school classrooms. The goal was to teach third through fifth graders about concepts of empathy and respect through education about prejudice and discrimination. The young students who were open and ready to learn would shape the future to be a more fair and equitable one. These presentations were effective and inspiring for everyone involved.

For the next school year, the focus was on elementary school presentations on the fifth-grade level, visiting each classroom three to four times.

Each presentation was interactive and covered major topics related to social justice and activism, such as racism, sexism, the LGBT community, and bullying. Each presentation had a strong focus on empathy development and increasing a sense of social responsibility.

Speak is focused on presentations, but it is not the only thing they do. The group of high schoolers meets two to three times a week to discuss current events within the community and world. There is a focus on educating oneself and being the best activist, and person, that one can be.

WORKPLACE/LEADERSHIP: CASE STUDY

During Deborah Levine's highly visible role as diversity and inclusion director at two Fortune 500 companies, she wrote internal articles read by people across the globe. She also had to make difficult decisions, sometimes with potentially significant financial consequences for the organization. Following is a major decision she made and the national fallout in one company. Following that are a few responses she received in response to internal articles. Note that topics of sexual orientation or Islam/Muslims seemed to generate these messages to her.

Situation #1: During the mid-1990s when issues around the inclusion of LGBT employees moved to the forefront of corporate diversity, she made the decision at a company to expand its worldwide diversity calendar to include Gay Awareness Month. That drew the immediate attention of an external national "family oriented" organization whose leader initiated a national boycott threat alleging that the company was supporting a "homosexual agenda" with mandatory "gay training" for supervisors, including a program that included the correct method for using different colored condoms. The company was inundated with hundreds of letters from irate customers, most of them canceling the company's services. Note that "family orientation" is often code language for socially conservative views, with no particular connection to families. Families can consist of a wide variety of close relationships, including varying degrees of sexual orientation.

Situation #2: An issue emerged in another organization with the strange disappearance of diversity-related posters, especially those that publicized LGBT events. During that time, she started receiving borderline harassing e-mails from an individual whenever she published something on or visibly supported activities initiated by the organization's Muslim employees. This came to a head when the person behind these acts berated a Muslim fellow car-pooler, which led to the harasser's termination. She was informed later that he was a member of a far-right external organization with a website with anti-gay and anti-Muslim propaganda.

Situation #3: An employee at a remote location sent strongly worded messages to her accusing her of being anti-white and anti-Christian based on her internal blog. Because of her, he refused to enter the office of anyone who he knew or suspected to be gay and successfully lobbied his management to allow him to meet with "gay suspects" only in conference rooms and never in his or their offices. This is how she responded:

> Like just about anyone, she was surprised and rattled by these missives. Her options were to (1) turn each one over to my management/security, (2) ignore them or (3) respond forcefully. Unless the message came across as physical threat, she ruled out the first option since she felt that she could handle it on her own. As much as she wanted to, the second option did not always work for her, given that she has always been unable to suppress things said that were incorrect, demeaning, bigoted or attacked her credibility. During those times when she did exercise the third option her hard-hitting responses sometimes exacerbated matters.[13]

RECOMMENDATIONS

Learn the Three-Step No-Hate Process[14]

Step #1: Develop Awareness: Recognize the emerging trends in hate groups. Understand the recruitment strategies of hate groups and their appeal.

Step #2: Expand Cultural Sensitivity: Increase knowledge of the diverse targets of hate and appreciate their cultural contributions and value.

Step #3: Solidify Competence: Learn how to combine awareness and sensitivity for individual ownership of the process. Develop an action plan to develop confidence and maximize the No-Hate Process for counteracting hate.

Advice for Community-School Efforts

Dispel stereotypes against marginalized groups, reduce hostility between and among groups, and encourage broader intercultural understanding and appreciation. It is important that school administrators, school boards, and classroom teachers confront harassment and denigration of those who are different. Anti-bias teaching should start in early childhood and continue through high school. Teachers must also have the backing of administrators and school board members to intervene against incidents of bias whether inside the school, on the playground, on athletic fields, and on field trips.

Use Anti-Bias Curricula and Resources in High Schools

Some sources of anti-bias school curricula:

- Southern Poverty Law Center's Teaching Tolerance program
- Facing History and Ourselves
- Anti-Defamation League
- Un-Bias Guide for Educators

Engage in Racial Healing

This is the process of engaging communities, organizations, and individuals to uproot and jettison the antiquated belief in the hierarchy of human value and its consequences. The healing comes through building authentic relationships and increasing the capacity for trust, honesty, and collective action within and across diverse groups to create policies and practices that foster a more equitable, fair, and just society.

Advice for Leadership

First, understand that given your role as a leader in the area of diversity, anticipate that you will be a target, often when you least expect it. Second, deal with each instance on a case-by-case basis. Third, quickly figure out the levels of support you can expect from management. Fourth, step back and do a best/worst case analysis with each of the options in addition to other possibilities. It is also recommended to seek advice from others in the field of diversity—preferably from outside your organization—for their perspective and experience with the issue at hand.

It's good to keep in mind that although we don't always know what really motivates people who behave in a hateful way, the one thing they all seek is attention. You must decide for yourself whether you want to give it to them. In the end, silence as your response may be your best option.[15]

NOTES

1. Diamond, "Essential Secrets of Psychotherapy."
2. Steinberg, Brooks, and Remtulla, "Youth Hate Crimes."
3. McDougald, "The Unflattering Familiarity of the Alt-Right in Angela Nagel's *Kill All Normies*."
4. Ury, *Getting to Peace*.
5. Ezekiel, *The Racist Mind*.
6. Hohensee and Derman-Sparks, "Implementing An Anti-Bias Curriculum in Early Childhood Classrooms."
7. Derman-Sparks and the A.B.C. Task Force, cited in Schwarz, "Anti-Bias and Conflict Resolution Curricula."
8. Derman-Sparks and the A.B.C. Task Force, cited in Schwarz, "Anti-Bias and Conflict Resolution Curricula."
9. Cited in Katz, "Development of Children's Racial Awareness and Intergroup Attitudes."
10. Southern Poverty Law Center, "Ten Ways to Fight Hate: A Community Response Guide."

11. Center for Community Engagement, "York County Human Relations Commission Feasibility Study."
12. Adapted from Levine, "The Challenge of Unconscious Bias."
13. Howard, "When Bias Comes Knocking."
14. Un-Bias Guide Series by Deborah Levine, https://americandiversityreport.com/diversity-resources/un-bias-guide-series/.
15. Derived from Howard, "When Bias Comes Knocking."

Chapter Twelve

The Special Responsibility of Schools

WHY THE FOCUS ON SCHOOLS?

Since the shooting at Parkland High School in Florida in 2018, there has been a school shooting approximately every twelve days.[1] Some of these were carried out by disaffected youth, mostly white boys, with psychological or organizational ties to neo-Nazi and far right-wing extremist groups. Some were self-radicalized. Shootings are not the only hate-filled incidents. Others include graffiti, neo-Nazi gestures, name calling (especially use of the N-word), performing in blackface, taunting of athletic teams with players of color, bullying, discrimination, and exclusion. Nonviolent incidents are sometimes dismissed as "boys will be boys" or "locker room talk."

We disagree and believe that everyone should be held to a higher standard. An example occurred in Baraboo, Wisconsin, in May 2018, when several dozen young men gathered on the steps of the courthouse to take pictures before their high school prom. The majority of them extended their right arms, mimicking the Nazi salute as a parent snapped a picture. The superintendent claimed that the students' actions were protected by the First Amendment and declined to discipline them.

While this is subject of much legal dispute, such incidents are a symptom of larger problems than thoughtless gestures. The larger issues include lack of knowledge of historical context, inculcation of hate as a gateway to violence, disrespect for members of a diverse society, retraction of parents and school officials from their duties to bring about social controls, and reinforcement of baser human instincts. These issues put key elements of schools at risk.

In fall 2018, about 56.6 million students enrolled in elementary and secondary schools in the United States, including 50.7 million students in public schools and 5.9 million in private schools. Of the public school students, 35.6 million are in prekindergarten through eighth grade and 15.1 million in ninth grade through twelfth grade. White students account for 24.1 million, of whom about half, or 12 million, are male. These are the potential targets for neo-Nazi and extreme right-wing group recruiting. They overwhelmingly use social media on a variety of platforms, and their use of the internet is largely unrestricted. Many are very savvy about such use, and they are exposed to inputs about which their parents and school officials have no idea. Their brains are still developing, and their filters may be low. Students are developing their identities and are open to a variety of influences. Many sources are trying to influence them in terms of buying habits, smoking/vaping, driving, environmental issues, drinking, dating, religion, and so forth.

Two of these sources are neo-Nazi and extreme right-wing groups. They may offer an avenue for anger, desire for belonging, companionship, and so forth. Childhood is a stressful time, and being a teenager is traditionally a period of maximum stress. An estimated 3.1 million adolescents aged twelve to seventeen in the United States had at least one major depressive episode. This number represented 12.8 percent of the U.S. population aged twelve to seventeen.[2] Teen mental disorders include substance use disorder. This is because teens use drugs and alcohol to self-medicate depression, anxiety, trauma, low self-esteem, and other underlying conditions.[3]

School officials and teachers today are being asked to do a great many things, while some of the older emphases, like civics education, are in decline or have disappeared. We are a bit leery about asking schools to do even more. Nevertheless, schools are central to our society and the threats are great. Therefore we have included in this book a chapter on the special responsibility of the 15,000 public school districts in the United States, as well as the 34,576 private schools.

COUNTERACT SCHOOL-BASED HATE INITIATIVES

Reassure members of the target group that the new, more diverse America is not threatening to them. Counteract efforts to foster racial segregation, fear, and hate among teenagers by neo-Nazi groups that break into high school campuses at night and plaster them with racial epithets and Nazi symbols. The next morning, when the Black or Latino students see the hateful symbols and words, they may blame the white students. At worst, for protection, each race may separate itself and the Nazis' mission is achieved. When students form their own groups on this basis, the school becomes racially divided.

Staff Training

All school employees, including teachers, administrators, support staff, bus drivers, and security staff, should be aware of the manifestations of hate and be trained to address hate incidents. Training should include anti-bias and conflict resolution; procedures for identifying and reporting incidents of racial, religious, and sexual harassment, discrimination, and hate crime; strategies for preventing such incidents from occurring; and resources available to assist in dealing with these incidents.

Student Training

Prejudice and discrimination are learned attitudes and behaviors. Neither is uncontrollable or inevitable. Teaching children that even subtle forms of hate such as ethnic slurs or epithets, negative or offensive name-calling, stereotyping, and exclusion are hurtful and inherently wrong can help to prevent more extreme, violent manifestations of hate. Through structured classroom activities and programs, students can begin to develop empathy while practicing the critical thinking and conflict resolution skills needed to recognize and respond to various manifestations of hate.

> I'd say the most effective strategy is to educate people about it, because it really thrives on being hidden and appearing to be something other than it is. Helping people understand how white supremacists operate in high schools, and the military, and all kinds of sectors of society gives people the resources and the understanding to not be pulled into those kinds of worlds.[4]

Unfortunately, there has been a decline in civics education in public schools. Retired U.S. Supreme Court Justice Sandra Day O'Connor founded iCivics to improve civics education for the nation's students. Her efforts led to its 2009 creation. It is a nonprofit that promotes learning about government through online games such as "We the Jury" and "Do I Have a Right?" As she has retired from public life, a new organization is being formed, CivXNow.org, that will focus on making civics a greater priority in schools. The new group has more than forty partnering organizations. Its opening statement reads as follows:

> In the wake of the 2016 election, people's knowledge of and trust in our government institutions are at near record lows. Now, more than ever, incivility and misinformation are growing. Communities are increasingly polarized; unable to respectfully disagree with each other or consider ideas from different perspectives. Unsurprisingly, given these low levels of trust in our institutions, engagement in civic life is low. Our American democracy is in crisis.
> We urgently need to build a national strategy that expands quality civic education standards at the elementary, middle, and high school levels to ensure that

future generations: gain a deep understanding of civic life; know how to engage as informed citizens; and understand why their civic participation matters. This common understanding and purpose—which must exist across partisan divides—is critical to a healthy civil society in a democracy.[5]

They also note the following:

> Young people especially are disconnected from civic life. Youth turnout in the 2016 election was lower than other age groups, with just 50% of eligible young voter turnout. Even worse: youth are dangerously uninformed about the basics of our democracy and politics. In a 2012 national survey, just 22% of 18-24 year olds correctly answered two factual questions (out of two) about the candidates' positions on the issues they cared about most. And in 2014, just 23% of students tested "proficient" on the 8th grade civics test in the Nation's Report Card. Civic ignorance is even greater for minority students: 50% of Latino 12th graders and over 60% of Black 12th graders do not even have a "basic" understanding of government.[6]

The goals include building a national strategy that expands quality civic education standards at the elementary, middle, and high school levels to ensure that future generations:

- Gain a deep understanding of civic life;
- Know how to engage as informed citizens;
- Understand why their civic participation matters.

These goals attempt to instill cognitive openness (willingness and ability to see different points of view, truths), emotional flexibility (ability to feel solidarity, identification, trust with people of different backgrounds, to negotiate the complicated "quest for significance in the modern world") and social variety (willingness and ability to negotiate and maintain relationships with people of different backgrounds).[7]

In the aftermath of the tragedy at Marjory Stoneman Douglas High School (a mass shooting in Florida), the nation has been impressed by the leadership, confidence, and poise of student leaders. They have emerged as eloquent advocates for political change at the local, state, and national levels. One of the reasons these students are able to express themselves so well is because they are the beneficiaries of what is arguably one of the nation's most comprehensive and successful efforts to teach civics.

Because of the extremely decentralized nature of American public education with over fifteen thousand public school districts, some schools may be breeding grounds for intolerance and violence. For example, resegregation by race is occurring in many U.S. schools, particularly through the charter school movement and the end of affirmative action. Some state school boards, such as Texas, have sharply reduced coverage of topics conducive to understanding, such as civil rights. A study has shown that most high school American history texts reduce coverage of the Civil Rights Movement to only a mention of Martin Luther King Jr. Some texts do not even ascribe slavery as a major cause of the Civil War.[8]

DEVELOP PARTNERSHIPS

Hate crime prevention cannot be accomplished by schools alone. School districts are encouraged to develop partnerships with parent groups, youth-serving organizations, criminal justice agencies, victim assistance organizations, businesses, advocacy groups, and religious organizations. These partnerships can help identify resources available to school personnel to address hate incidents, raise community awareness of the issue, ensure appropriate responses to hate incidents, and ensure that youth receive a consistent message that hate-motivated behavior will not be tolerated.

DEVELOP A HATE PREVENTION POLICY

Distribute the policy to every student, every student's family, and every employee of the school district. An effective hate prevention policy will promote a school climate in which racial, religious, ethnic, gender, disability, and other differences, as well as freedom of thought and expression, are respected and appreciated. The policy should be developed with the input of parents, students, teachers, community members, and school administrators. It should include a description of the types of behavior prohibited under the policy, the roles and responsibilities of students and staff in preventing and reporting hate incidents or crimes, the range of possible consequences for engaging in this type of behavior, and the locations of resources in the school and community where students can go for help. It should respect diverse viewpoints, freedom of thought, and freedom of expression. Every student should be informed of the contents of the school district's policy on hate crime on an annual basis. The policy should include a dispute resolution process and a compliance and grievance process.

PLAN CORRECTIVE ACTIONS

School districts are encouraged to take a firm position against all manifestations of hate, from ethnic slurs, racial epithets, and taunts to graffiti, vandalism, discrimination, harassment, intimidation, and violence. School districts can develop a wide range of nondisciplinary corrective actions to respond to incidents, including counseling, parent conferences, community service, awareness training, and student completion of a research paper on an issue related to hate, as well as disciplinary actions such as in-school suspension and expulsion. School officials should be prepared to contact local, state, or federal civil rights officials to respond to more serious incidents and, in cases involving criminal activity or threat of criminal activity, should call the police.

When members of a public school club were photographed making the Hitler salute, the superintendent of the school district stated that they were engaging in free speech and thus could not be punished. Unfortunately, the defense of "free speech" has been adopted by some neo-Nazi groups as protecting their right to hate speech. But in a lawsuit brought by the Southern Poverty Law Center, a federal district court judge in Montana rejected that defense for inciting followers on social media to violence. Such considerations show the difficult nature of choosing a proper and desired response. As in so many considerations in American society, legal liabilities can drive decision making. Thus, in choosing a path to follow, those who want to address neo-Nazi activities in their areas may want to consult with legal counsel before proceeding. It should be noted, however, that free speech is not designed to take away the rights of others.

COLLECT AND USE DATA

Collection of data on the occurrence of school-based hate incidents and crimes will assist administrators and teachers in identifying patterns and more effectively implementing hate prevention policies and programs. To obtain such data, school districts can include questions about hate crime on surveys they conduct related to school crime and discipline, as well as collect and analyze incident-based data on specific hate incidents and crimes. In the latter case, school districts are encouraged to work closely with local law enforcement personnel to collect uniform and consistent data on hate crimes.

PROVIDE SCHOOL INTEGRATION OPPORTUNITIES

Young people can begin to interact across racial and ethnic lines through school-supported organizations and activities. Multiethnic teams of students can work together on community service projects, organize extracurricular events, and complete class projects. High school students can participate in service-learning projects in which they tutor, coach, and otherwise assist younger students from diverse backgrounds.[9]

PROVIDE ALTERNATIVES

Positive messages and activities to groups targeted by the Nazis should be provided. Bad facts or fake news should be replaced with facts based on evidence and logic. Voltaire put it well when he said, "Those who can make you believe absurdities, can make you commit atrocities." Language shapes thought patterns on which actions are based. Parental guidance is essential to give direction to a potentially vulnerable young person. Such guidance provides a shield against propaganda that promotes the use of violence. More importantly, family members and close relations must maintain a bond with a young person who becomes radicalized. Parents facing this situation should seek support. "Some researchers have questioned whether today's youths have been cheated of the means to meet basic, profound human needs, including the need for security, positive identity, a sense of effectiveness and control, connection to other human beings, and a meaningful understanding of the world and their own place in it."[10]

> Isolate the source of the hatred . . . inoculate those constituencies which are potentially vulnerable . . . and help them understand the issue before the other side does.[11]

Counter Anti-Immigrant Rhetoric and Actions

The government, news media, and the public need to take a series of "intentional steps" to protect immigrants and refugees and address issues that generate student-based hate incidents. Such steps include the following:

- A pathway to citizenship for "Dreamers" (youth who were brought to the United States as children by undocumented parents), protection for refugees from Muslim majority countries, and protection for asylum seekers.
- Comprehensive immigration legislation that addresses the millions of undocumented individuals living in the United States and includes reforms to the current legal immigration system.
- Improve reporting of hate crimes to the FBI and provide more anti-bias training to law enforcement.
- Provide students with tools to combat hatred and bigotry and protect immigrant students.
- Expand efforts between the government and social media and other technology platforms to counter extremism and bigotry online.[12]

SCHOOL AND POLICE OFFICIALS SHOULD WORK TOGETHER

Hate crimes can be school related, community related, or a combination of both. Officials should consider prevention and response roles, identify potential trouble sites, and plan for phased police intervention. Tension can be eased by regular communication with parents, students, media, and other community organizations. Mediation and conflict resolution classes develop the capacity of youth to peacefully settle disputes and conflicts.

Keep law enforcement in the loop, reinforcing to them that your community members are the good people who are peacefully countering the neo-Nazi appearance with the true identity of your home. Neo-Nazis classically seek confrontation so there's the active possibility they'll make an appearance at any event you have. Keeping the police informed and allied will minimize the possibility of confrontation. If there is a confrontation, this relationship will help make sure the right people (that is, law enforcement officers who are paid and trained to do it) are the ones dealing with any flare-ups and violence.

RECOMMENDATIONS

Monitor and Report

Timely reporting on racist, anti-Semitic, and other bias crimes is an essential means to assess and respond to patterns of discrimination affecting particular population groups. There are few anti-bullying laws in the United States, and many are ill defined. (Note: Washington State has a strong Anti-Bullying Statute for schools, but it is not monitored or enforced as it should be. Other jurisdictions may be in similar situations.)

Particular note should be taken of how important it has been to victims of hate crimes whether others in the community cared about what had happened to them. "No one seemed to care" is reported by numerous persons of varied backgrounds, always with a deep sense of disappointment. When others seemed not to care, the effects on victims were intensified. Such a perceived lack of concern, whether from neighbors, strangers, officials, or others, added to a sense of isolation of the victims. When others do care, the trauma is softened. When others seemed not to care, victims experienced the incidents as portentous, calling into question their entire outlook on the world.[13]

One expert has advised the following when monitoring hate groups.

1. Do nothing alone.
2. If you don't feel safe, go somewhere you do.
3. Bring video/audio recording devices and spare batteries.

4. Don't get in shouting matches.
5. Try to associate and collaborate with some visibly identified clergy.
6. If approached by media, select the most coherent and calm of your group to speak (if at all) and keep it short.
7. Get together afterward with those who couldn't make it and talk about the experience (debriefing), take notes, and exchange names, phone numbers, and e-mails so you can report any harassment or suspicious events.
8. Get badge numbers and names of police officers you deal with; some might be far right sympathizers.
9. Film or note the license plate numbers of the neo-Nazis' vehicles.
10. Go easy on the caffeine; the adrenaline will do.[14]

Threat Assessment and Intervention

The U.S. Secret Service has provided recommendations about avoiding mass school shootings. While somewhat vague, they can form the basis for community discussion and policy development. In conjunction with physical security and emergency management, a threat assessment process is an effective component to ensuring the safety and security of schools.

- Threat assessment procedures recognize that students engage in a continuum of concerning behaviors, the vast majority of which will be nonthreatening and nonviolent but may still require intervention.
- The threshold for intervention should be relatively low so that schools can identify students in distress before their behavior escalates to the level of eliciting concerns about safety.
- Everyone has a role to play in preventing school violence and creating safe school climates. Students should feel empowered to come forward without fear of reprisal. Faculty and staff should take all incoming reports seriously and assess any information regarding concerning behavior or statements.[15]

The federal interagency study on school violence issued in December 2018 states, "Beyond the school building and campus, informed and alert communities play a critical role in keeping our schools safe. Prior to most attacks, other students had concerns about the attacker, yet most did not report what they knew to a parent or other responsible adult. Out-reach campaigns, such as 'If You See Something, Say Something' and similar state-specific programs, are essential to encouraging and facilitating the reporting of suspicious activities or other concerning behaviors. There are significant opportunities to customize or expand such efforts."[16]

Counter Implicit Bias in Students and Faculty

- Use storytelling to assist in efforts to integrate diverse groups, teams, and communities. Stories are an ancient form of communication that can express both historical information and emotional/psychological attitudes in digestible form. When we organize information and create the appropriate story, we can be understood across complex social geography categories and belief systems. Storytelling can clarify areas of conflict and remove the element of poor communication from them. See the Matrix Model Management System for details on structuring storytelling for clarity and impact.
- Deploy the four-step un-bias strategies for teacher training and classroom discussions (see Un-Bias Guide for Educators).
- Offer Holocaust education as a tool for educating students to the consequences of biases. See chapter 13 in this book for details, case studies, and recommendations for Holocaust education.

NOTES

1. Griggs and Walker, "In the Year Since Parkland There's Been a School Shooting, on Average, Every 12 Days."
2. "Major Depression," *National Institutes of Mental Health*.
3. Newport Academy, "A Guide to Teen Mental Disorders."
4. Blee, "Conservative and Rightwing Movements."
5. CivXNow, "Mission Statement."
6. CivXNow, "Mission Statement."
7. European Commission, "The Contribution of Youth Work to Preventing Marginalisation and Violent Radicalisation."
8. See, for example, Mannie et al., "Mississippi Textbooks Gloss Over Civil Rights Struggle."
9. U.S. Department of Education, "Preventing Youth Hate Crime."
10. Steinberg, Brooks, and Remtulla, "Youth Hate Crimes."
11. Burghart, cited in Taber, *Salvaging Democracy*, 34.
12. ADL, "Mainstreaming Hate."
13. Based on National Center for Victims of Crime, 2001, www.ncvc.org.
14. Taber, "Forms of Resistance."
15. Homeland Security, "Enhancing School Safety Using a Threat Assessment Model."
16. "Final Report of the Federal Commission on School Safety."

Chapter Thirteen

Holocaust Education

Given Oklahoma's array of hate groups, conspiracy theorists, neo-Nazi fans, and active militias [post–Oklahoma City bombing], I learned to expect the unexpected, and worse. Therefore, I wasn't entirely surprised to get a phone call informing me that Holocaust Denial was about to land on our doorstep.

The "who" coming to town was David Irving, Holocaust Denier extraordinaire. The "where" was a branch of Tulsa's public library located in our major shopping mall. Irving had reserved one of the library's meeting rooms under the fictitious title "Native American Constitution Party." I called the Cherokee Nation's offices and asked if there was any connection of Native Americans to such an organization or to David Irving. Their response was a moderately polite version of "Hell, no!"

My assignment was to go undercover to this meeting, observe what went on, and report back to the Jewish agency. . . . While we waited, the woman seated in front of me turned around and gushed, "Isn't he just the handsomest man you've ever seen?" . . . Irving began to speak, thanking the two dozen attendees for coming. . . . In a deep, mesmerizing voice, he shared that he was a besieged, beleaguered man because Jews everywhere heckled and defamed him. He spent considerable time going into detail about the Jews who tried to keep the truth from the world. There were no gas chambers at Auschwitz. Survivors tattooed their own arms so they could make false claims. Only a few hundred Jews died in WW II and they died of illness or were killed in Allied bombings.

Irving then went on to claim that Hitler was a friend of the Jews and he could prove it. Pulling a letter from his pocket, Irving unfolded it and read out loud what he claimed was personal correspondence from Hitler himself. The letter, supposedly to one of his army generals, expressed his deep respect for the Jewish people. Claiming that Hitler had been maligned, Irving explained that the reason anyone had gotten away with such defamation was that the letter was written in an ancient form of German that only he, David Irving, could read.[1]

The lessons of the Holocaust are increasingly applicable in today's contentious environment, but Holocaust survivors are scarce today. What happens to the moral lessons of the Holocaust in a world in which deniers gain traction and David Irving is a tour guide at the Auschwitz death camp?

> As the generation of Holocaust survivors gradually disappears, education about the Holocaust becomes ever more important. However, this is in contrast to the findings of recent surveys that show that growing numbers of young people place National Socialism and the Nazi persecution of the Jews firmly in the past, considering it to be irrelevant to the present. Correspondingly, knowledge about basic facts of the Holocaust is declining, according to a seven country survey recently conducted by TNS Sofres in Paris, commissioned by The American Jewish Committee.[2]

Some experts are unconvinced that Holocaust education is an effective tool for fighting hate and extremism. They question whether correct information is enough to discredit illegitimate arguments or organizing efforts. In *Anti-Semitism Today: How It Is the Same, How It Is Different, and How To Fight It*, Kenneth Stern, an award-winning author and the American Jewish Committee's expert on anti-Semitism and extremism, states, "There is simply no research-based proof that Holocaust education is an antidote to anti-Semitism. This solution is merely asserted and assumed to work."[3]

WHAT CAN BE ACHIEVED

Others are adamant that Holocaust education is vital to a society's ability to resist extremism and its violence. The Rev. Dr. John Pawlikowski, an original member of the U.S. Holocaust Commission, maintains the centrality of Holocaust remembrance and education in shaping contemporary ethics and behavior.

> The academic study of ethics, in light of the experience of the Holocaust, has witnessed rapid development in the last decade. In addition to research into ethical decision making during the Holocaust itself in such volumes as Rab Bennett's *Under the Shadow of the Swastika: The Moral Dilemmas of Resistance and Collaboration in Hitler's Europe*, more general reflections on the significance of the Holocaust for contemporary ethics have come to the fore from Jewish and Christian scholars alike. There have also been voices such as Herbert Hirsch who have questioned whether we can learn anything from the Holocaust in terms of the moral challenge facing us today given the sui generis nature of that event as well as the immense complexity of a modern, global society.
>
> I personally stand with those who do find the experience of the Holocaust significant for ethical reflection in today's global society. But Hirsch's pessimism does serve a purpose in reminding us that there is no simplistic transition

from the situation of the Shoah into today's complex social situation." (See appendix 8 for full article.)[4]

Pawlikowski emphasizes that Holocaust education must address the collectiveness encountered when respect for basic human dignity is supplanted by the notion that only correct belief entitles one to fundamental rights. Rather, our universe of moral concern must be broadened beyond the parameters of our own faith and national communities. There must be a realization of the consequences of our words and actions.

Violent religious language can greatly contribute to softening a society for genocide. Pawlikowski argues that this is what Christian anti-Semitism did during the Nazi era. Religion remains a powerful force in many present-day societies. If religious language in a given society demeans people who do not share the dominant faith system and denies them full rights of citizenship, it opens the door for physical assaults on such groups in times of social tension. On the other hand, positive religious language about the "religious other" can serve as a barrier against such assaults. It is especially necessary in the complex national societies that globalization has produced.

Many educators agree with Pawlikowski and are concerned that despite the benefits of Holocaust education, many states don't provide this education and few states mandate it.

> Only 12 states (CA, CT, FL, IL, IN, KY, MI, NJ, NY, OH, PA, and RI) have mandatory education about the Holocaust. A recent study shows that 65% of young people have no idea what Auschwitz is. Additionally, 31% of Americans believe that two million or fewer Jews were killed in the Holocaust. (This is far from the actual number.) . . . Holocaust education offers a lesson for humanity about too much government power in the wrong hands. It offers a slice of world history, which is filled with examples of tyrants and despots unleashing their brutal wrath on their subjects. It has personal stories of resisters to Nazi tyranny—righteous non-Jews who acted in heroic ways and Jewish partisans who hid in the forests to fight their oppressors head-on. Communities and towns were wiped out, but less than 10 years after the beginning of the Holocaust, Jews triumphed with the creation of the state of Israel—a diverse homeland for Jews from the Middle East and Europe, many of whom had just escaped the most rampant terror in modern history.[5]

HOLOCAUST DENIAL

Holocaust denial refers to any attempt to claim that the Holocaust/Shoah did not take place or to deny the extent of the extermination of the Jews and other victims by the Nazis and their accomplices during World War II. Holocaust denial may include publicly denying or calling into doubt the use of the principal mechanisms of destruction (such as gas chambers, mass shooting, starvation, and torture) or the intentionality of the genocide of the Jewish people and the deaths of other victims, such as the Roma, people with disabilities, and LGBT people. Holocaust denial in its various forms is an expression of anti-Semitism. The attempt to deny the genocide of the Jews is an effort to exonerate National Socialism and anti-Semitism from guilt or responsibility in the genocide of the Jewish people. Forms of Holocaust denial also include blaming Jews for either exaggerating or creating the Shoah for political or financial gain as if the Shoah itself was the result of a conspiracy plotted by Jews. In this, the goal is to make Jews culpable and anti-Semitism legitimate.

The goals of Holocaust denial often are the rehabilitation of an explicit anti-Semitism and the promotion of political ideologies and conditions suitable for the advent of the very type of event it denies. Distortion of the Holocaust refers to the following:

1. intentional efforts to excuse or minimize the impact of the Holocaust or its principal elements, including collaborators and allies of Nazi Germany;
2. gross minimization of the number of the victims of the Holocaust in contradiction to reliable sources;
3. attempts to blame the Jews for causing their own genocide;
4. statements that cast the Holocaust as a positive historical event — these statements are not Holocaust denial but are closely connected to it as a radical form of anti-Semitism and may suggest that the Holocaust did not go far enough in accomplishing its goal of "the Final Solution of the Jewish Question"; and
5. attempts to blur the responsibility for the establishment of concentration and death camps devised and operated by Nazi Germany by putting blame on other nations or ethnic groups.

Given the efforts by neo-Nazis to label Holocaust denial as freedom of speech, Holocaust educators must persevere in their efforts to educate. The Anne Frank Center plays a major role in advocating for Holocaust education and providing needed resources to educators. The center has launched an initiative to mandate this education in all fifty states.

> Two New Efforts Launched to Require Holocaust Education Nationwide, One Triggered by Spicer
>
> By Stav Ziv - 5/1/17 Newsweek quotes Steven Goldstein, Executive Director of the Anne Frank Center.
>
> The Anne Frank Center is very careful to differentiate between hate crimes and genocide, he says. Still, "history shows us that genocide begins with initial

steps of hate," he says. "There's no doubt effective genocide education includes the steps that unfortunately have led to genocide in history: the identification of oppressed people; demonizing them next; rounding them up next; isolating them next and then killing them. . . . There are different levels of stripping people of their humanity that eventually have led to genocides. All genocide begins with hate and prejudice. That's how it begins and then it escalates," Goldstein says. "Our schools need to be early sentinels of 'Never again' before 'Never again' becomes 'Once again.'"[6]

HOLOCAUST EDUCATION OPTIONS

Although the number of states with mandated Holocaust education is relatively small, there are alternatives that can be used. They include the use of Holocaust education resources such as books, movies, and videos, as well as class projects, elective courses, and invited speakers.

ELECTIVE HOLOCAUST COURSE: CASE STUDY

At the Chattanooga School for the Arts and Sciences in Tennessee, teachers are allowed to offer electives. Kevin Aslinger chose to create a course on the Holocaust. About twenty upper-class students chose to take the course. When asked why, their responses underscore the curiosity of senior high schoolers, the lack of Holocaust education, and the confusion surrounding it. Their statements included the following:

- I was genuinely interested in the Holocaust. I wanted to know what drove someone and his group of people to kill millions of others and what led up to the horrific event.
- The reason I took this class is because the Holocaust isn't talked about much, especially in schools. . . . I felt it was very important to be informed about what prejudice can turn into if combined with unchecked power. What factors went into causing the Holocaust.
- I chose to take the class because of all the conflicting information I've gotten about the Holocaust. I just want to know what really happened. Plus the Holocaust isn't really talked about much in any of the history classes I've taken so far.
- I chose to take this class to be more aware of the Holocaust and less of what is just the commercial view like a boy in the striped pajamas.

The curriculum that Aslinger used was both basic and broad. It defined religion and Judaism, anti-Semitism, genocide and the Holocaust, and stereotypes. The studies delved into the life of Jews in Europe in the Middle Ages before the Holocaust, the role of the Christian churches in developing anti-

Semitism, and the literature leading up to the Nazi regime. Using photographs, videos, music, and documentaries, the events prior to, during, and after the Holocaust were outlined.

When asked to describe the students' reaction to the course, Aslinger responded, "My own feeling is that they have been most overwhelmed by the sheer numbers of Germans (and Poles) who just 'went along' with the Holocaust; in a related issue, they have been shocked by the power of propaganda and also how bureaucrats willingly assisted in mass murder just because it 'was their job.'" Here are comments from the students when asked what affected them the most in the Holocaust course:

- Watching real Warsaw Ghetto footage and seeing how real, "alive" people are shaped like deformed, alien skeletons.
- Watching *The Pianist* and seeing a personal account of what happened in someone's life.
- Seeing the survivor (Eva Schloss) talk about what happened to her and how she survived.
- Learning about Treblinka and realizing that even though it was only open for a fraction of the time, almost as many people were killed there as were killed at Auschwitz.
- The thing that surprised me the most is how a lot of Poles refused to try to help the Jews and even turned them in to the Nazis. It also shocked me to learn how even within the camps the Jews and other prisoners were more against each other than trying to help each other.
- One of the things that had the largest impact on me was the amount of people that were murdered during the Holocaust, but also the many people that refused to do anything. There were homes right next to the camps and I know they could smell the burning flesh, but they went on with their lives like there was nothing going on. Then, when it came time to do something about it everyone said, "I didn't know what was going on."
- In the beginning of Holocaust Studies, I believed that only Jews were persecuted, but I was surprised to find out that there were more races and different kinds of " Non German " people involved.
- The thing that stood out most for me was how inhumane the SS officers were. They treated people in unspeakable ways and I never knew how brutal they could be. It is something that I have learned and will never be able to forget.

RECOMMENDATIONS

Learn from the Holocaust. Be wary of what you read and watch. Don't be swayed by lies and alternate facts or swept up in hate. Circumstances may have changed, but human nature has not, and a new normal is fast engulfing our humanity. Understand what didn't work for the victims and what may not work today.

- In the Holocaust, head in the sand and passive methods did not work.
- Cooperation with the Nazis did not work.
- Making concessions to the Nazis did not work.
- Staying neutral did not work. (Except for Switzerland.)
- The democratic system did not work. (Hitler was voted into power under the German Constitution.)
- The legal system did not work. (The German judiciary cooperated fully with Nazi rules, regulations, and statutes.)
- The types of victims expanded as groups were victimized.
- Many large corporations cooperated with the Nazis, including American-owned corporations.

Take advantage of any and all opportunities to see and hear from Holocaust survivors. While there are few left to tell their stories, and those who are left are quite elderly, it's a valuable experience for all ages to hear their testimonies.

If Holocaust survivors are not available in person, use videos and other resources from state Holocaust commissions and Holocaust museums, particularly the U.S. Holocaust Museum in Washington, DC. The museum has identified topic areas for students to consider while studying the Holocaust, along with documents and videos that can be accessed online and in person.

NOTES

1. Levine, *The Liberator's Daughter*, 127–29.
2. American Jewish Committee, "Thinking about the Holocaust 60 Years Later."
3. Stern, *Antisemitism Today*.
4. Pawlikowski, "Does the Holocaust Have Ethical Implications for Today?"
5. "If You Don't Have Mandatory Holocaust Education, DEMAND IT!"
6. Ziv, "Two New Efforts Launched to Require Holocaust Education Nationwide, One Triggered by Spicer."

Chapter Fourteen

Interfaith Efforts

As we sat in the library of the synagogue not long after the massacre at Pittsburgh's Tree of Life synagogue, we listened to the security suggestions from the local FBI director. Like many churches, mosques and other religious institutions, we are concerned that we will be targeted unexpectedly by violent extremists. It's no longer a surprise that religion is a major focus of their rage and we should be prepared for violent expressions of that hate.

> The role of religion in American culture is increasingly central to our relationships and our communities, influencing many aspects of intergroup relations. Those relations can be complex, challenging, and divisive as the diversity of religious groups grows exponentially. How can we successfully anticipate the impact of this religious diversity on service sectors, educational institutions, and urban planning and policies? How can we prepare ourselves for a world in which religions are a major element of public life and of the global economy?[1]

Preparation for religion's visible role as a target of violent extremism teaches us not only the value of awareness and security, but also the need to come together and invest in multifaith dialogue, coalitions, and programs. These initiatives have waxed and waned in the past, but are seeing a resurgence as hate groups increasingly target religious institutions. Interfaith efforts can take place in the community, workplace, and educational institutions and may be a response to an immediate threat, a conference, or a public statement. But the long-term nature of this work is where its greatest value lies.

The Parliament of the World's Religions was one of the earliest initiatives to cultivate harmony among the world's religious and spiritual communities in order to achieve a just, peaceful and sustainable world. In 1893, the city of Chicago hosted the World Columbian Exposition, which served as the birthplace of the 1893 World's Parliament of Religions. Held on the shores of

Lake Michigan, the Parliament marks the first formal gathering of representatives of Eastern and Western spiritual traditions. Today, the Parliament is recognized as the birth of formal interreligious dialogue. A variety of spiritual leaders from around the world came to share their perspectives and engage in dialogue.[2]

Much of the current focus of the Parliament is an annual conference where religious leaders speak on a wide range of topics, some of which are related to hate, prejudice, and bias. Attendees include religious leaders, scholars, and interfaith dialogue experts. The conference is intended to support ongoing projects and research and also enhance community interfaith efforts. However, it's at the local level that interfaith groups can do the most to counteract extremism and deal with incidents involving the Nazis and similar hate groups.

INTERFAITH CASE STUDY—LOCAL INTERFAITH COALITION

The DuPage Interfaith Resource Network (DIRN) was formed in 1990. As the technical corridor in Chicago's western suburbs became increasingly diverse and international, there were efforts to be inclusive that included repositioning the Christmas tree from the awning over the public school's front door to the lobby inside. The result was a street riot that ended up on the front page of the *Chicago Tribune*. The public library's move to rename its Christmas events as a holiday celebration resulted in death threats against the library's director, who removed his family for the month of December to keep them safe.

DIRN was created on the foundation laid by the National Workshop on Christian-Jewish Relations held in Chicago as well as the Catholic-Jewish program sponsored by the American Jewish Committee and Chicago's Archdiocese, which created small dialogue groups across the city. DIRN expanded to include a multi-faith network. "Our mission was to create a forum to discuss religious diversity and to explore issues in depth. Schools and libraries took advantage of the speakers, panels, and debates to defuse hostilities."[3] Tools were created to advance understanding of diverse faiths, including Quick Reference Religious Diversity Cards which were used by corporations, hospitals, and law enforcement. Built for sustainability, DIRN still exists as does its Interfaith Thanksgiving program, which has brought together diverse religious groups for more than twenty-five years.

One of the biggest hurdles in the formation of an interfaith organization is the decision about what faith traditions can be part of the effort. Groups like the DuPage Interfaith Resource Network struggled with this issue in its inception. DIRN struggled to find the appropriate degree of inclusion and turned to the interfaith council in Washington, DC, and its guidelines. That council had a written policy that stipulated established religions as partners. While not perfect, the policy was helpful to DIRN's executive committee in resolving issues over requests to join and gave members assurance that the group would not be hijacked while creating a forum for discussion of religious diversity.

CLERGY RESPONSE

Dialogue between faiths and religions often originates from among the leadership of these groups, and the ordained clergy in particular. As the visible representatives of an organization or congregation, these leaders can take the dialogue into the public sphere. The following article describes clergy efforts to combat extremism by working together.

> *The Christian Century*
> "Interfaith Clergy Group in Montana Counters Neo-Nazi Hate,"
> by Kimberly Winston
> May 15, 2018
>
> A clergy group formed supporting a rabbi in the ski resort town of Whitefish, where white supremacist groups targeted her and other local Jewish people.
> What do you do when anti-Semites, stirred up by a guy you see at the local coffee shop and the gym, send you doctored pictures of your child's face beneath the gates of Auschwitz? When they clog your phone lines with threats to "finish the job" for Hitler and gas you? When they promise to send an army of anti-Semites marching through your town?
> If you live in the small ski resort town of Whitefish, Montana—where neo-Nazi Richard Spencer, who has been called "a kind of professional racist in khakis," has put down roots—you fight back. But rather than match the haters slur for slur, you organize a kind of party for peace, one that draws on the faith traditions present across the Flathead Valley of northwestern Montana.

REGIONAL INTERFAITH ORGANIZATIONS

Regional interfaith groups that are both effective and sustainable are often registered as nonprofit organizations. One example of these organizations is the Interfaith Conference of Greater Milwaukee. Founded in 1970, this nonprofit organization involves eighteen member faiths and denominations, and also works with several nonmember faiths. Its mission is stated as "As the United States has become increasingly religiously diverse, we have been at the forefront of efforts to counter misunderstanding, fear, anxiety and hate while fostering interfaith, intercultural, and interracial understanding, tolerance and friendships across county and city-suburban lines."

INTERFAITH DIALOGUE—CASE STUDY

A key initiative of this interfaith nonprofit that can serve as a model for others is its Interfaith Restorative Practices Coalition which provides a forum for sharing and collaboration by representatives of eight agencies and institutions that use principle-driven restorative practices to heal individuals and communities affected by crimes and other harmful acts. The coalition emphasizes skills that offset hate and violence.

Restorative practices are listening and communication skills that honor the dignity of each individual. These practices can be used with adults, youth, and children to prevent and manage conflict and to heal broken relationships that have been hurt by conflict.

Restorative Practices address the heart of the issue—our way of thinking. People are coming to recognize restorative practices as ways to form trusting relationships, build community, and manage conflict.

By punishing and ostracizing, societies the world over practice violence as a way of combatting violence. It is not effective. Yet the belief that this is how we must treat wrongdoing is pervasive—not only in our criminal justice systems, but also in our homes, schools, churches, and community at large.

RELIGION IN THE WORKPLACE

Religious expression can be an emotional and divisive issue in the workplace. While some incidents are purposeful and end up in the legal sphere, many incidents are not intended to inflict pain. What can be done to avoid a hostile and offensive workplace when so many conflicts over religion are begun unintentionally? The bias is labeled "unconscious" when people have no cognizance of it, think it's harmless, and even fun, to joke about Jews and money, Muslims and head scarves, Sikhs and turbans. They're surprised when people feel harassed. They might feel it is their right to exercise their freedom of expression.

Some respond to the problem by insisting that no religious expression be allowed at all. Others consider that approach hostile and offensive to people of faith. How does begin to negotiate between such opposites? The first step is for organizations to develop written policies around religion. Without a written policy, every incident can become a matter of debate and personal preference. It doesn't take long for the resulting distrust and dislike to damage team cohesiveness.

Timing is everything. Well-meaning companies may find employees disengaged and distanced by ill-timed scheduling decisions. Simple steps include not holding a conference or essential meetings on a major holy day. And if you must, don't penalize those who can't attend. What happens when religious calendars aren't respected? If employees aren't able to spend time with their families on major holy days, they may feel undervalued and leave. The organization's talent pool is diminished and it incurs the expense of replenishing it.

Consider your partners and vendors, too. For example: Don't have a job fair on a day when diverse vendors can't set up booths. If vendors aren't able to observe their holy days, they may disappear. In that case, the organization not only loses needed vendors, but the communities that these vendors represent may remove themselves as customers. The organization now has fewer marketing options.[4]

RECOMMENDATIONS

Scheduling Strategies

A vital element of your company, organization, or school policy should be a multifaith calendar. Religious calendars vary with seasons, months, and days. Do not try to guess the dates of major holidays. Purchase a multi-cultural calendar or get an online version, many of which are free to users.

While we may not share the same holy days, and many of us aren't religious, respect for sacred time makes good business sense. Avoid insensitive scheduling and build credibility with employees, vendors, and customers onsite and online. Sensitivity generates good will year round. The trustworthiness you establish helps offset unintended mistakes.

School Strategies

Given the impressionability of young students, educating them to avoid hate based on religion is an essential element of any interfaith coalition's goals. Such a coalition can assist with (1) district policies, (2) teacher training, and (3) community feedback. Consider the following advice of Dr. Charles Haynes, formerly of the First Amendment Center/Vanderbilt University:

> If the school board appoints a task force, then representatives of the various leading faith traditions (and those with no "established" tradition) can be appointed without a theological ruling on what is and is not a religion. Then, various public forums can be an opportunity for others to have a voice. Members of various faith traditions can gather together to advise the school district on the role of religion in the schools. This is a helpful and useful step. However, the minefield of religion in schools may be best negotiated by a committee or task force that is appointed by the school district itself. (American Diversity Report 2013)

The political debate surrounding religion and the schools presents educators with many complex scenarios. The legal status of these issues is constantly changing and educators should seek legal counsel, establish a district policy, and stick to it rather than be guided by isolated suggestions in various pamphlets, or cave in to outside pressure. In the process, educators should consult with religious leaders and actively include them as part of the communal policy discussion.

NOTES

1. Levine, *Religious Diversity in Our Schools*.
2. Parliament of the World's Religions, "Fostering Interfaith Understanding for a More Peaceful, Just, and Sustainable World."
3. Levine, *Religious Diversity in Our Schools*.
4. Levine, "Policies, Faith, and Calendars."

Chapter Fifteen

Conclusions

While there are numerous studies and articles, it is notoriously difficult to study domestic neo-Nazi groups. It's a struggle for researchers to gain acceptance and to stay neutral. Further, many of the groups reject outsiders and resist infiltration. "Many have adopted a terrorist cell structure, where people in one cell don't even talk to people in other cells and there's not an overall organization. They just draw on the same ideas, often ideas that are circulated through the Internet, so if one cell is discovered, it doesn't lead to other cells."[1]

Despite the challenges, we are confident that effective steps can be taken to ameliorate and reduce the effects of neo-Nazi activities.

> The most resilient societies will also be those that unleash the full potential of individuals—including women and minorities—to create and cooperate. Such societies will be moving with, rather than against, historical currents, drawing upon the ever-expanding scope of human agency and skill to shape the future. In all societies, even in the bleakest circumstances, there will be those who choose to improve the welfare, happiness, and security of others—and who will use transformative technologies to do so at scale. The opposite will be true as well—destructive forces will be empowered as never before. The central choice before governments and societies is how to blend individual, collective, and national endowments in a way that yields sustainable security, prosperity, and hope.[2]

We realize that we've laid out a broad and sweeping set of necessary actions to successfully counteract the neo-Nazi threat. These actions cover many stakeholders and forms of infrastructure and require investment of social capital. Nevertheless, given the rightward drift internationally, the United States may be faced with existential threats to our democratic system and the American Dream. As Calvin Coolidge, not known to history as a very progressive president, said, "We cannot do everything at once, but we can do something at once."[3]

More work needs to be done to evaluate the various efforts to counteract neo-Nazi activities in the United States. There are many questions as to what is effective and how long any good results last. Projects that deradicalize are much needed, but there are also questions about their efficacy. Programs targeted to specific populations and needs are both ongoing and emerging. Some have a major impact and others are in the beginning stages. We encourage the funding, study, and analyses of these programs.

While many best practices are in the emerging category, there is evidence that clusters of programs are effective.

> The groups with the best approach . . . seem to be those that partner with a broad section of civil society—educators, social workers, those in health care and police—to tackle the full range of problems someone swept up into an extremist world might face. They may need additional schooling or employment training . . . or "maybe they have some housing needs, maybe they have some unmet mental health needs," such as past trauma or substance use problems. It's a more holistic approach that he says, in the end, is far more effective and less costly than prison and packing more people into the already overcrowded U.S. criminal justice system.[4]

The neo-Nazi and extremist right-wing threat is evolving. We therefore recommend working together not only to oppose and repel them but also to create and share novel approaches. The process will lead to a revitalization of the American Dream that can unite us rather than divide us.

While the United States had tragic faults such as slavery at its founding, we've made progress in overcoming these obstacles and challenges. Unfortunately in recent years there has been backsliding in terms of opportunity and tolerance. We must recapture the spirit of progress and create an atmosphere in which the neo-Nazi and extreme right-wing threat will be unacceptable. We have seen what happens when a nation allows itself to slide into hate as a national policy and program. Do not be a bystander. We must never stop trying to be a better nation. It requires the constant attention and devotion of all people in the United States. There is a story that upon exiting the Constitutional Convention, Benjamin Franklin was approached by a group of people asking what sort of government the delegates had created. His answer was, "A republic, if you can keep it." We believe that the Republic, a democracy with freedom and justice for all, is worth keeping and improving. We may stumble but must not let ourselves be tripped up by haters and by violence.

NOTES

1. Decker and Legers, "Interview with Kathleen Blee."
2. Director of National Intelligence, "The Near Future."
3. Coolidge, *Goodreads*.
4. Westervelt, "Is There a Cure for Hate?"

Chapter Sixteen

Postscript

As we finish writing this book and it prepares to go to press, yet another right-wing extremist/white supremacist-caused tragedy has occurred. In March 2019, a gunman from Australia who may have been acting alone killed fifty or more Muslims in two mosques in New Zealand. He used a semiautomatic rifle and wore a helmet with a head camera on which he broadcast to the internet the actual murders and woundings. He had traveled widely internationally, acknowledged the neo-Nazi mass murderer of African American church members in South Carolina, and used anti-immigrant language connected to a French far-right-wing philosopher. A question naturally arises: If the New Zealand community had read our book and implemented its recommendations, could this tragedy have been avoided or ameliorated?

We believe that the material in our book would have helped. While we advocate a whole community response to neo-Nazi and extreme right-wing threats, not everything can be done at once, in the same place, or by every stakeholder. Responses differ according to the level of institutional involvement and the degree of threat, risk, and potential harm. Potential victims in soft targets within a community that is not prepared for extreme right-wing threats are at greatest risk. Complacency is not a strategy and denial is not risk assessment. While Americans regard New Zealand and Australia as very similar or almost identical, there are cultural differences. For example, after a 1996 mass shooting tragedy in Australia, the nation strengthened its gun control laws extensively. Since then, there has not been another such incident. New Zealand, on the other hand, has relatively lax gun control laws, which were exploited by the shooter in the recent tragedy.

The New Zealand stakeholders could have prepared and responded in the following ways. This list is not complete.

1. The mosques could have been hardened with defensive architecture, layered protection, and security guards. There could have been an outer perimeter fence and security portals with scanners for weapons and biometric screening. Local and New Zealand police could have been posted outside the mosques. It is difficult to avoid being a target once far-right-wing haters have identified a group and its location. One's basic identity and characteristics cannot be shed without losing one's religion and culture. Assimilation into the larger culture can be tried as a way of hiding from enemies, but as we saw in the Holocaust in Germany and German-occupied Europe, assimilated Jews were still made victims of genocide.
2. A targeted group can engage in self-defense, posting armed guards. Against a large and determined enemy, this approach probably would not do more than buy time. Against a lone shooter, it might succeed in lowering deaths and casualties greatly.
3. New Zealand security and intelligence authorities could have implemented the domestic terrorist profile we have proposed and implemented preventive action. They could have scanned for the domestic terrorist profile that includes, for U.S. purposes, some or all of the following, and could have been modified for New Zealand use:

    a. White
    b. Male
    c. Young
    d. Ex-military
    e. Protestant
    f. Short hair
    g. A record of previous run-ins with the law, often involving domestic abuse of women
    h. Emotional and psychological trouble
    i. Precarious employment situation or underemployment
    j. Possession of many guns, much ammunition, and gun accessories
    k. Relationships with far-right-wing organizations
    l. Participation on far-right-wing websites
    m. Threats of violence
    n. Hate expressed for people of color, Jews, Muslims, women, and LGBT people
    o. Internet searches for information regarding location and dates of religious services of the above list of hated people
    p. Feelings of being ostracized and marginalized
    q. Extensive reading in hate literature

r. Seeking out propaganda and literature to support his or her beliefs
s. Almost every person in his or her life in some sense knew something was boiling inside of him or her
t. A feeling of moral outrage
u. Identification with an in-group perceived to be under threat
v. Relatively minimal education, especially minimal college
w. Low socioeconomic status

We recognize that the use of such profiling can run afoul of civil liberties protections in some countries. Nevertheless, as has been made clear in a debate going on since the founding of the United States, the Constitution is not a suicide pact. As we have noted elsewhere in this book, when a potential malefactor threatens or incites violence, shows his or her intent on social media, and acquires the means to carry out violence, he or she removes him- or herself from many legal protections. He or she gives up his or her right to the compassion of the law.

4. Regarding use of social media by far-right-wing violent and potentially violent haters, several actions are possible and within current technological capabilities by local and international internet and media companies:

- It is possible to stop, slow down, or interrupt the posting by hateful shooters of violent videos. For example, Wall Street has instituted "circuit breakers" to stop and delay the trading of stocks in which automated trades are occurring too fast. Key words, phrases, and images can be identified and the sound of gunshots can be identified (this is already done with acoustic recording devices in some cities that identify where shootings are occurring). Note, however, that social media platforms have also removed the New Zealand shooter's seventy-five-page "manifesto" from the internet. We have mixed feelings about this effort because it means that the shooter's writings are not available for examination, lessons learned, and education.
- Facebook, Amazon, Google, Microsoft, Apple, credit card companies, credit reporting companies, and others can get together and form a team to mine big databases using artificial intelligence to identify and profile these haters and killers before they strike. The European Union has already instituted requirements on a number of these large companies. There is tension between national laws and the fact that such companies operate across international boundaries; the internet leaps over such borders. Nevertheless, companies

operate in countries via a permitting process, and local law applies. That law can be beefed up. The location of the origin of the hateful video can be found, and local police notified.
- All material posted to the internet contains metadata including the location of the computer of origin. People leave tracks on the internet, often including purchases of items later used in mass crime. Twitter is already being used to identify outbreaks of flu, and studies of social media postings have been used to identify anti-Semitism; Alexa is being used to listen for people coughing and sneezing so advertisers know where to advertise antibacterial wipes; Amazon knows what books I read; Google knows I've been looking at short cars to take advantage of small parking spaces; my credit card company knows what I like to eat, and so on. At least six developments will improve violence forecasting. They include machine-learning techniques, more information about the wider causes of conflicts and their resolution, theoretical models that better reflect the complexity of social interactions and human decision making, better pattern recognition, and artificial intelligence.

5. Communities in New Zealand could have used our book to provide education and raise community awareness of the threat by working together in a "whole of community" effort. They could have instituted, at a minimum, an "If you see something, say something" program. Right-wing mass murderers inevitably leave tracks and clues; often they boast of what they plan to do.
6. National intelligence agencies in a number of countries are already collecting data on Islamic fundamentalist terrorists. They can collect such information on right-wing terrorists and potential terrorists and share such information with other countries. New Zealand is already part of the "Five Eyes" system of intelligence sharing among the United States, the United Kingdom, Canada, Australia, and New Zealand. Unfortunately such information sharing does not always work. For example, the Russia Foreign Intelligence Service (FSB) shared information with the U.S. FBI about the individuals who became the Boston Marathon bombers in 2013. The FBI did not follow up adequately, claiming that they were overwhelmed with reports from the FSB and did not have the staff power to surveille all the names individuals.
7. Gun control laws can be stiffened in advance of mass shootings. For special recommendations, see the paper on reducing gun violence in the United States, by one of our authors, Marc Brenman.[1]
8. Deterrence is possible through surveillance cameras and facial recognition software. Police car, street, and highway cameras that read car

license plates are in use. In the United States, "red light" cameras are already recording such information. Once again, the technology can be put to better use to deter and prevent right-wing terrorism. The Chinese are making extensive use of facial recognition.
9. Greater scrutiny of those arriving in a country from another country (in this case to New Zealand from Australia) can be instituted. A model is Israel's program of intense interviewing of non-Israelis who arrive in Israel. During the period of questioning, a simple internet search of the person can be conducted.
10. Law enforcement officials can conduct "wellness visits" to the residences of those who draw suspicion. If necessary, a variety of laws can be used to hold suspects until further information is discovered. Law enforcement, even in such advanced countries as the United States, often holds people in custody on relatively trivial charges, such as broken car tail lights. The law enforcement system must become oriented to real risks through extensive risk assessment programs. Those who have lots of guns and ammunition have the means to commit multiple murders very quickly. Predictive policing is already being used to identify likely spots for crime to occur. "Soft targets" like mosques can be identified. The city of San Francisco, California, already zones every neighborhood for risk from fire and dispatches the right amount of and number of pieces of equipment to each location.

These acts are not random but show patterns. The concept of the "lone wolf" is not particularly useful in today's interconnected world in which people can be influenced by people and groups they've never met, except online. John Cohen, a former senior official in the U.S. Department of Homeland Security, now a professor at Rutgers University, has said, "We know what the problem is, but every time there's another one of these attacks all we hear is, 'Oh, this is shocking, this is horrible, our prayers are with the people, who would have imagined this ever would have happened?' No, it's very imaginable because it's happening on a regular basis in this country. We're just not doing enough to stop it."[2]

NOTES

1. Brenman, "A Plan for Reducing Gun Violence in the US."
2. Thompson, "An Atomwaffen Member Sketched Map to Take the Neo-Nazis Down. What Path Officials Took Is a Mystery."

Glossary

14/88 = Common white supremacist code. 14 stands for the "14 words" slogan coined by David Lane, who is serving a 190-year sentence for his part in the assassination of a Jewish talk show host: "We must secure the existence of our people and a future for white children." 88 means "Heil Hitler," as H is the eighth letter of the alphabet.

28 = Shorthand for Blood and Honor, a skinhead group.

4chan = The internet's notoriously anarchic image board.

Act for America = A controversial group that urges legislators to pass bills banning Islamic sharia law in the U.S. Act for America, says its goal is to "protect and preserve American culture and to keep this nation safe," and has been labeled a "hate group" by the Southern Poverty Law Center.

action pathways = Also known as action scripts and refers to the process of engaging in terrorism or violent extremist actions.

active citizenship = "Active citizenship stands for an active participation of citizens in the economic, social, cultural and political fields of life. In the youth field much emphasis is on learning the necessary competences through voluntary activities. The aim is not only to improve the knowledge, but also motivation, skills and practical experience to be an active citizen."[1]

Agenda 21 = The Agenda 21 conspiracy claims that a UN document promoting sustainability and planning crafted in 1992 is a sinister plot to subvert property rights and enslave Americans. Planning efforts, especially public meetings, are being opposed, disrupted, and even taken over by groups who allege that planning agencies are following "Agenda 21" and taking away their freedom and liberty. Agenda 21 people have succeeded in tabling numerous projects with tactics described by someone who experienced them in the San Francisco Bay Area as "show[ing] up and intimidate[ing] people by filming their public comment and then posting it online, being the loudest in the room, stacking public comment, having the largest signs, disrupting others' comments."[2]

"America First" = President Trump announced during his campaign that this "will be the major and overriding theme of my administration." It is a phrase he has deployed repeatedly and to great effect. But seventy-seven years ago, "America First" had another distinctive meaning: it was the name of the organization formed to prevent the United States from entering World War II and battling the Nazis. One of the America First Committee's chief financiers was William Regnery's grandfather and namesake, the first William Regnery, who was born on a farm in Iowa and became a textile magnate, banker, and philanthropist in Chicago. The face of the original America First movement was Charles Lindbergh, better known for making the first nonstop solo flight across the Atlantic Ocean in 1927, who earned a reputation as an anti-Semite. "Our bond with Europe is a bond of race and not of political ideology," he said in a 1941 address.

antifa = Short for "antifascist action," with modern origins in the 1970s continental Europe and the United Kingdom, it emerged as a radical response to the neo-Nazi infiltration of sporting clubs and the underground music scene. Antifa involves more than just stated political opposition to antifascism: it is a radical reconceptualization of anti-fascist resistance that includes a critique of capitalism and aims for its total obliteration, along with the hierarchies and oppressions it engenders. The basic premise of antifa is to deny the political platform to all expressions of fascism and neo-Nazism. The wrongful assumption that "violence" stands alone as an antifa tactic underscores liberal critiques of antifa but is generally blind to the "construction" work performed by the broad band of communists, socialists, and anarchists. Their work allegedly includes mass mobilization, base building, reconstruction of the commons, critical pedagogy in education and training, and collective action. These are lynchpins of twenty-first-century resistance to fascism.

anti-Indian movement = This movement seeks to eradicate the treaty rights guaranteed to American Indians and uses tactics that amplify discrimination and bigotry toward American Indian community members. It seeks to deny legally established rights to American Indians by terminating treaty rights and tribal sovereignty while also erasing Indian culture in favor of white

European culture. See also anti-sovereignty movement. Another such group is the Citizens Equal Rights Alliance.

antisemitism = The Committee on Antisemitism and Holocaust Denial called the IHRA (International Holocaust Remembrance Commission) Plenary met in Budapest in 2015 to adopt the following working definition of antisemitism. The nonlegally binding working definition of antisemitism was done in the spirit of the Stockholm Declaration that states: "With humanity still scarred by . . . antisemitism and xenophobia the international community shares a solemn responsibility to fight those evils." "AntiSemitism is a certain perception of Jews, which may be expressed as hatred toward Jews. Rhetorical and physical manifestations of antisemitism are directed toward Jewish or non-Jewish individuals and/or their property, toward Jewish community institutions and religious facilities."[3]

anti-sovereignty movement = Organized anti-Indian movement dedicated to the termination of tribal governments and abrogation of the treaty-protected rights of indigenous peoples. Rather than seeking to resolve differences with tribes through tribal courts or respectful government to government relationships, anti-Indian groups seek to resolve issues by overturning tribal rights. This movement harkens back to periods such as conquest, removal, and termination in their opposition to tribal rights and the rhetoric they employ.

Atomwaffen Division = The Atomwaffen Division ("Atomwaffen" meaning "atomic weapons" in German) is a neo-Nazi terrorist organization based in the United States. Founded in 2013, the group's main base of operations is in Florida, but it has members in other states such as Texas and Montana. The group is part of the alt-right but is considered extreme even within that movement. Atomwaffen encourages members to burn the U.S. flag and Constitution and to attack the U.S. government and minorities. The group's membership is mostly young, and the Atomwaffen Division has been active on university campuses with recruitment postering.[4] The group promotes terrorist tactics and at least five murders were associated with them in 2018.

bias crime indicator = Objective facts, circumstances, or patterns attending a criminal act(s) that, standing alone or in conjunction with other facts or circumstances, suggest that the offender's actions were motivated, in whole or in part, by any form of bias.[5]

Blood and Soil = Video taken at the white supremacist rally in Charlottesville showed marchers chanting "blood and soil." The phrase is a nineteenth-century German nationalist term that connotes a mystical bond between the blood of an ethnic group and the soil of their country. It was used as a Nazi slogan in Germany during the 1930s and 1940s and since then has been used by neo-Nazi groups and other white supremacists around the world. It is one of several Nazi slogans that have been adopted by some members of the alt-right.

Christian Identity (CI) = A racist pseudo-theology that regards Jews as the literal descendants of Satan and nonwhites as nonhuman. CI adherents reject traditional Christianity as overly influenced by Jews, and they tend to be atheist or follow precepts of Odinism, occultism, or paganism.

Church of the Creator = An extremist quasi-Christian church with white supremacist beliefs.

coded messages = See also "dog whistle." For example, fears associated with "asylum seeking" become coded means of articulating anxieties about more diffuse "threats" and fears about economic competition and cultural pollution that may have heightened since 9/11.

codewords to avoid public detection = A 2016 4chan post detailed how minority groups are made into verbal targets: Alongside the codeword for Jews ("skypes"), African Americans become "googles," Mexicans are "yahoos," Muslims are "skittles," and liberals become "car salesmen" or "snowflakes." See also "dog whistle."

community cohesion = Community cohesion is what must happen in all communities to enable different groups of people to get on well together. A key contributor to community cohesion is integration, which is what must happen to enable new residents and existing residents to adjust to one another. This is based on three foundations: (1) people from different backgrounds having similar life opportunities; (2) people knowing their rights and responsibilities; and (3) people trusting one another and trusting local institutions to act fairly. This is also based on three key ways of living together: (1) a shared future vision and sense of belonging; (2) a focus on what new and existing communities have in common, alongside a recognition of the value of diversity; and (3) strong and positive relationships between people from different backgrounds.[6]

constitutionalists = Constitutionalists profess to be anti-government and anti-taxes rather than racist and anti-Semitic, like the Aryan Nations groups and skinheads. But many constitutionalists also belong to hate groups. Echoing their philosophy, as one told a reporter on television, "Jews are the children of Satan."[7]

constitutional sheriffs = The refusal of law enforcement officers to enforce the new gun control restrictions in Washington State plays into a longer history of so-called constitutional sheriffs resisting the gradual tightening of gun laws. There are also hints of the doctrine of "county supremacy," long nursed on the constitutionalist far right, that hold that county sheriffs are the highest constitutional authority in the country. Such notions have long been promoted by figures like Sheriff Richard Mack, who leads the Constitutional Sheriffs and Peace Officers Association. As gun laws throughout the West have gradually tightened in recent decades, resistance along these lines has become prevalent in areas with strong political support for gun rights.

coordination = A perversion of the normal use of the word by far right-wing extremists. Right-wing activists claim that "coordination" is how Montanans can overrule federal land-use policies and jumpstart local economies. Its supporters claim federal law allows county governments to force federal agencies to implement local directives. They stress the supposed ability of the county commission to control all the land within its boundaries and to ignore environmental regulation in favor of extractive industry. Other times they focus on claims that the county sheriff is charged with keeping federal agencies from enforcing tax, firearms, environmental, and other laws. Frequently, activists promote both versions of county supremacy at the same time. The basic idea is that county governments can adopt plans that contradict federal policy (that is, more logging in national forests or killing more wolves than allowed under the law). With this local plan in hand, according to "coordination" proponents, the county can force federal agencies to come to the table and "coordinate" on achieving the county's objectives. Proponents frequently claim their version of "coordination" is mandated by federal law.

cuckservative = Richard Spencer popularized the term "cuckservative," which has gained currency in the alt-right vernacular. In essence, a cuckservative is a conservative sellout who is first and foremost concerned about abstract principles such as the U.S. Constitution, free market economics, and individual liberty.

echo = Coincidence Detector, the Google Chrome internet browser extension, enclosed names that its algorithm deemed Jewish in triple parentheses, a symbol that allows white nationalists and neo-Nazis to more easily aim their anti-Semitic vitriol. It has been removed from the Chrome Web Store by Google, citing violation of its hate speech policy, which forbids "promotions of hate or incitement of violence." At least two far right-wing social media sites, The Right Stuff and its affiliated podcast The Daily Shoah, starting in 2014 used the symbol. On the blog and podcast, Jewish-sounding names received the sound effect of an echo, which then translated to a parenthesis in print as a visual pun. The echo has now emerged as a weapon in the arsenal of the alt-right, an amorphous conservative movement living primarily online. Some use the symbol to mock Jews and others seek to expose supposed Jewish collusion in controlling media or politics.

dog whistle = Coded race baiting used by Republican politicians and members of extreme right-wing groups to win elections and shape public policy debates. The hissing of the dog whistle, audible only to some, is a metaphor for the sophisticated and veiled racial appeals—about "illegal aliens," states rights, sharia law, personal responsibility—that trigger hostility against non-whites in many white Americans.

extremism = Extremism refers to political ideologies that oppose a positive society's core values and principles. In the context of liberal democracies this could be applied to any ideology that advocates racial or religious supremacy and/or opposes the core principles of democracy and human rights. The term can also be used to describe the methods through which political actors attempt to realize their aims, that is, by using means that show disregard for the life, liberty, and human rights of others.

freedom of speech = A right protected by the U.S. Constitution. It is not absolute. "Free speech" protections only apply to the actions of governmental bodies. The alt-right (neo-Nazis) have lately been appropriating the term "free speech." Limits on free speech include defamation, libel, slander, false advertising, incitement to violence, "shouting fire in a crowded theater," hate speech, using speech to harass, and speaking against the interests of one's employer. Government employees enjoy relatively little freedom of speech. A very clear First Amendment principle says that speech cannot be censored simply because listeners are offended by it.

Fully Informed Jury Association (FIJA) = FIJA has been part of the "patriot" movement for years. It claims that a jury has the right to "judge both the law and the evidence in the case before it," a tactic known as jury nullification. In essence, FIJA encourages juries to ignore laws they don't like and set defendants free regardless of evidence and rules to the contrary.

Gab = Gab is a website that acts as a forum for racism, white supremacy, and other forms of hate. Gab has since pledged to prevent incitement to violence on its platform, but failed to do so. The site features many posts and comments promoting the murder of Jewish , black, Latino, indigenous, Arab, and LGBTQ people, violence toward immigrants and political opponents, and rape against women.

Genocide = The definition of "genocide" as specified by the Convention on the Prevention and Punishment of the Crime of Genocide, adopted by the United Nations in 1948, and ratified by the United States in 1988, is as follows: Any of the following acts committed with the intent to destroy, in whole or in part, a national, ethnical, racial, or religious group, such as: (a) killing members of the group; (b) causing serious bodily or mental harm to members of the group; (c) deliberately inflicting on the group conditions of life calculated to bring about its physical destruction in whole or in part; (d) imposing measures intended to prevent births within the group; and (e) forcibly transferring children of the group to another group.

Goyim Defense League (GDL) = Using the Hebrew word for non-Jews, BuzzFeed News first reported this far right-wing organization. It is a play on the ADL, or Anti-Defamation League, a Jewish anti-discrimination organization.

GTKRWN = Stands for "gas the kikes, race war now."

Hammerskins = A nationwide skinhead syndicate, also known as Hammerskin Nation, with regional factions and chapters that once dominated skin-subculture nationwide. Confederate Hammerskins is the southern faction of Hammerskin Nation.

Hashtags like #tgsnt or "the greatest story never told" = Code for "Hitler was right."

identitarianism = Relating to or supporting the political interests of a particular racial, ethnic, or national group, typically one composed of Europeans or white people. Central to identitarianism is the rejection of liberal multiculturalism and the promotion instead of "ethnopluralism": the idea that different ethnic groups are equal but ought to live in separation from one another.

impulsive hate offenses = Committed by perpetrators who are looking for excitement. In the same way that some young men get together on a Saturday night to play a game of cards, youthful hatemongers gather to shout threats and obscenities, destroy property, or assault someone who is different. They look merely to have some fun and stir up a little excitement but at someone else's expense. In an impulsive thrill-seeking hate episode, there need not be a precipitating incident. The victim does not necessarily "invade" the territory of the assailant by walking across his or her campus or attending classes. On the contrary, it is the assailant or group of assailants, looking to harass those who are different, who searches out locations where the members of a particular group regularly congregate. The payoff for the perpetrators is psychological as well as social: in addition to gaining a sense of importance and control, the youthful perpetrators also receive a stamp of approval from their friends who regard hatred as "hip" or "cool." In impulsive thrill-motivated hate episodes, a group of young people typically travels to another area to find victims. Thus thrill-seekers might travel to a gay bar in the local community or target students at another college as something to do for fun when they are bored on a Saturday night.

incel rebellion = Some right-wing terrorists are "incel," or "involuntarily celibate." They claim to want relationships with women but can't, don't, or won't. They claim it's because of something wrong with women.

inclusivity = The conscious decision to create a nurturing climate in which similarities and differences are respected and supported by assuring the active, full participation of the entire community. Such inclusion increases our organizational capacity to create and deliver meaningful and relevant professional work.

intervention options = Include alternative pathways or "off-ramps" for individuals who appear to be moving toward violent action but who have not yet engaged in criminal activity.

Islamophobia = Prejudice against Muslims.

John Birch Society = Founded in 1958, the John Birch Society fought the perceived infiltration of communists in American society, even calling Dwight Eisenhower an "agent of the Communist conspiracy." Promoting an extreme right-wing ideology, the group vigorously opposed the Civil Rights Movement of the 1960s, claiming it was an effort to create a "Negro Soviet Republic" in the United States. The Birch Society was also a close ally of the segregationist Alabama governor George Wallace. As the Cold War subsided, the Birch Society took aim at the United Nations and became a purveyor of one-world government conspiracy theories, in addition to promoting Christian fundamentalism and the abolishment of numerous federal agencies.

leaderless resistance = A lone wolf operation in which an individual, or a very small, highly cohesive group, engages in acts of anti-state violence independent of any movement, leader, or network of support. This tactic makes it more difficult for law enforcement to detect potential threats because the small number of individuals involved and their isolation from organized entities allow them to "fly under the radar." "Lone wolf" is a similar term.

League of the South = A neo-Confederate hate group that advocates for the secession of Southern states, an ideology it refers to as Southern nationalism.[8]

militia movement = The militia movement is an anti-government extremist movement. It's part of a broader movement that's sometimes called the patriot movement, which also includes the sovereign citizen movement and the tax protest movement. The foundational belief of the militia movement is an anti-government conspiracy theory that posits that the rest of the world has essentially been taken over by a globalist tyrannical government. They often refer to it as the New World Order.

Minutemen = The Minutemen did not originate the dangerous spectacle of armed civilians taking the law into their own hands to keep immigrants at bay. The Knights of the Ku Klux Klan hatched the idea more than a quarter-century ago. Launched in 1977, the "Klan Border Watch" claimed to stretch from Texas to California and was part of the "battle to halt the flow of illegal aliens streaming across the border from Mexico." In shape, form, composition, and ideology, the Minutemen are also a mirror image of the militia groups of the mid-1990s, which left a legacy of violence, criminal plots, and domestic terrorism across the country. A number of Minutemen leaders are veterans of those militia, including the head of the Alabama Minutemen Support Team. While Minutemen leaders speak patriotically of enforcing law and order and deny racism and violence, their actions and words betray them. Their very existence is a stick in the eye of state laws that prohibit paramilitary activity. In 2004 Minuteman founder Chris Simcox was convicted of carrying a concealed weapon on federal land in his hunt for undocumented immigrants and then lying to a federal officer about it. James Gilchrist, the retired accountant who helped put Minutemen on the map, spoke last spring of building "an army-sized operation" by this fall and has publicly declared that he was "damn proud to be a vigilante." Gilchrist is fluent in the language of la reconquista outlandish conspiracy theories linking immigration with a plot to reclaim the southwestern United States for Mexico. Members of white nationalist groups like the neo-Nazi National Alliance and the Council of Conservative Citizens have participated in Arizona Minutemen maneuvers.

misogyny = Dislike, fear of, prejudice, and bias against women. Most commonly manifests in the United States as taking away basic health rights from women.

mud people = A negative term used by white supremacists for people of color and by the Nation of Islam for Jews.

multiculturalism = An approach to race and ethnic relations in society and education that explicitly acknowledges differences among groups and promotes the notion that differences associated with social identities should be valued.

National Socialist Movement (NSM) = "The organization is open about equating National Socialism with Nazism, as well as attributing its ideology to that of Adolf Hitler. One of the largest and most prominent neo-Nazi groups in the United States. It calls for the development of a nation made up of 'only those of pure white blood,' in which 'no Jew or homosexual may be a member of the nation.' The National Socialist Movement demands 'that all non-whites currently living in America' be forced to leave the country."[9]

neo-Confederates = White nationalist groups specifically in the U.S. Southeast. While the groups vary in mission and membership, neo-Confederates have a similar agenda that combines white supremacy, Christian dominance, an emphasis on traditional gender roles, and a view that justifies and affirms the Confederacy's role in the War between the States (Civil War). For that reason, they support the use of the Confederate flag and statues of Confederate heroes in public spaces.

New Anti-Semitism = Jews are targeted as Israel's agents or as payback for the Jewish state's perceived abuses. The main and possibly most troubling distinction of the latest new anti-Semitism is how it cuts across major religious and ideological differences among its propagators, uniting unlikely bedfellows such as neo-Nazis, communists, and jihadists under a single cause.

New Code of the West = An anti-Indian movement that seeks to eradicate the treaty rights guaranteed to Native Americans and uses tactics that amplify discrimination and bigotry toward American Indian community members. The movement believes that communists and the Muslim Brotherhood have conspired to establish a shadow government called the "counter state" using "Maoist insurgency doctrine." It believes that a shadowy Deep State is adversely affecting the western United States, trying to implement a one-world government that will enslave Americans. These theories trace back to the militia movement of the 1990s. Many of these militia conspiracies are modified only slightly from the anti-Semitic versions used by the white supremacist movement. The New Code of the West supporters held a conference in Whitefish, Montana, in 2018.

Oath Keepers = This group of anti-government "patriots" wants law enforcement officers and military personnel to sign onto their oath, which encapsulates many of the ideas promoted by the "patriot" movement's one-world government conspiracy theories. The organization frames itself as wanting to remind law officers and active duty soldiers that they swore an oath to defend the "Constitution against all enemies, foreign and domestic, so help us God." It asks active personnel to sign an oath to not follow "unconstitutional (and thus illegal) and immoral" orders that are "acts of war against the American people."[10] The oath encapsulates many of the one-world government conspiracy theories that undergird the "patriot" movement. These theories claim America will be invaded by troops acting on behalf of various international cabals and/or the federal government. In these theories, martial law is declared and Americans are rounded up and put in detention camps. Anti-government "patriots" believe they alone understand the truth about these upcoming developments, and it will be up to them to fight off this "New World Order" attack. Oath Keepers wants law officers and military personnel to stand on the frontlines with "patriots" for this battle. The group's oath is a "Declaration of Orders We Will NOT Obey." This includes not following orders to disarm citizens, place citizens in detention camps, or assist foreign troops on American soil.

Odinism = A neo-pagan religion that revives a pre-Christian pantheon of Norse gods and their leader, Odin. A legal religion in Norway, it is becoming popular among young urban white males as "Asatrú." While it may clash with the Christian beliefs held by extremist groups, a racist version of it appeals to some white supremacists because it mythologizes the virtues of early northern European whites as the tribe, or *folk*, strongly emphasizing genetic closeness. It credits whites with building civilization and an ethic of individual responsibility.[11]

Patriot Movement = A set of related extremist movements and groups in the United States whose ideologies center on anti-government conspiracy theories.

Posse Comitatus = An anti-Semitic white supremacist group that sprang up in the 1970s. Latin for "power of the county," the Posse Comitatus was founded in 1971 by retired army lieutenant colonel William Potter Gale. Gale "believed that all white, Christian men had an unconditional right to take up arms to enforce the principles of a 'Constitutional Republic,' and challenge various 'unlawful acts' of the federal government, including integration, taxation and the federal reserve banking system," according to Daniel Levitas.[12] Posse believers, like many white supremacists, maintain that the federal and state governments of the United States have been taken over by a worldwide

Jewish conspiracy, or "ZOG": the Zionist Occupation Government. The Posse views the sheriff as the highest legitimate law officer in the land. It believes citizens are not subject to state or federal authorities. The Posse was first organized in 1969 by Henry Beach, formerly of the Silver Shirts, a pro-Nazi U.S. group that operated in the 1930s. The Posse operates mostly in the Midwest and Western United States and has more recently spawned a number of anti-tax organizations in their region. Posse members have committed robberies and murders and issued numerous death threats. As an Identity organization, they are violently anti-Semitic.

premeditated hate episode = Those who engage in these are convinced that all out-group members are subhumans who are bent on destroying *our* culture, *our* economy, or the purity of *our* racial heritage. The offender therefore is concerned about much more than simply eliminating a few African Americans or Hispanics from his or her college or university. Instead he or she believes that he or she has a higher-order purpose in carrying out his or her crime. He or she has been instructed by God or, in a more secular version, by the Imperial Wizard or the Grand Dragon to rid the world of evil by eliminating *all* African Americans, Hispanics, Asians, or Jews, and he or she is compelled to act before it is too late. Premeditated mission hate offenders are likely to join an organized group such as the KKK, World Church of the Creator, or the White Aryan Resistance. The mission motivation is likely to result in the commission of a vicious, even deadly, hate crime. [13]

Proud Boys = The Proud Boys, founded by Gavin McInnes, are a right-wing "fraternity" who present themselves as proponents of mainstream conservative values but engage in extreme, often violent tactics to promote their agenda. Like conventional street gangs, many of the characteristics used by scholars and law enforcement to identify a member of the Proud Boys are used to identify members of a street gang. Members are initiated with violent rituals . They routinely gather to socialize in spaces guarded from outsiders. Members are encouraged to engage in criminal acts of violence.

racialism, race realism = "Racialism is the idea that humanity can be easily divided into well-defined categories ('races') that are both broad (each category should include many humans, such as entire continents) and clearly defined (the categorization method should rarely misidentify someone's 'race'). Racialism implies that these races are substantially different from each other and that these racial differences strongly determine the abilities and behavior of individuals and peoples. Essentially, racialism argues that human populations are substantially different from each other to a degree which necessitates biological classification below the species level. In short, racialism holds that biology divides humans. Very few racialists call themselves 'racialist.' Their preferred labels include scientific racism (pre–2000), race realism or racial realism (post–2000), and human bio-diversity or HBD (post–2010)."[14] These ideas are used by far right-wing groups to ascribe inferiority to people of color, and blame untoward social events on them.

radicalization = Refers to the process of developing extremist ideologies and beliefs.

RAHOWA = Short for "Racial Holy War," a slogan that originally came out of the neo-Nazi Church of the Creator; also the name of a defunct band.

reactive hate episodes = The hatemongers seize on what they consider a triggering incident to justify their expression of anger. They rationalize that by attacking someone they regard as an outsider they are in fact protecting their college, residence hall, fraternity, or group of friends. Indeed, they often cast their victims in the role of those actively threatening them, while they regard themselves as pillars of virtue on their campus. Moreover, the perpetrators of reactive hate episodes tend to target a particular individual or set of individuals who are perceived to constitute a personal threat—the African American student who has just moved into a previously all-Caucasian dormitory, the Caucasian college student who has begun to date her Asian classmate, or the Hispanic professor who introduces her students to a Hispanic American perspective. The reactive attack is meant to send a signal not only to the primary victim but also to every member of the victim's group: "you and others from your group do not belong on this campus."[15]

reconquista = The theory that the American Southwest belongs to Mexico. "Reconquista" is a term associated with El Plan Espiritual de Aztlán, the founding document of the Movimiento Estudiantil Chicano de Aztlán (Chicano Student Movement of Aztlán, or MEChA), a group with affiliates at numerous college campuses and several high schools that claims to work toward "improving the social and political situation of the Chicano/Latino community." Critics claim that El Plan Espiritual de Aztlán outlines a plan of recapturing the southwestern United States for Mexico. But Aztlán and reconquista are concepts promoted by "white supremacists and neo-Nazis" more than by Mexicans or Mexican Americans. The myth of reconquista stems from a misreading of one of the founding documents of the Chicano movement, "El Plan Espiritual de Aztlán."

red pill = The name is a reference to *The Matrix* and is used frequently by the white supremacist alt-right to indicate that its followers are the only ones who "know the truth" about what is really going on in America today.

Respect Washington = A statewide organization that the Southern Poverty Law Center has also labeled an anti-immigrant hate group that circulated a flyer with the names and addresses of alleged undocumented immigrants and the alleged crimes they had committed. Craig Keller, a Republican who ran for Congress last year against U.S. Rep. Pramila Jayapal (D-Washington), founded the group. At the time, Keller was attempting to repeal the so-called sanctuary status of both Burien and Spokane by putting measures to roll back the cities' sanctuary status on their respective November ballots. His effort ultimately failed.

right-wing = The more intellectually rigid, uncompromising, and sometimes intolerant division of conservative political thought expressed in political parties or as movements opposed to socialism and communism, dogmatically committed to narrow interpretations of American political history, proponent of or at least sympathetic with ideas of social Darwinism, and intent on radically altering social, economic, and political institutions to reflect these views, achieved through forced change or political change.

right-wing extremism = Can be defined as the various movements that either by tradition, patriotism, nationalism, fascism, or adhesion to a counter-revolutionary ideology are hostile to both the socialist and liberal conceptions of society. Right-wing extremism encompasses a large, loose, heterogeneous collection of groups and individuals espousing a wide range of grievances and positions; these groups can sometimes be in conflict with each other. In general, members of extreme right groups are proud of the ideology behind their movement and tend to keep a high profile.

right-wing libertarian anarchist community = These anarchists blatantly oppose democracy, labeling America's system of government as: "unconstitutional totalitarian cults of parasites, criminals, and terrorists—opposed to liberty, freedom, self-determination, sovereignty, and nature—that pretend to be some form of unanimously elected majority in order to tax, rob, indebt, and enslave the individuals of a society through denying and usurping their life, liberty, property, and natural rights."[16]

Bitcoin is much liked by these anarchists because they believe that they can bypass the normal monetary system.

Rise Above Movement (RAM) = A far right-wing, violent, white supremacist group that was active in Charlottesville, with origins in California. "RAM operates like an alt-right street-fighting club," said Oren Segal, director of the Anti-Defamation League's Center on Extremism. For public events, RAM has developed its own menacing signature look, with members often wearing skull masks and goggles to ward off pepper spray. At times,

RAM fighters have tied American flag bandanas around their faces to conceal their identities. The group portrays itself as a defense force for a Western civilization under assault by Jews, Muslims, and brown-skinned immigrants. The RAM logo features a medieval sword with a cross on the pommel—a symbol of the crusades—and an evergreen tree. On T-shirts they wear while training, the logo appears above three words, "courage, identity, virtue." At rallies, members have waved red-and-white crusader flags and carried signs saying "Rapefugees Not Welcome" and "Da Goyim Know," an anti-Semitic slogan meant to highlight a supposed conspiracy by Jews to control the globe and subjugate non-Jews. One RAM banner, which depicts knights on horseback chasing after Muslims, reads "Islamists Out!"

"Shrinky Dinks" = Being used by neo-Nazis as a substitute phrase for "Jewish people"—another example of how the most innocent-looking language can be co-opted as an anti-Semitic slur.

small hats = Anti-Semitic slur for yarmulkes, the head covering that observant Jewish men wear.

social desirability bias = A polling results problem. That is, some respondents may not be providing their honest opinions, given the social stigma attached to racism. This is particularly problematic if the prevalence of social desirability bias differs systematically across different groups. In this case, it is possible that wealthier and better-educated respondents were simply more likely to lie about their real attitudes.

Sovereign Citizen Movement (SCM) = Far right-wing group that "engages in harassing tactics such as filing lawsuits, false liens, and restraining orders as a method to harass government and financial institutions. This is known as 'paper terrorism.' The modern SCM has its roots in the Posse Comitatus movement and in racialist philosophies such as the Christian Identity Movement. It was primarily a movement embraced by right-wing Caucasians. Over time, the SCM has morphed from a primarily racialist platform to a more inclusive anti-government platform."[17]

strategic frames = Help far right-wing groups articulate the problems they identify and the solutions to those problems; they also help them identify their allies and their enemies. Those in charge of communication for these groups and movements intend their messages to resonate widely with those whose support they want, mobilizing these supporters to take action on behalf of the groups.

Strausserism = A form of neo-Nazism that is considered to be further left and more heavily emphasizes the socialist aspects of the fascist philosophy.

street gang = Criminal codes usually define a street gang as an ongoing group, club, or association composed of five or more individuals who participate in either a felony, simple assault, or destruction of property.

targeted harassment and violence = Any unwanted conduct, violence, harassment, or abuse directed toward a person or group because of their age, disability, gender, race, religion or belief, sexual orientation, transgender status, or a combination of these characteristics.

terrorism = The FBI defines terrorism as: "The unlawful use of force or violence against persons or property to intimidate or coerce a government, the civilian population, or any segment thereof, in furtherance of political or social objectives" committed by a group. The FBI's terrorism definition excludes important categories of crimes: excludes nonfederal (that is, state) prosecutions; excludes ideologically motivated crimes committed by lone-wolf perpetrators; excludes incidents where a group did not claim responsibility; excludes nonviolent ideologically motivated crimes; excludes non-ideological/routine crimes; and state and local municipalities that subscribe to a broader definition.

Third Position = Blends ideological principles from World War II–era German Nazism, in particular support for a white working class understood to be facing economic destruction from corporate power and monopoly capitalism and obsessive attention to purported Jewish conspiracies, with standard white supremacist philosophies that are broadly shared by a number of organized white supremacist groups in the United States today. These include Thomas Metzger's emphasis on racial separatism (an attempt to suggest that the Third Position is not a racial supremacist movement) and his insistence that white "race suicide" will be the inevitable effect of higher birth rates among non-whites than whites.[18]

Traditionalist Worker Party = "Self-described as a political party seeking to 'establish an independent white ethno-state in North America' in which immigration is 'limited to members of the White European Race,' the Traditionalist Worker Party is a relatively new group. It formed a couple of years ago under the leadership of Matt Parrott and Matthew Heimbach of Indiana after they started the Traditionalist Youth Network. At Unite the Right and other protests, members have outfitted themselves with shields, wearing masks and often all-black clothing. The group opposes capitalism and colonialism, as well as 'international Jewry,' calling instead for a 'National Socialist government, economy and society for our people,' according to its website."[19]

(((triple parentheses))) = Used by neo-Nazi groups and individuals to brand another online user as Jewish, marking them as targets for harassment.

turbokike = "Jews."

Unforgiven = The Unforgiven gang favors Nazi-styled imagery, and is listed as a hate group and prison gang by the Anti-Defamation League. It has been active in Florida with explosive devices.

USS *Liberty* = A U.S. Navy spy ship that was accidentally fired upon by Israel Defense Forces in 1967 off the coast of Israel. Israel maintains that it mistook the ship for an Egyptian one during that year's war with Egypt. Since then, extremist anti-Semites have used the incident as an accusation against Jews.

Vanguard America = Previously operating under the name American Vanguard and Reaction America. "A white supremacist group that opposes multiculturalism and believes America is an exclusively white nation, primarily targeting college-aged men in its recruitment efforts."[20]

white ethnostate = A white ethnostate is a type of state or nation proposed by far right-wing racists in which residence or citizenship would be limited to white people.

"wise use" or "multiple use" anti-environmental movement = began in the 1980s with funding and guidance from the extractive (such as oil and gas) industry, which created astroturf (false) community groups to promote the industry's agenda. While the movement's agenda is focused on opposing conservation and environmental interests, it has long intersected with the anti-Indian and militia movements, especially at the local levels. "Wise use" is code language for use by people and industry in a way that does not take environmental concerns into consideration.

xeno-racism = A form of cultural racism with "racialization" of certain ethnic and cultural groups. In these racialized constructions, stigmatized groups are presented in contradictory ways—so that they are regarded both as inferior, and potentially polluting, and also as powerful, hence a threat to the "host" or "majority" community.

youth work = "The values of youth work are: respect, dialogue approach, relation work (trust), inclusive approach, positive approach, tailor-made intervention, flexibility, voluntary based, non-formal and informal learning methodology, resource perspective (building on the young person's potential), youth advocacy."[21]

ZOG = Shorthand for Zionist Occupation (or Occupied) Government, reflecting the neo-Nazi conspiracy theory that the American government is secretly controlled by a powerful Jewish cabal. Neo-Nazis believe it works on behalf of Jewish overlords to take away the rights and guns of white, Aryan citizens.

NOTES

1. European Commission, "The Contribution of Youth Work to Preventing Marginalisation and Violent Radicalisation."
2. Solange Gould, personal communication with author, January 22, 2015.
3. International Holocaust Remembrance Alliance, "Working Definition of Anti-Semitism."
4. Wikipedia, "Atomwaffen Division."
5. Massachusetts Model Protocol for Bias Crime Investigation, "Responding to Hate Crime: A Multidisciplinary Curriculum."
6. The National Archives, "Hate Crime —The Cross-Government Action Plan."
7. Rosenblatt, "Their Finest Minute."
8. Allison, "4 Extremist Groups that Will be Part of Weekend's White Lives Matter Rallies."
9. Allison, "4 Extremist Groups that Will be Part of Weekend's White Lives Matter Rallies."
10. Neiwert, "Oath Keepers' Chief Points to Katrina Response to Justify Paranoia."
11. Southern Poverty Law Center, "New Brand of Racist Odinist Religion on the March."
12. Levitas, *The Terrorist Next Door.*
13. U.S. Department of Justice, "Community Relations Service."
14. RationalWiki, "Racialism."
15. U.S. Department of Justice, "Community Relations Service."
16. Lyons, "Rising above the Herd."
17. Bell, "The Sovereign Citizen Movement."
18. Blee, "White Supremacy as Extreme Deviance."
19. Allison, "4 Extremist Groups that Will be Part of Weekend's White Lives Matter Rallies."
20. Allison, "4 Extremist Groups that Will be Part of Weekend's White Lives Matter Rallies."
21. European Commission, "The Contribution of Youth Work to Preventing Marginalisation and Violent Radicalisation."

Resources

Active Shooter: Recommendations and Analysis for Risk Mitigation
   New York City Police Department
   Counterterrorism Bureau 2012
   The Adam and Gila Milstein Family Foundation
   16027 Ventura Boulevard, Suite 550
   Encino, CA 91436
   contact@hello.milsteinff.org

Anti-Defamation League (ADL)
   www.adl.org

Michael Lieberman, Washington Counsel
   Director, Civil Rights Policy Planning Center
   mlieberman@adl.org
   (202) 261-4607 (office)
   (202) 296-2371 (fax)

Mark Pitcavage
   National Fact-Finding Director
   ADL Regional Director
   Pacific Northwest Region
   600 Stewart Street, Suite 720
   Seattle, WA 98101
   (206) 448-5350 (office)
   (206) 448-5355 (fax)

ADL Center on Extremism Database

This database provides an overview of many of the symbols most frequently used by a variety of white supremacist groups and movements, as well as some other types of hate groups.
https://www.adl.org/education-and-resources/resource-knowledge-base/hate-symbols

Against Violent Extremism
  YouTube Channel
  https://www.youtube.com/user/AgainstVE

American Association of Colleges and Universities (AAC&U)
  A Systematic Plan to Fight Hate on Campus (2004)
  American Civil Liberties Union Briefing Paper Number 16, Hate Speech on Campus
  American Jewish Committee (AJC)
  https://www.ajc.org/

Kenneth Stern (award-winning author and the American Jewish Committee's expert on anti-Semitism and extremism)
  "Anti-Semitism Today: How It Is the Same, How It Is Different, and How to Fight It"

Steven Z. Koplin
  AJC Research Assistant
  165 East 56th Street
  New York, NY 10022
  (212) 891-6753 (phone)
  (212) 891-1495 (fax)
  koplins@ajc.org

American Psychological Association (September 15, 1999)
  "Hate Crimes: Causes, Consequences, and Current Policy: What Does Social Science Research Tell Us?"
  http://www.apa.org/ppo/pi/hatecrime.html

Anne Frank Webguide
  Learn about how to put together a really great project, talk, or photo story and how to make a website or a PowerPoint presentation.
  http://www.annefrankguide.net/en-AU/bronnenbank.asp?oid=404278

Albert Bandura
  "Selective Moral Disengagement in the Exercise of Moral Agency," *Journal of Moral Education* 31, no. 2 (2002)

https://web.stanford.edu/~kcarmel/CC_BehavChange_Course/readings/Additional%20Resources/Bandura/bandura_moraldisengagement.pdf

Building Democracy Initiative (BDI)
Center for New Community
Devin Burghart, Director
http://www.buildingdemocracy.org/
P.O. Box 479327
Chicago, IL 60647
(312) 266-0319 (office)
(312) 266-0327 (fax)

BDI gets calls from individuals looking for guidance or advice. "They want to speak to someone who has experienced some of the same problems that they're going through in their local community, and can possibly talk them through some of the different things they're dealing with." The training conducted by BDI involves a mixture of opposition research, propaganda analysis, and investigative techniques, depending on the needs and the interests of the people involved and what they're facing in their community, as well as putting it into a framework of how to look at the situation and what good research can do for them. The training has helped BDI establish a regional network of organizations that keep an ear to the ground doing local research while continuing to develop themselves organizationally.

"Responding to Hate Crimes: A Roll Call Training Video for Police Officers"
Bureau of Justice Assistance (BJA)
U.S. Department of Justice

The video has an excellent eight-minute segment on hate crime indicators. The International Association for Chiefs of Police (IACP) created a brochure to accompany the video.

For information about the video, contact the BJA at (800) 688-4252.

To order the brochure, call the National Criminal Justice Reference Service at (800) 851-3420 or download it from the IACP web site at www.theiacp.org.

Promising Practices Against Hate Crimes
Hate Crimes Series #2; No Date
Jason Carmel
Global Chief Data Officer
#WeCounterHate
A program run by the advertising agency Possible.
Seattle, Washington
https://www.possible.com/people/jason-carmel

https://wecounterhate.com/

The campaign uses A.I. to detect hate speech on Twitter before "countering" it. "Countering" involves replying to toxic messages with a tweet explaining that every time the hateful post is retweeted, a donation will be made to an organization supporting diversity and equality. The project has had success—"countered" posts see a 64 percent reduction in retweets, according to the agency.

Center for American Progress
"Curbing Hate Online: What Companies Should Do Now"
Henry Fernandez, October 2018
https://www.americanprogress.org/issues/immigration/reports/2018/10/25/459668/curbing-hate-online-companies-now/

For the article's detailed appendix on corporate policies, see https://cdn.americanprogress.org/content/uploads/2018/10/24111621/ModelInternetCompanies-appendix.pdf

Center for the Prevention of Hate Violence
Steve Wessler, Executive Director
stevew@preventinghate.org
68 High Street
Portland, ME 04101
(207) 780-4756

A group that develops curricula and conducts trainings to combat prejudice.

Charlottesville, Virginia
Final Report: Independent Review of the 2017 Protest Events in Charlottesville, Virginia
Prepared by consultants Hunton and Williams, LLP, 2017
"Common Shock: Witnessing Violence Every Day: How We Are Harmed, How We Are Healed"
Kaethe Weingarten
burghart@newcomm.org

Community Relations Service
U.S. Department of Justice
www.usdoj.gov/crs

A specialized federal conciliation service available to state and local officials to help resolve and prevent racial and ethnic conflict. CRS offers its services to governors, mayors, police chiefs, and school officials in their efforts to defuse racial crises. CRS assists local officials and residents in designing locally defined resolutions when conflict and violence threaten community stability and well-being. As directed by the Civil Rights Act of 1964, CRS conciliators use specialized crisis management and violence reduction techniques to provide assistance in identifying the sources of conflict and violence and creating a more cohesive community environment. CRS has no law enforcement authority and does not impose solutions, investigate or prosecute cases, or assign blame or fault. However, CRS conciliators are required by law to conduct their activities in confidence, without publicity, and are prohibited from disclosing confidential information.

Responding to Hate Crimes and Bias Motivated Incidents on College and University Campuses (2000)
    Community Oriented Policing Office
    U.S. Department of Justice
    https://ric-zai-inc.com/
    Response Center at (800) 421-6770
    The COPS Office publishes materials for law enforcement and community stakeholders to use in collaboratively addressing crime and disorder challenges.
    Violent Victimization of College Students (2003)

L. Derman-Sparks and the A.B.C. Task Force. *Anti-Bias Curriculum: Tools for Empowering Young Children.* Washington, DC: National Association for the Education of Young Children, 1989 (ED 305 135).

Steven M. Chermak, Joshua D. Freilich, and Michael Suttmoeller. "The Organizational Dynamics of Far-Right Hate Groups in the United States: Comparing Violent to Non-Violent Organizations." Final Report to Human Factors/Behavioral Sciences Division, Science, and Technology Directorate, U.S. Department of Homeland Security. College Park, MD: START, December 2011.

EXIT USA
    With the tagline "No judgment. Just help." EXIT USA is a nongovernmental organization developed and run by former white-power extremists. It performs outreach work dedicated to helping those involved with white-power and far-right extremist groups in the United States to exit and start new lives. EXIT USA provides a safe place for people to reach out and seek help, either for themselves or for someone they know exiting a white-power group.

Facing History and Ourselves
    https://www.facinghistory.org/contact-us

The mission is to engage students of diverse backgrounds in an examination of racism, prejudice, and anti-Semitism in order to promote the development of a more humane and informed citizenry. By studying the historical development of the Holocaust and other examples of genocide, students make the essential connection between history and the moral choices they confront in their own lives.

FBI et al. Report: White Supremacist Threats
Final Report of the Federal Commission on School Safety, December 18, 2018
Education Department, Department of Justice, Department of Homeland Security, Department of Health and Human Services

Extremist Crime Database
Joshua D. Freilich, Co-Director
Joshua D. Freilich, Steven M. Chermak, Roberta Belli, Jeff Gruenewald, and William S. Parkin. "Introducing the United States Extremist Crime Database (ECDB)." *Terrorism and Political Violence* 26 (2014): 372–84. http://www.tandfonline.com/doi/full/10.1080/09546553.2012.713229?mobileUi=0
Open-source database of violent and financial crimes committed by political extremists.

Joel Finkelstein
Director and Co-Founder
Network Contagion Research Institute
Researching anti-Semitic language on social media sites 4chan and Gab.
http://ncri.io/
joel@ncri.io

Brittan Heller
ADL's Center for Technology and Society
Silicon Valley, California
Its objective is to bring civil rights into the digital age. Brittan formerly served in the Department of Justice, Human Rights and Special Prosecutions section, where she specialized in the intersection of human rights and technology. Before government service, Brittan practiced international human rights law overseas, where she built a law school in Kabul, Afghanistan, assisted North Korean refugees throughout Asia, and prosecuted the first cases at the International Criminal Court. During law school, Brittan spearheaded groundbreaking impact litigation to combat cyber-harassment and advocated for cyber civil rights. She is a graduate of Stanford University and Yale Law School.
bheller@cyber.harvard.edu

J. B. Hohensee and L. Derman-Sparks. *Implementing an Anti-Bias Curriculum in Early Childhood Classrooms.* ERIC Digest. Urbana, IL: ERIC Clearinghouse on Elementary and Childhood Education, 1992. (ED 351 146).

Hope Not Hate
  hopenothate.com
  2129 N. Western Ave.
  Chicago, IL 60647

iCivics
  iCivics.org
  1035 Cambridge Street, Suite 21B
  Cambridge, MA 02141
  (617) 356-8311 (phone)

Improving Security by Democratic Participation (ISDEP)
  Goal: Prevent terrorism by tackling the factors that can lead to radicalization and recruitment, in Europe and internationally. Training programs based on the EU Commission's Counter Terrorism strategy.
  maria.ladu@agenformedia.com

P. A. Katz. "Development of Children's Racial Awareness and Intergroup Attitudes." In *Current Topics in Early Childhood Education*, volume IV, edited by L. G. Katz. Norwood, NJ: Ablex, 1982 (ED 250 100).

JD Journal for Deradicalization
  www.journal-derad.com
  Peer-reviewed periodical for the theory and practice of deradicalization with an international audience.

Josephson Institute of Ethics
  Goal: Increase ethical commitment, competence, and practice in all segments of society.
  http://josephsoninstitute.org/
  8117 W. Manchester Ave. #830
  Playa del Rey, CA 90293
  (310) 437-0827 (phone)
  (310) 846-4858 (fax)

German Institute on Radicalization and De-Radicalization Studies
  http://girds.org/
  Daniel Koehler, Founder and Director

A transparent network of experts both from practical backgrounds and the academia aiming to foster the theoretical and practical development of deradicalization methods, evaluation tools, training manuals, and concepts.

Muslim Jewish Advisory Council
mjac@ajc.org
https://global.ajc.org/secure/contact-us
A joint initiative of AJC and the Islamic Society of North America (ISNA).
David Harris, AJC CEO
The Muslim-Jewish Advisory Council brings together recognized business, political, and religious leaders in the Jewish and Muslim American communities to advocate jointly for issues of common concern. Stanley Bergman, chairman of the board and CEO of Henry Schein, Inc., and Farooq Kathwari, president and CEO of Ethan Allen, co-chair the national council. The American Jewish Committee and the Islamic Society of North America are its co-conveners. The council has two policy objectives: to combat the rise in hate crimes and to promote the positive image of Muslim and Jewish citizens of the United States.

A Night at the Garden
A short film by Marshall Curry.
About a 1939 American Nazi rally.
https://www.niot.org/blog/oscar-nominated-short-night-garden?fbclid=IwAR34NPrhqeeD-_BmE3CaEH-G-yGETOoksAksAnacCzSwqovOOZGQ6XSHV68

The Opportunity Agenda
https://opportunityagenda.org/approach/our-values
(212) 334-5977 (phone)
(212) 334-2656 (fax)
Alan Jenkins, President and Co-Founder
568 Broadway, Suite 701
New York, NY 10012

Organization of Chinese Americans
Responding to Hate Crimes: A Community Action Guide
www.ocanatl.org
1001 Connecticut Ave., NW, Suite 601
Washington, DC 20036
oca@ocanatl.org

Designed as a practitioner's guide, the manual offers the general public step-by-step guidelines, checklists, internet resources, and best community response practices to hate crimes.

The Turner Diaries by William L. Pierce
A novel about a race war that consumes America. (Timothy McVeigh, who carried out the 1995 Oklahoma City bombing, had pages from the book in his possession when he was captured.)

Mica Pollock, ed. *Everyday Antiracism: Getting Real About Race in School*. New York: The New Press, 2008.
How should teachers and parents respond when children ask challenging questions about race? How should teachers handle the use of the "N-word" or discuss "achievement gaps" with colleagues? How can teachers avoid unwittingly making children of color speak on behalf of their entire group? While numerous books exist about race and race theory, *Everyday Antiracism* puts theory into practice by offering specific strategies for combating racism in the classroom.

The Prejudice Institute
2743 Maryland Ave.
Baltimore, MD 21218
prejinst@aol.com
(410) 243-6987 (phone)
Howard Ehrlich, Director
Experts on ethnoviolence (hate crimes) and media.

Program on Extremism: George Washington University
https://extremism.gwu.edu/
2000 Pennsylvania Ave. NW
Washington, DC 20052
(202) 994-2437 (phone)
extremism@gwu.edu
Focuses on Islamism, but much of its work on methodology is applicable to non-Islamic extremist groups.

Radicalisation Awareness Network (RAN)
A network of professionals whose work focuses on radicalization leading to violence. It is funded by the European Commission and its purpose is to encourage people to share knowledge and practices in this field. Every year, RAN publishes a report detailing counter-radicalization initiatives that have been undertaken.

Religious Diversity at Work by Deborah Levine
   https://www.amazon.com/Religious-Diversity-Work-Deborah-Levine/dp/1533526036

Religious Diversity in Our Schools by Deborah Levine
   https://www.amazon.com/Religious-Diversity-Schools-Deborah-Levine/dp/1492144215

Royal Canadian Mounted Police
   Terrorism and Violent Extremism Awareness Guide
   http://www.rcmp-grc.gc.ca/en/terrorism-and-violent-extremism-awareness-guide
   (See chapters on right-wing extremism.)

U.S. Secret Service, National Threat Assessment Center (NTAC)
   Enhancing School Safety Using a Threat Assessment Model
   www.SecretService.gov
   https://www.dhs.gov/sites/default/files/publications/18_0711_USSS_NTAC-Enhancing-School-Safety-Guide.pdf

I. Siraj-Blatchford. *The Early Years: Laying the Foundations for Racial Equality*. Stoke-on-Trent, Staffordshire, England: Trentham Books, 1994.

Bias
   This digest is based on *A Directory of Anti-Bias Education Resources and Services* by Wendy Schwartz with Lynne Elcik.
   http://www.ericdigests.org/1995-2/bias.htm

Southern Poverty Law Center
   https://www.splcenter.org/

Intelligence Project/ Report
   400 Washington Ave.
   Montgomery, AL 36104
   (334) 956-8200
   mark@splcenter.org

Teaching Tolerance: Responding to Hate and Bias at School
   Tolerance.org

Responding to Hate at School, a Guide for Teachers, Counselors and Administrators (1999)

Facing History and Ourselves
www.facing.org
16 Hurd Road
Brookline, MA 02445
(617) 232-1595 (phone)
(617) 232-0281 (fax)
info_boston@facing.org

Lawyers' Committee for Civil Rights Under Law
Stop Hate Project
Working to combat hate by offering a resource and reporting hotline, 844-9-NO-HATE, and hosting an online resource hub at 8449nohate.org where users can access free legal resources.

Un-Bias Guide for Leaders: Unconscious Bias to Conscious Choices Workbook by Deborah Levine
https://www.amazon.com/Bias-Guide-Leaders-Unconscious-Conscious/dp/1720853878

Un-Bias Guide for Educators by Deborah Levine
https://www.amazon.com/Bias-Guide-Educators-Unconscious-Management/dp/1721666524

The Liberator's Daughter by Deborah Levine
https://www.amazon.com/Liberators-Daughter-Deborah-J-Levine/dp/1519321082

Montana Human Rights Network
www.mhrn.org
A grassroots, state-based human rights nonprofit organization in Montana working to promote democratic values such as pluralism, equality, and justice; challenge bigotry and intolerance; and organize communities to speak out in support of democratic principles and institutions. The network uses a multifaceted approach to expand the base for human rights in Montana, including pursuing progressive public policy, exposing the radical right, and supporting local community organizing. The network has researched and reported on the activities of the radical right for more than twenty-five years.
https://mhrn.org/right-wing-research/.
You can find more of the network's reports and issue briefs here: https://mhrn.org/resources/.
P.O. Box 1509
Helena, MT 59624
network@mhrn.org

Angela Nagle. *Kill All Normies: Online Culture Wars from 4Chan and Tumblr to Trump and the Alt-Right*. Alresford, Hants, UK: Zero Books, June 30, 2017.

National Association of Student Personnel Administrators
    Diversity on Campus: Report from the Field (2000)

National Center for Hate Crime Prevention
    Education Development Center, Inc.
    Office for Victims of Crime, U.S. Department of Justice
    Responding to Hate Crime: A Multidisciplinary Curriculum for Law Enforcement and Victim Assistance Professionals
    55 Chapel Street
    Newton, MA 02458-1060
    (800) 225-4276
    (617) 969-7100
    www.edc.org/HHD/hatecrime/
    https://www.ncjrs.gov/ovc_archives/reports/responding/files/ncj182290.pdf

Not in Our Town
    The Working Group
    www.theworkinggroup.org
    1611 Telegraph Ave., Suite 1400
    Oakland, CA 94612
    (510) 268-9675
    Patrice O'Neill
    poneill@theworkinggroup.org

Bureau of Justice Assistance
    U.S. Department of Justice
    Hate Crimes Series #2: Putting the Far Right into Perspective
    http://www.nwcitizen.us/publicgood/reports/spectrum/

Paul de Armond, Research Director, Public Good Project
    GroundView Productions
    P.O. Box 96
    Wauna, WA 98395
    (253) 225-6571
    dave@groundviewproductions.org

John F. Kennedy School of Government

https://www.hks.harvard.edu/
Saguaro Seminar: Civic Engagement in America
[Social Capital]
Thomas Sander
Executive Director
saguaro@harvard.edu
Harvard University
www.ksg.harvard.edu/saguaro

Christian Picciolini. *White American Youth*. New York: Hachette Book Group, 2017.
Co-Founder, Life Against Hate
Director and producer, public service campaign, "There Is Life After Hate," aimed at helping deradicalization.

Simon Wiesenthal Center
www.wiesenthal.com
9760 West Pico Boulevard
Los Angeles, CA 90035
(310) 553-9036

Annie Steinberg, MD, Jane Brooks, MEd, and Tariq Remtulla, BA. "Youth Hate Crimes: Identification, Prevention, and Intervention." *American Journal of Psychiatry* 160 (2003): 979–89.

Community Relations Service, U.S. Department of Justice
http://www.usdoj.gov/crs/pubs/prevyouhatecrim.htm
Preventing Youth Hate Crime: A Manual for Schools and Communities

10 Ways to Fight Hate on Campus, a Response Guide for College Activities (1999)
Stop Repeating History

Jay Hirabayashi, Holly Yasui, and Karen Korematsu. "A Call to Action: Reject the Shameful Legacy of Japanese American Incarceration and Call Upon the U.S. Supreme Court to Fulfill Its Role as Defender of the Constitution." *Stop Repeating History*. No date. Accessed August 8, 2019, https://stoprepeatinghistory.org/calltoaction/
Children of the Japanese American defendants Gordon Hirabayashi, Min Yasui, and Fred T. Korematsu who challenged the forced removal and incarceration of Japanese Americans during World War II before the U.S. Supreme Court.
#StopRepeatingHistory

https://stoprepeatinghistory.org/
Toolkit: https://stoprepeatinghistory.org/toolkit/

Tactical Community Policing for Homeland Security
Virginia Center for Policing Innovation
The Virginia Center for Policing Innovation (VCPI) is a nonprofit organization based in Richmond, Virginia, that provides training and assistance to law enforcement organizations throughout the United States.
413 Stuart Circle, Suite 200
Richmond, VA 23220
info@vcpionline.org
(804) 644-0899 (phone)
(804) 644-0309 (fax)
https://copstrainingportal.org/tactical-community-policing-for-homeland-security/
e-Learn course in which participants explore the following topics:

- community partnerships
- practical problem-solving strategies
- proactive prevention, intervention, and interdiction strategies
- values-based policing in the climate of terrorism
- the process of intelligence development

This course is ideal for all law enforcement and criminal justice professionals, as well as any community-policing stakeholders.

Washington State Human Rights Commission
www.hum.wa.gov
711 S. Capitol Way, Suite 402
Olympia, WA 98504-2490
(360) 753-6770

White Right: Meeting the Enemy
A film by Deeyah Khan
US/UK/Norway, 2017, 55 minutes, Color, DVD
Order No. W181227

In this Emmy-winning documentary, acclaimed Muslim filmmaker Deeyah Khan meets U.S. neo-Nazis and white nationalists, including Richard Spencer, face to face and attends the now-infamous Unite the Right rally in Charlottesville, Virginia, as she seeks to understand the personal and political motivations behind the resurgence of far-right extremism in the United States. Speaking with fascists, racists, and proponents of alt-right ideologies, Deeyah attempts to discover new possibilities for connection and solutions.

As she tries to see beyond the headlines to the human beings, her own prejudices are challenged and her tolerance tested. When she finds herself in the middle of America's biggest and most violent far right rally in recent years, Deeyah's safety is jeopardized. Can she find it within herself to try and befriend the fascists she meets? With a U.S. president propagating anti-Muslim propaganda, the far-right gaining ground in German elections, hate crime rising in the United Kingdom, and divisive populist rhetoric infecting political and public discourse across Western democracies, *White Right: Meeting the Enemy* asks why. The film is an urgent, resonant, and personal look at race wars in America.

The Witnessing Project
  http://www.witnessingproject.org/what.html
  The Witnessing Project has two primary goals: (1) to make people aware of themselves as everyday witnesses to violence and violation, and (2) to provide people with the tools to cope with the biological, psychological, interpersonal, and societal effects of witnessing.

Appendix 1

Know Your Enemy

Twenty-Five Points of American National Socialism

1. We demand the union of all Whites into a greater America on the basis of the right of national self-determination.
2. We demand equality of rights for the American people in its dealings with other nations, and the revocation of the United Nations, the North Atlantic Treaty Organization, the World Bank, the North American Free Trade Agreement, the World Trade Organization, and the International Monetary Fund.
3. We demand land and territory (colonies) to feed our people and to settle surplus population.
4. Only members of the nation may be citizens of the state. Only those of pure White blood, whatever their creed, may be members of the nation. Non-citizens may live in America only as guests and must be subject to laws for aliens. Accordingly, no Jew or homosexual may be a member of the nation.
5. The right to vote on the State government and legislation shall be enjoyed by citizens of the state alone. We therefore demand that all official appointments, of whatever kind, whether in the nation, in the states or in smaller localities, shall be held by none but citizens. We oppose the corrupting parliamentary custom of filling posts merely in accordance with party considerations and special interests-without reference to character or abilities.

6. We demand that the State shall make it its primary duty to provide a livelihood for its citizens. If it should prove impossible to feed the entire population, foreign nationals (non-citizens) will be deported.
7. All non-White immigration must be prevented. We demand that all non-Whites currently residing in America be required to leave the nation forthwith and return to their land of origin: peacefully or by force.
8. All citizens shall have equal rights and duties, regardless of class or station.
9. It must be the first duty of every citizen to perform physical or mental work. The activities of the individual must not clash within the framework of the community and be for the common good.

   We therefore demand:
10. The abolition of incomes unearned by work. The breaking of interest slavery.
11. In view of the enormous personal sacrifices of life and property demanded of a nation by any war, personal enrichment from war must be regarded as a crime against the nation. We therefore demand the ruthless confiscation of all war profits.
12. We demand the nationalization of all businesses which have been formed into corporations (trusts).
13. We demand economic reform suitable to our national requirements:

    - The prohibition of pro-Marxist unions and their supplantation with National Socialist trade unions;
    - The passing of a law instituting profit-sharing in large industrial enterprises;
    - The creation of a livable wage;
    - The restructuring of social security and welfare to include drug testing for welfare recipients;
    - The immediate discontinuation of all taxes on things of life's necessity, such as food, clothing, shelter, medicine, etc.;
    - The replacement of the current tax system with a flat-rate tax based on income.

14. We demand the treasonable system of health care be completely revolutionized.

    We demand an end to the status quo in which people die or rot away from lack of proper treatment due to the failure of their medical coverage, Health Maintenance Organization, or insurance policy.

    We further demand the extensive development of insurance for old age and that prescription drugs be made both affordable and accessible.

Appendix 1 187

15. We demand the creation and maintenance of a healthy middle class, the immediate communalizing of big department stores and their lease at a cheap rate to small traders, and that the utmost consideration shall be shown to all small trades in the placing of state and municipal orders.
16. We demand a land reform suitable to our national requirements, that shall be twofold in nature:

    The primary land reform will be to ensure all members of the nation receive affordable housing. The party as such stands explicitly for private property.

    However, we support the passing of a law for the expropriation of land for communal purposes without compensation when deemed necessary for land illegally acquired, or not administered in accordance with the national welfare.

    We further demand the abolition of ground rent, the discontinuation of all taxes on property, and the prohibition of all speculation in land.

    The secondary land reform will be to ensure the environmental integrity of the nation is preserved;

    - By setting aside land for national wildlife refuges;
    - By cleaning the urban, agricultural, and hydrographical (water) areas of the nation;
    - By creating legislation regulating the amount of pollution, carbon dioxide, greenhouse gases, and toxins released into the atmosphere;
    - And for the continued research and development of clean burning fuels and energy sources.

17. We demand the ruthless prosecution of those whose activities are injurious to the common interest. Murderers, rapists, pedophiles, drug dealers, usurers, profiteers, race traitors must be severely punished, whatever their creed or race.
18. We demand that Roman edict law, which serves a materialistic new world order, be replaced by Anglo-Saxon common law.
19. The state must consider a thorough reconstruction of our national system of education with the aim of opening up to every able and hardworking American the possibility of higher education and of thus obtaining advancement.

    The curricula of all educational establishments must be brought into line with the requirements of practical life.

    The aim of the school must be to give the pupil, beginning with the first sign of intelligence, a grasp of the state of the nation through the study of civic affairs.

We demand the education of gifted children of poor parents, whatever their class or occupation, at the expense of the state.
20. The state must ensure that the nation's health standards are raised by protecting mothers, infants, and the unborn:

- By prohibiting abortion and euthanasia, except in cases of rape, incest, race-mixing, or mental retardation.
- By prohibiting child labor and ending the rudiments of child abuse, alcoholism, and drug addiction.
- By creating conditions to make possible the reestablishment of the nuclear family in which the father works while the mother stays at home and takes care of the children if they so choose.
- By taking away the economic burden associated with childbirth and replacing it with a structured system of pay raises for those that give birth to healthy babies, thereby returning the blessing associated with children.

To further ensure that the nation's health standards are raised, legislation shall be passed promoting physical strength and providing for compulsory gymnastics and sports, and by the extensive support of clubs engaged in the physical training of youth.

21. We demand the right to bear arms for law-abiding citizens.
22. We demand the abolition of the mercenary army, the end to the overuse of our military as a "Meals-on-Wheels" program in foreign lands of no vital interest to our nation; and the formation of a true national service for the defense of our race and nation. One that excludes: non-Americans, criminals, and sensitivity training.
23. We demand legal warfare on deliberate political mendacity and its dissemination in the press. To facilitate the creation of a national press we demand:

   a. That all editors of and contributors to newspapers appearing in the English language must be members of the nation;
   b. That no non-American newspapers may appear without the express permission of the State. They must not be written in the English language;
   c. That non-Whites shall be prohibited by law from participating financially in or influencing American newspapers, and that the penalty for contravening such a law shall be the suppression of any such newspapers, and the immediate deportation of the non-Americans involved.
   d. The publishing of papers which are not conducive to the national welfare must be forbidden. We demand the legal

prosecution of all those tendencies in art and literature which corrupt our national life, and the suppression of cultural events which violate this demand.

24. We demand absolute religious freedom for all denominations in the State, provided they do not threaten its existence nor offend the moral feelings of the White race. The Party combats the Jewish-materialistic spirit within and without us, and is convinced that our nation can achieve permanent health only from within on the basis of the principle: The common good before self-interest.
25. To put the whole program into effect, we demand the creation of a strong central national government for the nation; the unconditional authority of the political central parliament over the entire nation and its organizations; and the formation of committees for the purpose of carrying out the general legislation passed by the nation and the various American States.

The leaders of the movement promise to work ruthlessly if need be to sacrifice their very lives to translate this program into action.[1]

NOTE

1. National Socialist Movement, "Twenty-Five Points."

Appendix 2

National Socialist Rally: Press Release

The National Socialist Movement is holding a RALLY in Olympia, Washington on Monday, July 3rd 2006. We are doing this to make White People aware of THE SLOW GENOCIDE OF OUR PEOPLE BY DIVERSITY. When a country has more than one Race of People inhabiting it, there will be a certain amount of interracial mating; over time, this will have the effect of reducing the number of WHITE PEOPLE WITH PURE RACIAL BACKGROUNDS and also introduces the idea of "tolerance" towards other Races, which speeds up the race-mixing process. This is happening in White Nations such as England, France, Germany, Australia, Russia, the United States, and all others. All White Nations are experiencing a negative birthrate for the White People there, and all the Governments involved are BRINGING IN NON-WHITES TO REPLACE THEM. The National Socialist Movement stands against this anti-White future, these anti-White policies, and SEEKS TO INITIATE a National Awakening of White People: We must secure the existence of our People and a Future for our Children. The Rally will be held on the steps of the State Capitol Building from 2 p.m. until 4 p.m. There will be a Press Conference the day before the Event. Media will be notified about its time and location.[1]

NOTE

1. For more information, see http://www.nukeisrael.com/seattleprotest/olympiarally.htm. All Pro-White supporters are welcome to attend and stand with the NSM in Solidarity. www.nsm88.com.

Appendix 3

Compassionate Witnessing and Rehumanizing the Enemy

I have since developed a set of questions that I have used in workshop settings all over the world that takes people through a series of steps similar to the ones that got set in motion for me in South Africa. People work in small groups to talk with each other about their responses to each of the questions. However, I have also had people tell me that reading the questions on their own, and thinking through their responses, has had powerful effects.[1]

These are the questions developed by Weingarten to help individuals consider actions that they may take to interrupt the unthinking ways that they pass on antagonistic impressions of another group.

The questions stimulate self-reflection about something we often think very little about: the many opportunities we have to inflame or bridge differences by what we say and do. These questions assist in rehumanizing the other.

1. What is your large group identity (choose a religious, ethnic or national group identity)?
2. What is your group's historical or "chosen" trauma?
3. How has the knowledge of the trauma passed to you?
4. How do you pass it to others? Exactly? With modifications? What aspects of it are you aware of? What ways might you pass it of which you are relatively unaware?
5. What effects are there of passing on the large group's chosen trauma for

    - You?
    - Your family?

- Your community?
- Your country?

6. What would you wish to do with regard to passing on the historical trauma?
7. Whose support and what kind of support would you need to enlist to accomplish your preferred relationship to the chosen trauma?

NOTE

1. Weingarten, "Compassionate Witnessing and the Transformation of Societal Violence."

Appendix 4

Example of Anti-Nazi Resolution

RESOLUTION: RESISTING NAZI INCURSIONS
IN WASHINGTON STATE

American Nazis, especially those from the National Socialist Movement (NSM), are organizing in Washington State. In recent months, they have held rallies in several cities in the State, including Olympia, to try to spread their message of lies, hate and intolerance. Their numbers are small, but they have a vigorous new leader in Washington State, sophisticated in manipulating the media to obtain publicity.

After consulting with the Anti-Defamation League (ADL), the Japanese-American Citizen's League (JACL), the Southern Poverty Law Center (SPLC), and many other groups, it is agreed that the Nazis will not go away simply by ignoring them. We fully realize their rights to freedom of speech and assembly. In the marketplace of ideas, we need to make a persuasive case that tolerance, nondiscrimination, equity, and fairness are much truer and more valuable American ideals than the ones the Nazis promulgate.

The Nazi message is a hateful one, against people of color, Jews, gays and lesbians, and people with disabilities. The Commissioners and staff of the Washington State Human Rights Commission are deeply troubled to learn of the appearance of Nazis in Washington State. They are a shocking reminder that racism and hate crimes continue to seek a foothold in the Pacific Northwest.

For the Commission, which has been tasked with preventing and eliminating discrimination in the state of Washington since 1949, the appearance of Nazis is a disturbing and painful reminder that there is still much work to be done in human and civil rights.

The Commission urges individuals and groups to take a peaceful stand against the Nazis and engage in lawful efforts to speak out against them; demonstrate the superiority of fairness, diversity, and equity; and especially talk to young people about the dangerous, destructive, and anti-democratic path taken by Nazis. We will continue to counter the efforts of the Nazis through contact with local groups such as Unity in the Community, sponsoring showings of films such as *Not in Our Town* (recounting the efforts of Billings, Montana, when Nazis invaded in 1995); and by interacting with local law enforcement and community-based chapters of civil rights organizations.

Other community efforts include a speakers' bureau, reaching into the schools, a diversity fair, and dialog circles. The point is to take positive and life-enhancing action, while avoiding confrontation with the Nazis and giving them the publicity they seek. We urge all Washingtonians to take a stand in favor of respect, peace, and justice. Together we can show that the best spirit of Washington stands strongly against the discredited and violent Nazi ideology.

For these reasons, we, the Commissioners of the Washington State Human Rights Commission, sign this resolution.

May 26, 2006 [Commissioners and Executive Director Signature Block]

Appendix 5

Sample Hate Crime Policy

Policy Statement on Hate Crimes and Hate-Related Conduct
June 2001

As well as constituting violations of federal criminal laws and, in many cases, state laws, hate crimes have an incendiary effect and we must combat them with the full array of tools that we have available. In the Department of Transportation, zero tolerance is the only acceptable response to hate crimes or related conduct that may occur in our workplace and we must be diligent to ensure that these violations to human dignity do not occur here.

A hate crime is a crime in which the perpetrator intentionally selects a victim or, in the case of a property crime, the property that is the object of the crime because of the actual or perceived race, color, religion, national origin, ethnicity, gender, disability, or sexual orientation of any person. These bias-motivated crimes are intended to provoke fear in, alienate, and intimidate victims. They have a corrosive effect on our communities and workplaces and must be dealt with swiftly and effectively.

Each management official must set the proper leadership tone by acting swiftly and appropriately to hate crime allegations, which includes taking appropriate steps needed to enhance workplace security and assuring the thorough investigation of allegations. Investigating and taking action swiftly and deliberately with respect to hate crimes will promote a sense of safety for victims and encourage witnesses to come forward. Employees can also report instances of hate-related misconduct to their management, their Security Office, the Departmental Office of Civil Rights, their operating administration's civil rights office, or the Inspector General Hotline ([202] 366-1461 in Washington, DC; [800] 424-9071 nationwide).

Department of Transportation employees determined to have engaged in hate crimes and hate-related conduct will be subject to appropriate disciplinary action. All of our employees are entitled to work in an environment that is free from fear. We must ensure that we have a safe environment for their sake and the sake of our customers who expect an effective and efficient transportation system.

Appendix 6

Sample Bias Incident Response Protocol

INTERIM BIAS RELATED INCIDENT RESPONSE
PROTOCOL: POLICY AND PROCEDURES

The Evergreen State College (TESC), Olympia, Washington, 2006

The reality for Evergreen students is that hate crimes and bias incidents can occur in their living communities, in their classrooms, at co-curricular activities, in employment situations, and at off-campus college-related activities. The college already has policies, procedures, and protocols in place to respond to different kinds of incidents, enabling the college to attend to the health and safety of students, manage individual complaints or grievances, and adjudicate possible violations of college policies or local, state, or federal laws. Examples of such policies, procedures, and protocols include:

1. Living communities: the housing contract, the Student Conduct Code, the Peer Arbitration Board, the college Non-Discrimination Policy, and local, state, and federal civil rights laws and regulations
2. Classrooms: program covenants, the Faculty Handbook, college Non-Discrimination Policy, academic administrative policies, and deans
3. Co-curricular activities: the Student Conduct Code, college Non-Discrimination Policy and local, state, and federal civil rights laws and regulations
4. Employment settings: student employment agreements, policies and procedures, college Non-Discrimination Policy, and local, state, and federal civil rights laws and regulations
5. Case Coordinating Protocol

6. Sexual Assault Protocol

Protocol for Bias Incidents

The following protocol is to ensure a timely, efficient, and effective response to campus incidents involving Evergreen students, which may be characterized as hate crimes or bias incidents. The protocol should be implemented whenever a hate crime or bias incident is believed or perceived to have occurred. This protocol is specific to addressing hate crimes or bias incidents directed at Evergreen students. The protocol does not cover faculty and staff. The protocol may apply in incidents off campus. This proposed interim protocol is not in lieu of and does not override established college or external processes and services available to students.

CIRCUMSTANCES WHEN THE PROTOCOL IS TO BE INITIATED — DEFINITIONS

The bias incident protocol is initiated in cases of what may be a hate crime, bias incident, or when it is clear that the incident would have a serious impact on groups by virtue of their race, color, religion, ethnic/national origin, gender expression, sex, age, disability, or sexual orientation identities. The purpose of convening the protocol response team is not to respond to more private incidents, especially when victims are uncomfortable with a public response, but rather to deal with more visible incidents that are likely to significantly affect the community.

A hate crime is an actual criminal offense motivated in whole or in part by the offender's bias toward the victim's status based on race, color, religion, ethnic/national origin, gender expression, sex, age, disability, or sexual orientation identities.

A bias incident is conduct, speech, or expression that is motivated by bias based on perceived race, color, religion, ethnic/national origin, gender expression, sex, age, disability, or sexual orientation identities but does not rise to the level of a crime. To constitute a bias incident, sufficient objective facts must be present to lead a reasonable and prudent person to conclude that the actions in question may be motivated by bias toward the status of a targeted individual or a group.

REPORTING OF BIAS INCIDENTS

Students who experience or witness and staff or faculty members who become aware of a possible hate crime or bias incident are asked to report the crime or incident immediately to a designated college office or official:

- Vice President for Student Affairs
- Police Services
- Director of Housing and Food Services
- Campus Grievance Officer
- Dean of Student and Academic Support Services
- Director of First Peoples' Advising Services
- Civil Rights Officer
- Provost Office
- President's Special Assistant for Diversity Affairs

Notification of the report will then be made to the Office of the Vice President for Student Affairs. The Vice President will ensure that the complaint is investigated by the appropriate investigative official as well as convene the response team.

This protocol will be used twenty-four hours a day, seven days a week. During regular business hours, the Vice President for Student Affairs, the Dean of Student and Academic Support Services, Police Service, the Director of Housing and Food Services, or Academic Dean should be notified immediately of any incidents that have the potential to be characterized as hate crimes or bias incidents.

During evening and weekend hours, Police Services or housing staff will notify the Vice President for Student Affairs or the Vice President's designee. In the case of incidents in the living community, Police Services or housing staff will first notify the Director of Housing and Food Service or the director's designee, who will then notify the Vice President for Student Affairs.

PROCEDURAL STEPS

1. Frontline respondents to the incident should (a) assess and determine the need for emergency services, which may include emergency medical or psychological treatment; (b) determine if there continues to be a threat to parties involved and provide appropriate protection to the targeted individual or group through Police Services. A list of student affairs practitioners who can be contacted to assist will be available in the Office of the Vice President for Student Affairs and in the Police Services office.
2. Once an incident has been reported the Vice President for Student Affairs or the Vice President's designee will initiate the case-coordinating protocol, and a student affairs practitioner will be assigned to coordinate services for the student(s) involved. The assigned coordinator will be responsible for maintaining contact with the student(s)

throughout the process, from the initial crisis through subsequent periods as needed to address academic and personal issues that may have developed as a result of the hate crime or bias incident. If the student(s) shows any signs of being distraught, contact with the counseling center or crisis center should be made immediately. Based on interactions with the student(s) it may be determined appropriate to assign case coordinators who may be from the individual's affinity group if possible. If this is not possible, every effort should be made for the case coordinator to identify who within the college community could assist as additional support to the student(s).

3. Documentation of the incident should begin immediately. Police Services should be contacted to document possible hate crimes or bias incidents through such activities as photographing physical injuries, offensive graffiti, and evidence of vandalism. Depending on where the incident occurs (in the living community, in the classroom, in a co-curricular program, or on the job), the appropriate documentation procedure should be implemented. Reports should include important details such as when and where the incident occurred and who was involved in or witnessed the incident. Any physical evidence of the incident (messages written on doors, physical objects, etc.) should be retained and secured for police to investigate and crime scenes should not be disturbed prior to the arrival of Police Services.

4. Targeted students may feel uncomfortable about cooperating with an investigation due to fear of retaliation by the perpetrator(s). Impacted students should be assured by investigating authorities that their safety and security are important and that every effort will be made to ensure that their safety is protected, and measures, such as relocation and when possible anonymous reporting, can be utilized to minimize potential threats. Any retaliatory behavior by the student suspected of the violation or by his or her supporters may constitute an independent violation of college policy.

5. Students who have been identified as suspects in a bias incident or hate crime will be assigned a case coordinator to work with regarding the impact of the incident and the student's rights and responsibilities and the steps for due process that he or she will be afforded under the Student Conduct Code.

6. Intake investigation of complaints of hate crimes and bias incidents will be conducted by the appropriate investigative teams (Police Services, Campus Grievance Officer, and Civil Rights Officer). Investigations will be conducted to determine possible violations of college policies and local, state, and federal laws and regulations. Students suspected of violations may be accountable under the criminal justice system, Student Conduct Code, and Non-Discrimination Policy.

7. Once the immediate needs have been addressed, the Vice President for Student Affairs or designee will convene the response team composed of

   - Vice President for Student Affairs
   - Dean of Student and Academic Support Services
   - Director, Housing and Food Services and designees
   - Academic Dean (Provost will refer to the appropriate dean)
   - Director of First Peoples' Advising Services
   - Director of Police Services
   - Campus Grievance Officer
   - Civil Rights Officer
   - Executive Associate to the President
   - Associate Vice President for Human Resource Services
   - Director of College Relations
   - Director of Access Services
   - President's Special Assistant for Diversity Affairs
   - Director of Student Activities
   - Students

8. The response team will identify the needs of the affected communities as well as those of the larger Evergreen community. Informing the affected communities as well as the larger community regarding the incident, as appropriate, will be a major function of the response team.
9. An email will be sent to the college community describing the incident and the steps that are being taken, the status of the investigation, and that the response team has been assembled. An update should follow once the response team has had an opportunity to assess the situation and determine next steps.
10. The response team may organize open forums within the affected communities as well as the larger community to provide information regarding those details of the incident that can be revealed outside of the investigation, to gather suggestions, to denounce such incidents, to reaffirm Evergreen's values and standards around diversity and equal respect, and to educate about hate and bias.
11. The response team will be provided with progress reports of the investigation. Given that criminal and judicial investigations are confidential, the team will be kept informed of the investigation's progress to the extent allowable. Whenever possible, the team will provide assistance to ensure that all aspects of bias-related activities are examined and that the investigation is handled in a manner that is efficient, effective, and culturally sensitive. The intent is to send a clear message that the college has zero tolerance for hate crimes and bias inci-

dents and will act swiftly and effectively when such incidents are reported.
12. The response team will also determine topic program areas for additional trainings for students, staff, and faculty. All efforts should be made to develop trainings for the community that will enhance and encourage intergroup dialogue that focuses on how conversations around issues of racism and discrimination of all types enable all students to be more socially integrated into the campus.[1]

Division of Student Affairs Case-Coordinating Protocol

In crises and emergencies the Division of Student Affairs activates the case-coordinating protocol to ensure direct services and support to students in crisis. The case coordinator is a student affairs practitioner trained in crisis management and emergencies. The coordinator assists the student(s) in accessing campus and local support services and resources and intervenes or facilitates in matters related to the student's(s') academic and personal well-being. The case coordinator is assigned to the student(s) until the crisis is resolved. When requested by the student(s), the case coordinator will accompany the student(s) to appointments when appropriate, as well as advise the student(s) regarding college policies. Students residing in the residence halls are assigned a case coordinator by the Director of Housing and Food Service, and students living off campus are assigned a case coordinator by the Dean of Student and Academic Support Services.

The case coordinator also works with students who may not have been directly involved in the crisis but who have felt its impact. Another form of support the case coordinator lends is to students who are involved in the college judicial system, assisting them in understanding their rights and responsibilities and due process guidelines.[2]

NOTES

1. Policies and protocols for Evergreen State College can be found at www.evergreen.edu.
2. Permission granted by Syracuse University to adopt selected text from Syracuse's Bias Related Incidents Protocol.

Appendix 7

CRS Efforts to Defuse Hate Crime Activity

When hate crimes threaten racial and ethnic relations or escalate community-wide tensions, Community Relations Service (CRS) offers five types of services. To determine the best service(s), CRS conciliators meet with elected officials and community leaders, analyzing a variety of indicators, including causes, potential for violence or continued violence, extent of dialogue, communication, and interest in working cooperatively to restore harmony and stability. The five services are:

1. Mediation and Conciliation. Mediation and conciliation are two techniques used by CRS to help communities resolve tensions and conflicts arising from hate crimes. CRS conciliators help community groups and local government leaders work together to help restore stability and harmony through orderly dialogue and clarification of the issues. CRS establishes with the parties the ground rules for discussion and facilitates the meetings.
2. Technical Assistance. CRS can assist local officials and community leaders on developing and implementing policies, practices, and procedures to respond to hate crimes and garner the support of residents and organizations to ease tensions.
3. Training. CRS can conduct training sessions and workshops to teach police officers and residents how to recognize a hate crime, gain support of the community early in the investigation, and begin the identification of victims and witnesses to the crime. CRS can teach community leaders and volunteers how to prevent the likelihood of more hate crimes and how to work cooperatively with law enforcement.

Volunteers can help with rumor control, community watch patrols, and information programs on hate crimes and those who perpetrate such offenses.
4. Public Education and Awareness. CRS can also conduct hate crime prevention and education programs in schools, colleges, and the community. These programs break down barriers, build bridges of trust across racial lines. The Center, the National Association of Attorneys General, and the International Association of Directors of Law Enforcement Standards and Training and other U.S. Department of Justice agencies have developed four model hate crime training curricula. The four curricula are specifically designed for patrol officers, investigating officers, and supervising officers and along ethnic lines develop mutual respect and reduce fear. CRS helps to address conflicts and violence, reduce tensions, develop plans to avoid potential incidents, and conducts training programs for students, teachers, administrators, and parents.
5. School-Based Programs. CRS offers school-based conflict resolution and prevention programs. One example is the Student Problem Identification and Resolution (SPIR) program, a conflict resolution program designed to identify and defuse racial tensions involving students at the middle and high school levels. SPIR assists school administrators in addressing racial and ethnic tensions through a carefully structured process that involves students, teach, administrators, and parents. A further expansion of this successful program, call Student Problem Identification and Resolving It Together (SPIRIT), involves local law enforcement agencies as key partners in the design of an action plan. CRS now trains school officials and police officers to conduct the SPIRIT Program as a part of the process to strengthen cooperation among law enforcement and school officials.

EVENT CONTINGENCY PLANNING

CRS, at the request of either local officials or demonstration organizers, can assist in contingency planning to ensure that marches, demonstrations, and similar events occur without exacerbating racial and ethnic tensions and minimize the prospect of any confrontations. CRS can also train community residents to plan and monitor local events. CRS assistance is often requested when demonstrations and marches are scheduled. CRS has helped scores of municipalities with contingency planning for successfully preparing for Ku Klux Klan and white supremacist rallies and counter-demonstrations.

HATE CRIME TRAINING CURRICULUM

CRS and the FBI's Hate Crime Unit, working with the Department of the Treasury's Federal Law Enforcement, train mixed audience of officers and command staff. This effort was undertaken to provide state and local law enforcement officers with the skills and knowledge that are crucial to the identification, reporting, investigation, and prosecution of and education about hate crimes.

As part of the Attorney General's Hate Crime Initiative, CRS and the FBI's Hate Crime Unit, working with the Department of the Treasury's Federal Law Enforcement Training Center, the National Association of Attorneys General, and the International Association of Directors of Law Enforcement Standards and Training and other USDOJ agencies, are developing four model hate crime training curricula. The four curricula are specifically designed for patrol officers, investigating officers, supervising officers, and a multilevel audience of officers. This effort was undertaken to provide state and local law enforcement officers with the skills and knowledge that are crucial to the identification, reporting, investigation, and prosecution of and education about hate crimes.

The new courses are approximately eight hours in length, can be taught at a training academy or on site at a department, and have been field tested at law enforcement academies and departments across the country. The curricula will contain the best policies, procedures, practices, and materials used to train law enforcement officers and provide an equitable balance of instruction on enforcement, victim assistance, and community relations.

CRS BEST PRACTICES TO PREVENT ESCALATION OF RACIAL AND ETHNIC TENSIONS

From years of experience with hundreds of hate crime cases that have caused or intensified community-wide racial and ethnic tensions, CRS recommends certain "best practices" to prevent hate crimes and restore harmony in the community.

HATE CRIME ORDINANCES ARE A DETERRENT

A core responsibility of government is to protect the civil rights of its citizens and to advance its inherent obligation to ensure good race and ethnic relations. This tenet should not be abrogated and such a commitment requires no special funding. A government can confirm its commitment to the safety and well-being of its citizens by establishing an ordinance against hate crime activity or enhancing the punishment for hate crime. It can also encourage compliance with existing equal opportunity statutes.

A local government may establish an ordinance against hate activity modeled on existing hate crime law in that state. Punishment is enhanced by promulgating guidelines or amending existing guidelines to provide varying offense levels for use in sentencing. There should be reasonable consistency with other guidelines, avoidance of duplicative punishments for the same offense, and consideration of mitigating circumstances.

Compliance with existing statutes can be achieved by training law enforcement officers to enforce existing statutes, impose fines or penalties when ordinances are violated, review licenses or privileges, review tax exempt status, and provide incentives or awards. Local governments may establish commissions to review and analyze hate crime activity, create public service announcements, and recommend measures to counter hate activity. In September 1994, Congress enacted a federal hate crime penalty enhancement statute (Public Law 103-322 § 28003) that increased penalties for federal crimes where victims were selected "because of the actual or perceived race, color, religion, national origin, ethnicity, gender, disability, or sexual orientation."

LOCAL ACTIONS TO IMPROVE COMMUNICATION

An unresolved hate crime may escalate unresolved racial and ethnic friction into a community-wide conflict or civil disturbance. Communication and interaction between majority and minority groups are key factors in easing tensions or restoring harmony.

A Human Rights Commission (HRC) can facilitate and coordinate discussions, training, and events for the benefit of everyone. An HRC can create a forum for talking about racial and ethnic relations and encourage citizens to discuss their differences, commonalities, hopes, and dreams. Forums could focus on the common features of community life, including economic development, education, transportation, environment, cultural, and recreational opportunities, leadership, community attitudes, and racial and ethnic diversity. The commission can use multicultural training and special events to promote harmony and stability. Also see *A Policymaker's Guide to Hate Crimes*, published by the Bureau of Justice Assistance (BJA), U.S. Department of Justice. Contact BJA at 1-800-688-4252, or visit their home page at www.ojp.usdoj.gov/BJA .

COALITIONS CREATE A POSITIVE CLIMATE

Racial and ethnic tensions increase during periods of economic downswing. Hate crimes may occur when unemployed or underemployed workers vent anger on available scapegoats from minority groups.

Coalitions of representatives from political, business, religious, and community organizations help create a positive climate in the community and encourage constructive dialogue. Coalitions can recommend initiatives to help racial and ethnic communities affected by loss of jobs, including programs and plans to help local government ensure equitable disbursement of public and private finds, resources, and services.

PREVENTING HATE CRIMES WITH POLICIES DESIGNED TO PROMOTE RACIAL AND ETHNIC RELATIONS

Local governments can assure that everyone has access to full participation in the municipality's decision-making processes, including equal opportunity for minorities to be represented on appointed boards and commissions. Local governments might institute a policy of inclusion for appointments on boards and commissions. The policy could require listing all appointive positions and notifying all racial and ethnic groups of open seats throughout minority media.

SCHOOLS AND POLICE MUST WORK TOGETHER

Racial and ethnic tensions may increase in schools when there are rapid demographic or socioeconomic changes. Tensions may result from the perception of unequal educational opportunities or disparate practices in hiring faculty and school staff.

Preventing and dealing with hate crimes and hate-based gang activity in schools are the responsibility of school and police officials, who should work together to develop a plan to handle hate crimes and defuse racial tensions. Hate crimes can be school related, community related, or a combination of both. Officials should consider prevention and response roles, identify potential trouble sites, and plan for phased police intervention. Tension can be eased by regular communication with parents, students, media, and other community organizations. Mediation and conflict resolution classes develop the capacity of young people to peacefully settle disputes and conflicts. For more information on how to prevent and counter hate crime in schools, contact the Office for Juvenile Justice and Delinquency Prevention (OJJDP), U.S. Department of Justice. See also OJJDP's *A National Hate Crime Pre-*

vention Curriculum for Middle Schools . Contact OJJDP at 1-800-638-8736, or visit their home page at www.ncjrs.gov/ojjhome.htm .

RUMORS FUEL RACIAL TENSIONS AND CONFLICT

Law enforcement officers believe rumors aggravate more than two-thirds of all civil disturbances. When racial or ethnic tensions may become heightened by exaggerated rumors, a temporary rumor control and verification center is an effective mechanism to ensure accurate information.

A temporary rumor control and verification center typically is operated twenty-four hours a day during the crisis period by a local government agency. It is staffed by professionals and trained volunteers. The media and others should publicize the telephone number.

THE MEDIA CAN BE A HELPFUL ALLY

The influence of print and broadcast media is critical in shaping public attitudes about the hate crime, its perpetrators, and the law enforcement response.

The media can play an important role in preventing hate crimes from increasing community tensions. Local officials should designate an informed single point of contact for hate crime information. Accurate, thorough, and responsible reporting significantly improves the likelihood that stability and harmony will be restored. The media can promote public understanding of mediation and conflict resolution processes and help alleviate fear, suspicion, and anger.

HATE CRIMES MUST BE INVESTIGATED AND REPORTED

Findings on the exact number of hate crimes and trends are difficult to establish and interpretations about hate crimes vary among individuals, law enforcement agencies, public and private organizations, and community groups.

A municipality should assure that its law enforcement agencies adopt the model policy supported by the International Association of Chiefs of Police (call [703] 836-6767) for investigating and reporting hate crimes. This model policy uses the standard reporting form and definition of hate crime developed by the FBI after passage of the Hate Crime Statistics Act (HCSA), 28 U.S.C. 534, enacted April 1990, as amended by the Church Arson Prevention Act of June 1996 (the HCSA also requires collection of data on crimes based on religion, sexual orientation, ethnicity, and disability). The FBI offers training for law enforcement officers and administrators on developing data collection procedures.

For more information, contact the FBI at 1-888-UCR-NIBR. The FBI recommends a two-tier procedure for accurately collecting and reporting hate crime case information. It includes: (1) the officer on the scene of an alleged bias crime making an initial determination that bias motivation is "suspected"; and (2) a second officer or unit with more expertise in bias matters making the final determination of whether a hate crime has actually occurred For more information, see the FBI's *Training Guide for Hate Crime Data Collection and Hate Crime Data Collection Guidelines*. See also Hate/Bias Crimes Train-the-Trainer Program, conducted by the National Center for State, Local, and International Law Enforcement Training, Federal Law Enforcement Training Center (FLETC), U.S. Treasury Department. Contact FLETC at 1-800-743-5382, x 3343.

HATE CRIMES AND MULTIJURISDICTIONAL TASK FORCES

Multijurisdictional or regional task forces are an effective means of sharing information and combining resources to counter hate crime activity.

Some local governments have institutionalized sharing of expertise and agency resources through memorandums of understanding. For example, creating a coalition of public and private agencies and community organizations will give communities in the county or region a thorough range of resources and information to promote racial and ethnic relations and counter hate crimes. This network or consortium can also work with coalitions created especially to investigate and prosecute hate crimes. Such a coalition might include the district attorney, the city attorney, law enforcement agencies, and civil rights, community, and educational organizations. This partnership links prosecutory and law enforcement agencies and community-based response organizations.

VICTIMS, WITNESSES, AND OFFENDERS NEED HELP

Nearly two-thirds of all known perpetrators of hate crimes are teenagers or young adults. When appropriate, a victim-offender restitution program or offender counseling program can be an effective sanction for juveniles.

Educational counseling programs for young perpetrators of hate crime can help dispel stereotypes, prejudice, fears, and other motivators of hate crime. Counseling may include sessions with members of minority groups and visits to local correctional facilities. In addition, "restorative justice," the concept of healing both the victim and the offender while regaining the trust of the community, may be appropriate. The offenders are held accountable and are expected to repair both the physical and emotional damage caused by their actions.

To ensure a comprehensive response to hate crimes, the needs of the victims must be served. For more information on how to meet the diverse needs of both the immediate and secondary victims of hate crimes, contact the Office for Victims of Crime (OVC), U.S. Department of Justice. OVC also provides funding for state offices to provide victim assistance and compensation services. See also OVC's National Bias Crimes Training: For Law Enforcement and Victim Assistance Professionals. Contact OVC at www.ojp.usdoj.gov/ovc/ .

Appendix 8

Holocaust Ethical Implications

"Does the Holocaust Have Ethical Implications for Today?" (With permission of author John T. Pawlikowski, OSM, PhD.)[1]

April 12, 2015

The academic study of ethics, in light of the experience of the Holocaust, has witnessed rapid development in the last decade. In addition to research into ethical decision making during the Holocaust itself in such volumes as Rab Bennett's *Under the Shadow of the Swastika: The Moral Dilemmas of Resistance and Collaboration in Hitler's Europe*, more general reflections on the significance of the Holocaust for contemporary ethics have come to the fore from Jewish and Christian scholars alike. There have also been voices such as Herbert Hirsch who have questioned whether we can learn anything from the Holocaust in terms of the moral challenge facing us today given the sui generis nature of that event as well as the immense complexity of a modern, global society.

I personally stand with those who do find the experience of the Holocaust significant for ethical reflection in today's global society. But Hirsch's pessimism does serve a purpose in reminding us that there is no simplistic transition from the situation of the Shoah into today's complex social situation.

In beginning any study of ethics in the shadow of the Holocaust a caution is always in order. Such an academic study can never substitute for continued remembrance of the victims of the Nazis. Elie Wiesel's oft-quoted statement that to forget the actual victims is in fact to kill them a second time must always remain implanted in our personal and communal templates. Otherwise such an academic study can become a barren exercise.

As we face the ethical challenges of our global society today three basic perspectives must become foundational for our reflections: (1) respect for basic human dignity must supplant any notion that only correct belief entitles one to fundamental rights; (2) our universe of moral concern must be broadened beyond the parameters of our own faith and national communities; and (3) acknowledgment of past failings on the part of our religious and national communities is a necessary pre-condition for development of the internal integrity necessary for genuine and consistent moral commitment.

Let me offer a brief commentary on each of these perspectives. For centuries in my own Roman Catholic tradition correct belief was an absolute requirement for full human dignity. After a bitter struggle at the II Vatican Council over the document on religious liberty, Catholicism underwent a major turn-about in its understanding. In the vision of Vatican II human dignity, not merely right belief, became the fundamental cornerstone of a just society. To be sure, belief remains important. But no longer is it the absolute barometer for human rights. In some ways this reality was also recognized in secular society. As the late Gerhard Riegner has shown in his memoirs, the experience of the Nazi era was crucial in the development of international legal codes on human rights and genocide after the end of World War II.

The lack of a human rights perspective significantly curtailed the Catholic institutional response to Nazism. Now that we are coming to recognize that, at the level of institutional Christianity, fear of liberalism and concern for the loss of the Church's influence over the public order were in fact stronger motives for acquiescence or even collaboration with Nazism and Fascism than classical Christian anti-Semitism itself, we are in a position to ask seriously whether the Church's response would have been different if those Christian voices who advocated incorporation of dimensions of the liberal vision into Christianity, including liberalism's human rights vision, had been heeded. And what if Church leaders had made a concerted effort to establish a working relationship with the liberal opposition to Nazism despite that opposition's widespread hostility to religious belief?

There are those who are asking, and I support their question, whether the return to fundamentalist religious perspectives in nearly all religious traditions might well erode the commitment to basic human dignity as the ground of global society resulting from the ethical reflections on the Nazi era during the past decade or so. There could be such stress on particularistic identity that the developing focus on common human dignity may be lost. That would clearly represent a failure to take the moral challenge of the Holocaust with utter seriousness.

I recognize that hindsight can never reproduce the difficulty of the actual challenge faced by the churches during the Nazi era. Still I must ask whether some embrace of liberalism's fundamental stress on human rights by Catholicism and other churches might not have generated the possibility of an anti-

Nazi coalition between the churches and the liberal secularists despite the latter's strong critique of religion. Clearly the unmitigated opposition to the values espoused by liberalism, including its stress on human rights, undercut such a possible coalition, particularly in the case of the Catholic Church. There were Catholic voices such as Felicite de Lamennais and Henri Lacordaire who urged such an integration of certain liberal values, including the focus on human rights, into mainstream Catholic consciousness. But they were berated for such proposals, much to the ultimate detriment of the Church.

Whether such a coalition would have resulted in the survival of many more Jews, Poles and Roma is an open question. Some prominent historians such as Michael Marrus and Gunther Lewy do not believe that active, public opposition to Nazism on the part of the Christian leadership would have made much difference in terms of the survival of people targeted for extermination by the Nazis, principally the Jews. But on the level of protecting the Church's basic moral integrity, it likely would have proven quite significant.

This is a point I first learned from the teacher who first introduced me to issues of the Church and the Holocaust as an undergraduate student at Loyola University in Chicago. That professor was Dr. Edward Gargan, an historian, who taught a very popular course on modern German history. Speaking as a committed Catholic, he felt that the Church had seriously compromised its future moral integrity by not standing up more directly and openly to Hitler whatever the impact and consequences might have been. That perspective remains deeply ingrained in me until today.

Another aspect of the human rights question in light of the Holocaust is how we state our own faith understanding. Michael Berenbaum has made this point quite strongly. If we do so in a way that fundamentally denigrates another religious tradition, as was the case for centuries especially in terms of the Jewish tradition, we are transforming our faith into an instrument of potential violence. We have seen far too often in past history and even in the present day how powerful and destructive such religious identification can be in terms of instigating or abetting social violence.

Violent religious language can greatly contribute to softening a society for genocide. I would argue that this is precisely what Christian anti-Semitism did during the Nazi era. Religion remains a powerful force in many present-day societies. If religious language in a given society continues to demean people who do not share the dominant faith system and even denies them full rights of citizenship it certainly opens the door for physical assaults on such groups in times of social tension. On the contrary, positive religious language about the "religious other" can serve as a barrier against such assaults. It is especially necessary in the complex national societies that globalization produces.

The emphasis on human rights as a central moral imperative after the Holocaust also impacts our understanding of ecclesiology. Any post-Holocaust definition of the Church (or any religious tradition for that matter) must make human rights integral to that definition.

The vision of the Church that needs to prevail is one that sees the survival of all persons as integral to the authentic survival of the Church itself. The desire for self-preservation, as legitimate as it is, can never be sustained by indifference to human rights abuses against the outside "other." I have argued that Pope Pius XII was regrettably affected by such a "limited" ecclesiology as he tried to keep the institutional Church operational under very trying political circumstances.

There definitely appears to be some understanding of the need for a shift in ecclesiological vision after the Holocaust. I can cite several examples, such as the stance of many of the churches in South Africa in the face of the brutal apartheid political system, the strong support given by local church leaders to the revolution that brought down the Marcos regime in the Philippines, and the courageous stance taken by the Catholic bishops of Malawi when the late Dr. Hastings Banda threatened the human rights of many of the country's citizens. The last situation is especially relevant because the bishops were willing to risk institutional church survival when President Banda made a serious threat to murder them and their catechists if they continued in their protest on behalf of people who, in most instances, were not Catholic or even Christian. Clearly ecclesiology with a human rights bent had become part of the template in Malawi.

But other situations show the need for considerable development of a human rights-based ecclesiology. In the Philippines and in South Africa, Catholic bishops had to go against the papal representatives who urged caution and even support for the existing oppressive regimes. The situations . . . show a Catholic leadership far down the learning curve in terms of moral lessons in light of the Holocaust.

The second ethical principle emerging from reflections on the Holocaust experience involves the extension of our parameters of moral concern. It follows directly from the first principle just discussed. The well-being and even the survival of our own community can never come at the indifference to the sufferings of others. As some Holocaust commentators have put it, we cannot make others "unfortunate expendables" in the process of self-preservation, as many people in the churches seemed to do with regard to the Jews during the period of the Holocaust. Ignoring the plight of others may not be as heinous an offense as outright hatred, but it remains morally unacceptable nonetheless. Allowing some to become "expendable," may in fact rebound eventually on those who take on such an attitude. We, too, may at some point find ourselves "expendable" by some other dominant group if we allow such marginalization of human dignity to go unchallenged. Put another way, the greatest protection of our own human dignity comes ultimately through the uncompromising effort to protect the dignity of all.

There is another dimension of the need for expansion of moral concern as a response to the Holocaust. It has to do with what I have termed the "neutralization" of people, particularly those we may regard rightly or wrongly as our enemy. I remain convinced that religion has a vital role to play in [ensuring] that groups in a society are not "neutralized" in terms of their fundamental humanity. The Holocaust scholar, Henry Friedlander, showed some years ago how the neutral language in reporting daily death counts in the Nazi extermination camps paralleled the language used by the United States military in reporting Vietnamese casualties during the Vietnam War. I myself have examined some of the death camp reports on their daily "activities." If one had no inkling from where they came, one could easily assume they were reporting on the daily production of radios in a manufacturing facility rather than on the daily death count of Nazi victims. The reports were totally devoid of any language that would indicate that human beings were involved at the level of "production."

To understand how easily such "neutralization" of victims, especially those regarded as enemies, can infiltrate human consciousness I would report on a situation in the Hyde Park neighborhood at the University of Chicago where my home institution is located during the Vietnam War era. The Museum of Science and Industry, at the time the most visited tourist attraction in the Midwest, put up an exhibit sponsored by the U.S. armed forces which depicted a mock Vietnamese village. As a pioneering interactive museum, the exhibit had a "hands-on" dimension for children. They could enter a recreated American helicopter gunship and shoot down at the Vietnamese village. It took a group of local clergy people one night in jail to force the closure of the exhibit. This total insensitivity on the part of museum and military officials reflected a much wider disturbing phenomenon as the sanctioning of the term "gooks" for the Vietnamese people which robbed them of all human dignity and hence greatly reduced the sense of moral culpability in the process of killing them.

The Iraqi war generated some similar patterns. Torture and human degradation of prisoners was given at least tacit approval by some military commanders. And the wider public, whether in the United States or in the United Kingdom, has shown little or no moral concern over the high number of Iraqi civilian casualties during this conflict. This total moral indifference extends to the church leadership in both countries who have never challenged their membership on this dimension of contemporary warfare.

Historian Peter Hayes of Northwestern University has further illuminated this "expendable" category of people during the Nazi era in his continuing research on German business leaders during the period of the Third Reich. Hayes concludes that in the end German big business was willing "to walk over corpses." The importance of economic success gradually eroded any sense of the human dignity of those relegated to forced labor in German industry.

There were many factors internal to Germany that contributed to this process of moral numbing. But above all, says Hayes, was the fact that "the Third Reich constructed a framework of economic policy in which the effective pursuit of corporate survival or success had to serve, at least outwardly, the goals and the ideological requirements of the regime." The indifference of German businessmen during the Third Reich, Hayes continues, reveals the all-too-common penchant in the contemporary world to hide behind so-called professional responsibilities in the face of deep moral challenges. "The obligation to achieve the best possible return for the firm and those who own or work for it to secure their long-term prospects, which in decent contexts can be a guarantee against personal corruption or frivolous management, became an excuse for participating in cruel, eventually murderous acts, indeed a mandate to do."

Most alarming about this development was not even the complicity in murder through direct participation in the Nazi program of forced labor, but a sense of innocence about such complicity on the part of very many of the businessmen. They were able to subdue any moral hesitations with the response, "What else can I do?" losing sight of the far more important question, according to Hayes, "what must I never do."

Clearly these German businessmen had "neutralized" the humanity of the people forced by the Nazis into their labor program.

Hayes' studies provide solid data for the perspectives of a number of Jewish and Christian ethicists regarding the erosion of a sense of personal responsibility within Nazi culture. The "system" became the dominant reality, not human dignity. Regrettably we have not learned a lesson from the Nazi experience in this connection. Today we often see a similar process taking place within the context of globalization. "What else can I do?" has in fact become a stock phrase in the vocabulary of global capitalism.

The dynamics of the market must reign supreme no matter what the cost in human terms, no matter that, as a European Union report of several years ago showed, some two hundred and fifty million children around the world are used to support this system living in conditions, in many instances, of virtual slavery. They have become a new form of Nazi forced labor. The late Pope John Paul II, in what may prove in the end to be his most prophetic concern, warned that the global ideology of the market, which has tended to replace the competing Cold War ideologies in recent years, cannot insure the preservation of human dignity:

> The rapid advance toward the globalization of economic and financial systems also illustrates the urgent need to establish who is responsible for guaranteeing

the global common good and the exercise of economic and social rights. The free market by itself cannot do this, because in fact there are many human needs which have no place in the market. (Pope John Paul II)

NOTE

1. Pawlikowski, "Does the Holocaust Have Ethical Implications for Today?"

Appendix 9

Human Rights First

TEN-POINT PLAN FOR COMBATING HATE CRIME[1]

Human Rights First calls on all governments to implement the following Ten-Point Plan for combating violent hate crimes:

1. Acknowledge and condemn violent hate crimes whenever they occur. Senior government leaders should send immediate, strong, public, and consistent messages that violent crimes which appear to be motivated by prejudice and intolerance will be investigated thoroughly and prosecuted to the full extent of the law.
2. Enact laws that expressly address hate crimes. Recognizing the particular harm caused by violent hate crimes, governments should enact laws that establish specific offenses or provide enhanced penalties for violent crimes committed because of the victim's race, religion, ethnicity, sexual orientation, gender, gender identity, mental and physical disabilities, or other similar status.
3. Strengthen enforcement and prosecute offenders. Governments should ensure that those responsible for hate crimes are held accountable under the law, that the enforcement of hate crime laws is a priority for the criminal justice system, and that the record of their enforcement is well documented and publicized.
4. Provide adequate instructions and resources to law enforcement bodies. Governments should ensure that police and investigators—as the first responders in cases of violent crime—are specifically instructed and have the necessary procedures, resources and training to identify,

investigate and register bias motives before the courts, and that prosecutors have been trained to bring evidence of bias motivations and apply the legal measures required to prosecute hate crimes.
5. Undertake parliamentary, inter-agency or other special inquiries into the problem of hate crimes. Such public, official inquiries should encourage public debate, investigate ways to better respond to hate crimes, and seek creative ways to address the roots of intolerance and discrimination through education and other means.
6. Monitor and report on hate crimes. Governments should maintain official systems of monitoring and public reporting to provide accurate data for informed policy decisions to combat violent hate crimes. Such systems should include anonymous and disaggregated information on bias motivations and/or victim groups, and should monitor incidents and offenses, as well as prosecutions. Governments should consider establishing third party complaint procedures to encourage greater reporting of hate crimes and conducting periodic hate crime victimization surveys to monitor underreporting by victims and under-recording by police.
7. Create and strengthen anti-discrimination bodies. Official anti-discrimination and human rights bodies should have the authority to address hate crimes through monitoring, reporting, and assistance to victims.
8. Reach out to community groups. Governments should conduct outreach and education efforts to communities and civil society groups to reduce fear and assist victims, advance police-community relations, encourage improved reporting of hate crimes to the police and improve the quality of data collection by law enforcement bodies.
9. Speak out against official intolerance and bigotry. Freedom of speech allows considerable latitude for offensive and hateful speech, but public figures should be held to a higher standard. Members of parliament and local government leaders should be held politically accountable for bigoted words that encourage discrimination and violence and create a climate of fear for minorities.
10. Encourage international cooperation on hate crimes. Governments should support and strengthen the mandates of intergovernmental organizations that are addressing discrimination—like the Organization for Security and Cooperation in Europe, the European Commission against Racism and Intolerance, and the Fundamental Rights Agency—including by encouraging such organizations to raise the capacity of and train police, prosecutors, and judges, as well as other official bodies and civil society groups to combat violent hate crimes. Governments should also provide a detailed accounting on the incidence and

nature of hate crimes to these bodies in accordance with relevant commitments.

NOTE

1. http://www.humanrightsfirst.org/our-work/fighting-discrimination/ten-point-plan/.

Appendix 10

Financial Help with Security of Institutions

EXAMPLE OF FAITH-BASED FACILITIES SECURITY OPERATING GRANTS

Montgomery County has approved funds to be used for faith-based communities experiencing hate crimes or at significant risk of becoming targets of hate crimes. These grants are available to augment costs for security personnel or other security planning measures for faith-based organizations located in Montgomery County, Maryland. To be eligible to receive funds, individual organizations must:

- Be an IRS registered 501(c)3 tax-exempt nonprofit organization.
- Be in good standing with the Maryland State Department of Assessments and Taxation.
- Be physically located in Montgomery County.
- Be a faith-based organization experiencing hate crimes or at significant risk of becoming a target of hate crimes.

Organizations may use the funds for:

- Current security personnel or to augment current security personnel.
- To pay for a security assessment or plan.
- To conduct security training.
- To develop and execute a security drill.

Organizations may not use the funds for:

- Equipment purchases
- Facility upgrades
- Supplies

The following terms and conditions will apply to the administration of this grant:

- Funds must be used within one year of the date of execution of a contract with the county. No grant funds can be used for expenses beyond these dates.
- All awards will be made on a reimbursement basis. The organization must first incur the expenses and be subsequently reimbursed by the county. The county cannot reimburse for any expenses incurred before the date of a signed and executed contract.
- This is a one-time program for security personnel. Organizations may request further grants through the standard County Executive and County Council grants processes. Information and deadlines for FY20 are available at http://montgomerycountymd.gov/government/grants.html.

In addition, the following conditions apply to applicants for this grant:

- Only one application per organization will be accepted.
- Applicants may request up to a maximum of $20,000.
- Umbrella organizations applying for grant funding on behalf of multiple organizations or institutions will be asked to provide the names of those member organizations or institutions.
- Umbrella organizations may request up to a maximum of $100,000.
- If an individual organization applies for a grant but is also represented by an umbrella organization applying for grant funding on their behalf, funding may be limited to one grant only, depending on funding availability.
- All applications will be accepted and reviewed.

Applications are subject to the Maryland Public Information Act (MPIA) and the county must comply with the disclosure requirements of the MPIA when a request for documents is received. This application must be completed in one sitting. You may not save your information and return later. It is advised that you craft your responses in a separate Word document and copy and paste them into this form. Once submitted, it cannot be changed. Questions? Contact: OEMHS.grants@montgomerycountymd.gov.

Appendix 11

Bomb Threat Checklist

DEPARTMENT OF HOMELAND SECURITY

Most bomb threats are received by phone. Bomb threats are serious until proven otherwise. Act quickly, but remain calm and obtain information by using this checklist.

Note: If a bomb threat is received by phone:

1. Remain calm. Keep the caller on the line for as long as possible. DO NOT HANG UP, even if the caller does.
2. Listen carefully. Be polite and show interest.
3. Try to keep the caller talking to learn more information.
4. If possible, write a note to a colleague to call the authorities or, as soon as the caller hangs up, immediately notify them yourself.
5. If your phone has a display, copy the number and/or letters on the window display.
6. Complete the Bomb Threat Checklist immediately. Write down as much detail as you can remember. Try to get exact words.
7. Immediately upon termination of call, DO NOT HANG UP, but from a different phone, contact authorities immediately with information and await instructions. Do not delete the message.

Note: Signs of a suspicious package:

- No return address
- Excessive postage

- Stains
- Strange odor
- Strange sounds
- Unexpected delivery
- Poor handwriting
- Misspelled words
- Incorrect titles
- Foreign or large amounts of postage
- Restrictive notes

Refer to your local bomb threat emergency response plan for evacuation criteria.

Do not:

- Use two-way radios or cellular phones. Radio signals have the potential to detonate a bomb.
- Touch or move a suspicious package.

Note:

- Date:
- Time:
- Time caller hung up:
- Phone number where call received:

Ask caller:

- Where is the bomb located? (building, floor, room, etc.)
- When will it go off?
- What does it look like?
- What kind of bomb is it?
- What will make it explode?
- Did you place the bomb?
- Why?
- What is your name?

Report exact words of threat:
Information about caller:

- Where is the caller located? (background/level of noise)
- Estimated age:
- Is voice familiar? If so, who does it sound like?

Appendix 11 229

Note: Caller's voice:

- Female/male
- Accent
- Angry/calm
- Clearing throat
- Coughing
- Cracking voice
- Crying
- Deep breathing
- Disguised
- Distinct
- Excited
- Laughter
- Lisp
- Loud
- Nasal
- Normal
- Ragged
- Rapid
- Raspy
- Slow
- Slurred
- Soft
- Stutter

Note: Background sounds:

- Animal noises
- House noises
- Kitchen noises
- Street noises
- Booth
- PA system
- Conversation
- Music
- Motor
- Clear
- Static
- Office machinery
- Factory machinery

Note: Threat language:

- Incoherent
- Message read
- Irrational
- Profane
- Well spoken
- Odd pronunciations
- Taped message
- Disguised voice
- Local/long distance
- Other information:

Bibliography

Aboud, Frances E. *Children and Prejudice*. Hoboken, NJ: Blackwell, 1988.
ADL. "Funding Hate: How White Supremacists Raise Their Money." No date. Accessed March 2019. https://www.adl.org/resources/reports/funding-hate-how-white-supremacists-raise-their-money.
———. "Hate Crime Laws—The ADL Approach." 2012. Accessed March 2019. https://www.adl.org/sites/default/files/documents/assets/html/combating-hate/Hate-Crimes-Law-The-ADL-Approach.html.
———. "Mainstreaming Hate: The Anti-Immigrant Movement in the U.S." November 2018. Accessed March 2019. https://www.adl.org/the-anti-immigrant-movement-in-the-us.
Alesina, Alberto, and Eliana Ferrara. "Participation in Heterogeneous Communities." *Quarterly Journal of Economics* 115, no. 3 (August 2000): 847–904. https://academic.oup.com/qje/article-abstract/115/3/847/1828162?redirectedFrom=fulltext.
Allison, Natalie. "4 Extremist Groups that Will be Part of Weekend's White Lives Matter Rallies." *The Tennessean, USA Today*. October 25, 2017. Accessed March 2019. https://www.usatoday.com/story/news/nation-now/2017/10/25/groups-behind-white-lives-matter/798600001/.
American Jewish Committee. "Thinking about the Holocaust 60 Years Later. A Multinational Public-Opinion Survey." 2005. Accessed March 2019. http://www.policyarchive.org/handle/10207/13667.
American Psychological Association. "Hate Crimes Today: An Age-Old Foe in Modern Dress." *Texas NAACP*. http://www.texasnaacp.org/hatec.htm#apatop.
Barrelle, K. "Pro-Integration: Disengagement from and Life after Extremism." *Behavioral Sciences of Terrorism and Political Aggression* 7, no. 2 (2015): 129–42.
BBC. "YouTube's Neo-Nazi Music Problem." March 20, 2018. https://www.bbc.com/news/blogs-trending-43416117.
BBC Radio Four. "What You Can Do to Spot and Stop Unconscious Bias." Accessed March 2019. https://www.bbc.co.uk/programmes/articles/21wxrfj5S79pz6CMCdHmVL3/what-you-can-do-to-spot-and-stop-unconscious-bias.
Beckwith, Dave, and Christina Lopez. "Community Organizing: People Power from the Grassroots." *Center for Community Change*. No date. Accessed March 2109. https://comm-org.wisc.edu/papers97/beckwith.htm.
Bell, Devon M. "The Sovereign Citizen Movement: The Shifting Ideological Winds." *Naval Postgraduate School*. March 2016. Accessed March 2019. http://hdl.handle.net/10945/48519.

Bellagio. "Bellagio Principles." *Health and Pollution Fund.* May 2017. Accessed March 2019. https://sustainabledevelopment.un.org/content/documents/15591Bellagio_principles_on_valuing_water_final_version_in_word.html.

Blazakis, Jason M. "American Terrorists: Why Current Laws Are Inadequate for Violent Extremists at Home." Lawfare . December 2018 . Accessed March 2019. https://www.lawfareblog.com/american-terrorists-why-current-laws-are-inadequate-violent-extremists-home.

Blee, Katherine. "Conservative and Rightwing Movements." Department of Sociology, University of Pittsburgh. 2010. Accessed March 2019. https://www.annualreviews.org/doi/pdf/10.1146/annurev.soc.012809.102602.

———. "Our Misconceived Picture of Racists." *UiO: Department of Sociology and Human Geography.* October 23, 2015. Accessed March 2019. https://www.sv.uio.no/iss/english/about/news-and-events/news/2015/our-misconceived-picture-of-racists.html.

———. "The Stigma of Racist Activism." In *Coping with Minority Status: Responses to Exclusion and Inclusion,* edited by Fabrizio Butera and John M. Levine, 222–42. Cambridge: Cambridge University Press, 2009. doi:10.1017/CBO9780511804465.011.

———. "US Holocaust Memorial Museum; Voices on Antisemitism." January 2013. https://www.ushmm.org/confront-antisemitism/antisemitism-podcast/kathleen-blee.

———. "White Supremacy as Extreme Deviance." In *Extreme Deviance,* edited by E. Goode and D. A. Vail, 108–17. Thousand Oaks, CA: Pine Forge Press/Sage Publications Co.

Blumenthal, Paul, Jessica Schulberg, and Luke O'Brien. "Mass Shooters Have Exploited the Internet for Years. New Zealand Took It to a New Level." *Huffpost.* Accessed March 16, 2019. https://www.huffpost.com/entry/new-zealand-shooting-columbine-breivik-rodgers-roof-bowers_n_5c8c4b79e4b0d7f6b0f38e58.

Braswell, Sean. "Could Robots Develop Prejudice on Their Own." *OZY.* December 12, 2018. Accessed March 2019. https://www.ozy.com/acumen/could-robots-develop-prejudice-on-their-own/91165?utm_source=dd&utm_medium=email&utm_campaign=12122018&variable=d736864af7133f9b501084b35405d47b.

Brenman, Marc. "A Plan for Reducing Gun Violence in the US." *Urban Planning and Economic Development News,* iss. 5. (January 15, 2013): 38–39. https://issuu.com/urbanplanninganddevelopment/docs/issue_five.

Center for Community Engagement. "York County Human Relations Commission Feasibility Study." *York County Community against Racism.* August 2006. Accessed August 10, 2010. https://www.yorkcity.org/city-services/human-relations-commission-2/.

Chabin, Michele. "Facing Anti-Semitism at Her California School, This Jewish Teen Takes Matters into Her Own Hands." Jewish Telegraphic Agency. November 29, 2018. Accessed March 2019. https://www.jta.org/2018/11/29/news-opinion/facing-anti-semitism-at-her-california-school-this-jewish-teen-takes-matters-into-her-own-hands?utm_source=JTA%20Maropost&utm_campaign=JTA&utm_medium=email&mpweb=1161-7215-16949.

Chakraborti, Neil, David Gadd, Paul Gray, Sam Wright, and Marian Duggan. "Research Report 74." UK: Equality and Human Rights Commission. 2011. Accessed March 2019. https://www.equalityhumanrights.com/sites/default/files/rr74_targeted_harassment.html.

Chamberlin, Jamie. "Lost Boys." *Monitor on Psychology.* June 2008. Accessed March 2019. https://www.apa.org/monitor/2008/06/boys.aspx.

Charles, J. Brian. "A Growing Response to School Shootings: Panic Buttons— on Phones." *Governing.* December 12, 2018. Accessed March 2019. https://www.governing.com/topics/public-justice-safety/gov-school-shooting-panic-button.html.

Chermak, Steven M., Joshua D. Freilich, and Michael Suttmoeller. "The Organizational Dynamics of Far-Right Hate Groups in the United States: Comparing Violent to Non-Violent Organizations, Final Report to Human Factors/Behavioral Sciences Division, Science and Technology Directorate." College Park, MD: U.S. Department of Homeland Security, START, December 2011.

CivXNow. "Mission Statement." No date. Accessed July 5, 2019. https://civxnow.org/mission.

CNN. "ISIS Goes Global: 143 Attacks in 29 Countries Have Killed 2,043." February 12, 2018. https://www.cnn.com/2015/12/17/world/mapping-isis-attacks-around-the-world/index.html.

Coolidge, Calvin. *Goodreads.* No date. Accessed June 17, 2019. https://www.goodreads.com/quotes/38913-we-cannot-do-everything-at-once-but-we-can-do.

Council for European Studies. "We Are Patriots: Uses of National History in Legitimizing Extremism." *Europe Now.* Accessed October 2, 2018. https://www.europenowjournal.org/2018/10/01/we-are-patriots-uses-of-national-history-in-legitimizing-extremism/.

Counter-Narrative Toolkit. http://www.counternarratives.org/custom/plan/best-practices.

Davidson-Hiers, C. D., and Julie Hauserman. "Florida Authorities Make Another Big Arrest Involving White Supremacists and Bombs." Florida Phoenix. November 27, 2018. Accessed March 2019. https://www.floridaphoenix.com/2018/11/27/florida-authorities-make-another-big-arrest-involving-white-supremacists-and-bombs/?fbclid=IwAR1Ii-caqSR7c7w-Ao6unOQE3EwzqLY0sWgJ34yzcvMz9dUHpPaJ0XkC2VY.

Dawson, Kate Pound. "US Military Commanders Reject Extremists in the Ranks." *Voice of America.* August 23, 2017. Accessed March 2019. https://www.voanews.com/a/us-military-commanders-reject-extremists-in-the-ranks/3997458.html.

Decker, Stephanie, and Liz Legers. "Interview with Kathleen Blee." *Social Thought & Research* 28. Accessed March 2019. https://kuscholarworks.ku.edu/bitstream/handle/1808/5222/STARV28A2.html.sequence=1.

DeMilto, L. "Turning Point: Collaborating for a New Century in Public Health: A Premise Paper." *National Association of County & City Health Officials (NACCHO).* May 13, 2008. Accessed March 2019. https://www.rwjf.org/en/library/research/2008/05/turning-point-.html.

Diamond, Stephen A. "Essential Secrets of Psychotherapy: What Is the 'Shadow'?" *Psychology Today,* April 20, 2012. Accessed March 2019. https://www.psychologytoday.com/us/blog/evil-deeds/201204/essential-secrets-psychotherapy-what-is-the-shadow.

Dilawar, Arvind. "'Hate Is Just Exhausting': Growing Up With—And Running Away From—The Ku Klux Klan." *Pacific Standard Magazine,* November 28, 2018. https://psmag.com/news/jvonne-hubbard-growing-up-with-the-ku-klux-klan.

Director of National Intelligence. "The Near Future: Tensions Are Rising." 2018. Accessed March 2019. https://www.Dni.Gov/Index.Php/Global-Trends/Near-Future.

European Commission. "The Contribution of Youth Work to Preventing Marginalisation and Violent Radicalisation. A Practical Toolbox for Youth Workers & Recommendations for Policy Makers." Luxembourg: European Union Work Plan for Youth for 2016–2018. 2017. Accessed March 2019. https://publications.europa.eu/en/publication-detail/-/publication/0ad09926-a8b1-11e7-837e-01aa75ed71a1.

Ezekiel, R. S. *The Racist Mind: Portraits of American Neo-Nazis and Klansmen.* New York: Viking, 1995.

Federal Bureau of Investigation. "Uniform Crime Reporting Program's Hate Crime Frequently Asked Questions." April 2018. https://ucr.fbi.gov/hate-crime-faqs.

Fernandez, Henry. "Curbing Hate Online: What Companies Should Do Now (Appendix)." Center for American Progress. October 2018. Accessed March 2109. https://cdn.americanprogress.org/content/uploads/2018/10/24111621/ModelInternetCompanies-appendix.html.

"Fighting Discrimination: Ten Point Plan." *Human Rights First.* No date. Accessed March 2019. http://www.humanrightsfirst.org/our-work/fighting-discrimination/ten-point-plan/.

"Final Report of the Federal Commission on School Safety." December 18, 2018. https://www2.ed.gov/documents/school-safety/school-safety-report.pdf.

Florida, Richard. *The Rise of the Creative Class.* New York: Basic Books, 2014.

Frankl, Viktor. *Man's Search for Meaning.* New York: Pocket Books, 1997.

Gallup-Healthways. "State of American Well-Being: 2013 State, Community, and Congressional District Analysis." 2014. Accessed March 2019. www.well-beingindex.com.

Gore, Jeanine. "Former Neo-Nazi Shares Stories of Hatred at Cal State–Chico." *The Orion.* November 14, 2001. https://culteducation.com/group/1071-neo-nazis/15042-former-neo-nazi-shares-stories-of-hatred-at-cal-state-chico.html.

Goss, Jennifer L. "History of the Nazi Party." ThoughtCo. 2018. https://www.thoughtco.com/history-of-the-nazi-party-1779888.

Grattet, Ryken. "Hate Crimes: Better Data or Increasing Frequency?" No date. Accessed March 2019. http://www.prb.org/Template.cfm?Section=PRB&template=/ContentManagement/ContentDisplay.cfm&ContentID=6926.

Griggs, Brandon, and Christina Walker. "In the Year Since Parkland There's Been a School Shooting, on Average, Every 12 Days." CNN.com. February 14, 2019. Accessed March 2019. https://www.cnn.com/2019/02/14/us/school-shootings-since-parkland-trnd/index.html.

Hamm, M. S. "Apocalyptic Violence: The Seduction of Terrorist Subcultures." *Theoretical Criminology* 8, no. 3 (2004): 323–39.

———. "Terrorist Recruitment in American Correctional Institutions: An Exploratory Study of NonTraditional Faith Groups Final Report." *National Institute of Justice*. December 2007. Accessed March 2019. https://www.ncjrs.gov/html.files1/nij/grants/220957.html.

Hate on Display™. "Hate Symbols Database." Accessed March 2019. ttps://www.adl.org/education-and-resources/resource-knowledge-base/hate-symbols.

Hatley, James. *Suffering Witness: The Quandary of Responsibility after the Irreparable*. Albany: SUNY Press, 2000.

Hawley, George. *Making Sense of the Alt-Right*. New York: Columbia University Press, 2017.

Herek, G. M., and K. T. Berrill. *Hate Crimes: Confronting Violence Against Lesbians and Gay Men*. Newbury Park, CA: Sage Publications, 1992.

Hermansson, Patrik. "My Time Undercover with the Alt-Right." *New York Times*, September 27, 2017. Accessed March 2019. https://www.nytimes.com/2017/09/27/opinion/alt-right-neo-nazis.html.

Hernández, Tanya Katerí. "Black-on-Mexican Violence in Staten Island, NY: The Untold Tale of Turf Defense." *Guest Commentary; National Institute for Latino Policy*, August 24, 2010. Accessed March 2019. www.latinopolicy.org.

HG.org Legal Resources. "RICO Law." No date. Accessed March 2109. https://www.hg.org/rico-law.html.

Hohensee, J. B., and L. Derman-Sparks. "Implementing an Anti-Bias Curriculum in Early Childhood Classrooms." *ERIC Digest*. Urbana, IL: ERIC Clearinghouse on Elementary and Childhood Education. 1992 (ED 351 146).

Hollywood, John S. "Suppressing Motivation, Legitimacy Can Help Avoid Political Violence." *Rand*. November 28, 2018. Accessed March 2019. https://www.rand.org/blog/2018/11/suppressing-motivation-legitimacy-can-help-avoid-political.html.

Homeland Security. "Enhancing School Safety Using a Threat Assessment Model." *National Threat Assessment Center*. 2018. Accessed March 2019. https://www.dhs.gov/publication/enhancing-school-safety-using-threat-assessment-model.

Howard, Terry. "When Bias Comes Knocking." *America Diversity Report*. December 2018. Accessed March 2019. https://americandiversityreport.com/category/when-bias-comes-knocking-by-terry-howard/.

Hunton and Williams LLP. "Final Report: Independent Review of the 2017 Protest Events in Charlottesville, Virginia." November 24, 2017. http://www.charlottesville.org/home/showdocument?id=59691.

Hurley, Katie. "Social Media and Teens: How Does Social Media Affect Teenagers' Mental Health." Psycom. No date. Accessed November 30, 2018. https://www.psycom.net/social-media-teen-mental-health.

"If You Don't Have Mandatory Holocaust Education, DEMAND IT!" No date. Accessed March 2019. https://chelm.freeyellow.com/Holocaust_education.html.

International Holocaust Remembrance Alliance. "Working Definition of Antisemitism." No date. Accessed March 2019. https://www.holocaustremembrance.com/working-definition-antisemitism.

International Institute for Justice and the Rule of Law. October 2017. "Toolkit on Juvenile Justice in a Counter-Terrorism Context, 1st edition." https://theiij.org/wp-content/uploads/IIJ-TOOLKIT-JUVE-NILE-JUSTICE.pdf.

Karahan, Fatih, and Darius Li. "What Caused the Decline in Interstate Migration in the United States?" *Federal Reserve Bank of New York: Liberty Street Economics*. October 17, 2016. Accessed March 2019. https://libertystreeteconomics.newyorkfed.org/2016/10/what-caused-the-decline-in-interstate-migration-in-the-united-states.html.

Kaufman, George W. *The Lawyer's Guide to Balancing Life & Work*. Chicago: American Bar Association 2006.

Katz, P. A. "Development of Children's Racial Awareness and Intergroup Attitudes." In *Current Topics in Early Childhood Education*, edited by L. G. Katz. Norwood, NJ: Ablex, 1982.

Koehler, D. Understanding Deradicalization. Methods, Tools and Programs for Countering Violent Extremism. Oxon/New York: Routledge, 2016.

Kotch, Alex. "How the Right-Wing Koch and DeVos Families Are Funding Hate Speech on College Campuses Across the U.S." April 2017. Accessed March 2019. https://www.alternet.org/right-wing/rightwing-billionaires-are-intentionally-funding-hate-speech-college-campuses.

Leamer, Nathan, and R. Street. "A Chance to Fix Civil Asset Forfeiture." *Spotlight on Poverty and Opportunity*. October 26, 2016. Accessed March 2019. https://spotlightonpoverty.org/spotlight-exclusives/chance-fix-civil-asset-forfeiture/.

Leat, Chad. "Commentary: We're Not in Kansas Anymore." *U.S. News and World Report*. April 11, 2018. Accessed March 2019. https://www.usnews.com/news/best-states/articles/2018-04-11/commentary-were-not-in-kansas-anymore.

Lenz, Ryan. "Life after Hate." *Cult News 101*. May 2016. Accessed March 2019. https://www.cultnews101.com/2016/03/life-after-hate.html.

Levin, J., and J. McDevitt. *Hate Crimes: The Rising Tide of Bigotry and Bloodshed*. New York: Plenum Press, 1993.

Levine, Deborah. "The Challenge of Unconscious Bias." *American Diversity Report*. March 2018. Accessed March 2019. https://americandiversityreport.com/category/the-challenge-of-unconscious-bias-by-deborah-levine/.

———. "Holocaust Lessons at Memorial Auditorium." *American Diversity Report*. October 28, 2018. Accessed March 2019. https://americandiversityreport.com/category/category/about-us/editor-and-advisors/about-deborah-levine/newspaper-opinion-columns-by-deborah-levine/.

———. "The Liberator's Daughter." 2016. *American Diversity Report*.

———. "Pandora's Box of Hate." *Chattanooga Times Free Press*. March 20, 2018. Accessed March 2019. https://www.timesfreepress.com/news/opinion/columns/story/2018/mar/20/levine-deborah-levine/466314/.

———. "Policies, Faith, and Calendars." *American Diversity Report*. 2018. Accessed March 2019. https://americandiversityreport.com/category/policies-faith-and-calendars-by-deborah-levine/.

———. Religious Diversity in Our Schools. Deborah Levine Enterprises, LLC, 2013.

———. "Shelley Rose: Council Against Hate." *American Diversity Report*. March 2019. https://americandiversityreport.com/category/shelley-rose-trends-in-hate-and-anti-semitism/.

Levitas, Daniel. *The Terrorist Next Door: The Militia Movement and the Radical Right*. New York: St. Martin's Press, 2002.

Ling, Justin. "Follow the Money." *Vice News*. August 22, 2017. Accessed March 2019. https://news.vice.com/en_ca/article/wjz73q/inside-rebel-medias-big-money-anti-islam-crusade.

Liphshiz, Cnaan. "The Latest Poll on Anti-Semitism in Europe Looks Bad. Trust Me: It's True." *Jewish Telegraphic Agency*, December 2018. Accessed March 2019. https://www.jta.org/2018/12/10/global/the-latest-poll-on-anti-semitism-in-europe-looks-bad-trust-me-its-true?utm_source=JTA%20Maropost&utm_campaign=JTA&utm_medium=email&mpweb=1161-7525-14426.

Lyons, Matthew N. "Rising above the Herd: Keith Preston's Authoritarian Anti-Statism." *New Politics*. April 29, 2011. https://newspol.org/rising-above-herd-keith-prestons-authoritarian-anti-statism/.

"Major Depression." *National Institutes of Mental Health*. No date. Accessed March 2019. https://www.nimh.nih.gov/health/statistics/major-depression.shtml.

Mannie, Sierra, *Reveal Hechinger*, and *Clarion-Ledger*. "Mississippi Textbooks Gloss Over Civil Rights Struggle." *Education Week*, October 4, 2017. Accessed March 2019. https://www.edweek.org/ew/articles/2017/10/04/why-students-are-ignorant-about-the-civil.html.

Marsden, Victor E. *Protocols of the Zionist and Masonic Elite for a Big Brother Police State and a New World Order*. Spicewood, TX: RiverCrest Publishing, 2011.

Massachusetts Model Protocol for Bias Crime Investigation. "Responding to Hate Crime: A Multidisciplinary Curriculum." National Center for Hate Crime Prevention, U.S. Department of Justice, 2000. https://www.ncjrs.gov/ovc_archives/reports/responding/files/ncj182290.pdf.

May, Rob. "Hearing Hate: White Power Music." *Europe Now*. October 1, 2018. Accessed March 2019. https://www.europenowjournal.org/2018/10/01/hearing-hate-white-power-music/.

McCord, Mary, and Michael Signer. "This Legal Tactic Can Keep Neo-Nazi Protests Out of Your City." *Washington Post*, August 10, 2018. https://www.washingtonpost.com/outlook/this-legal-tactic-can-keep-neo-nazi-protests-out-of-your-city/2018/08/10/c80bc240-9c07-11e8-8d5e-c6c594024954_story.html.?utm_term=.8876b391951b.

McDougald, Park. "The Unflattering Familiarity of the Alt-Right in Angela Nagel's Kill All Normies." *New York*, July 13, 2017. http://nymag.com/intelligencer/2017/07/angela-nagles-kill-all-normies-the-alt-right-and-4chan.html.

McManus, John C. "Beware of the Strong Cities Network." *The New American*, May 6, 2016. Accessed March 2019. https://www.thenewamerican.com/reviews/opinion/item/23122-beware-of-the-strong-cities-network.

The National Archives. "Hate Crime—The Cross-Government Action Plan." *Home Office UK.gov.* October 13, 2009. Archived April 8, 2010. 2010. https://webarchive.nationalarchives.gov.uk/20100408151451/http://www.homeoffice.gov.uk/documents/hate-crime-action-plan/.

National Socialist Movement. "Twenty-Five Points." No date. Accessed June 17, 2006. http://www.nsm88.com/25points/25pointsengl.html.

Newport Academy. "A Guide to Teen Mental Disorders." October 30, 2018. Accessed March 2019. https://www.newportacademy.com/resources/mental-health/teen-mental-disorders/.

Neiwert, David. "Oath Keepers' Chief Points to Katrina Response to Justify Paranoia: 'They Disarmed Americans Over Some Bad Weather.'" *Crooks and Liars*, February 2, 2010. https://crooksandliars.com/david-neiwert/oath-keepers-chief-points-katrina-re.

Nietzsche, Friedrich. *Ecce Homo*. *Goodreads*. No date. https://www.goodreads.com/quotes/822482-another-thing-is-war-i-am-naturally-warlike-attacking-is.

NSW Government. "Healthy Urban Development Checklist: A Guide for Health Services When Commenting on Development Policies, Plans and Proposals." NSW Department of Health . 2009. Accessed March 2019. www.health.nsw.gov.au.

Ogawa, Brian. *Color of Justice: Culturally Sensitive Treatment of Minority Crime Victims*. Boston: Allyn and Bacon, 1990.

Olmstead, Elena. "Racist Fliers Dropped in Neighborhood." *Grandview Herald*. August 8, 2006.

Opportunity Insights. "The Opportunity Atlas: Mapping the Childhood Roots of Social Mobility." *Harvard University*. No date. Accessed March 2019. https://opportunityinsights.org/.

Parliament of the World's Religions. "Fostering Interfaith Understanding for a More Peaceful, Just, and Sustainable World." No date. Accessed March 2019. https://parliamentofreligions.org/.

Pawlikowski, John T. "Does the Holocaust Have Ethical Implications for Today?" *American Diversity Report*. April 12, 2015. Accessed March 2019. https://americandiversityreport.com/category/does-the-holocaust-have-ethical-implications-for-today-by-john-t-pawlikowski-osm-ph-d/.

Perry, Barbara. "The Psychological Harms of Hate: Implications and Interventions." *Hate Crimes* 3. Santa Barbara, CA: Greenwood Publishing Group, 2009.

Piazza, J. A. "The Determinants of Domestic Right-Wing Terrorism in the USA: Economic Grievance, Societal Change and Political Resentment." *Conflict Management and Peace Science* 34, no. 1 (2017): 52–80.

Putnam, Robert D. *Bowling Alone: The Collapse and Revival of American Community*. New York: Simon and Schuster, 2000.

RationalWiki. "Racialism." No date. Accessed March 2019. https://rationalwiki.org/wiki/Racialism.

Ray, Paul H., and Sherry Ruth Anderson. *The Cultural Creatives: How 50 Million People Are Changing the World*. Portland, OR: Broadway Books, October 2, 2001. Accessed March 2019.

Reeves, Richard V., and Eleanor Krause. "Raj Chetty in 14 Charts: Big Findings on Opportunity and Mobility We Should All Know." *Brookings*, January 11, 2018. https://www.brookings.edu/blog/social-mobility-memos/2018/01/11/raj-chetty-in-14-charts-big-findings-on-opportunity-and-mobility-we-should-know/.

Reilly, Claire. "Dark Web 101: Your Guide to the Badlands of the Internet." *CNET*, November 17, 2017. Accessed March 2019. https://www.cnet.com/news/darknet-dark-web-101-your-guide-to-the-badlands-of-the-internet-tor-bitcoin/.

Reitman, Janet. "All-American Nazis." *Rolling Stone*, May 2, 2018. Accessed March 2019. https://www.rollingstone.com/politics/politics-news/all-american-nazis-628023/.

Robins-Early, Nick. "Facebook and Instagram Let Neo-Nazis Run Clothing Brands on Their Platforms." *Huffington Post*, August 2, 2018. Accessed March 2019. https://www.huffingtonpost.com/entry/facebook-nazi-clothing-extremism_us_5b5b5cb3e4b0fd5c73cf2986.

Romm, Tony. "Russia-Purchased Ads on Facebook during the 2016 Election Were Aimed at Stoking Social Tensions." *Recode*, September 25, 2017. Accessed March 2019. https://www.recode.net/2017/9/25/16363920/facebook-russia-ads-interference-election-social-divisions-tensions.

Rosenberg, Marshall. "Speak Peace in a World of Conflict." *Puddle Dancer Press*. No date. Accessed June 13, 2019. https://www.nonviolentcommunication.com/freeresources/article_archive/emotional_healing_mrosenberg.htm.

Rosenblatt, Roger. "Their Finest Minute." *New York Times*, July 3, 1994. https://www.nytimes.com/1994/07/03/magazine/their-finest-minute.html.

Roskie, Jamie Baker. "Values as Part of the Clinical Experience." *Pace Environmental Law Review Online Companion* 2, no. 1 (July 2011). https://core.ac.uk/download/pdf/46710347.pdf.

Roston, Aram, and Joel Anderson. "The Man Behind the Alt-Right." *BuzzFeed News*. Accessed March 2019. https://www.buzzfeednews.com/article/aramroston/hes-spent-almost-20-years-funding-the-racist-right-it.

Ruhl, Stefan, and Gisela Will. "RAXEN Focal Point for the UK; National Analytical Study on Racist Violence and Crime." University at Bamberg. European Forum for Migration Studies (EFMS). No date. Accessed March 2019. http://eumc.europa.eu/.

Saez, Emmanuel. "Income Inequality." *UC Berkeley*. No date. Accessed March 2019. https://inequality.org/facts/income-inequality/.

Sander, T. H. "Still Bowling Alone? The Post-9/11 Split." *Journal of Democracy* 21, no. 1 (January 2010): 9–16.

Scanlon-Monash Index. https://www.monash.edu/__data/assets/html_file/0009/1585269/mapping-social-cohesion-national-report-2018.html.

Schulberg, Jessica. "Controversial Trump Aide Katharine Gorka Helped End Funding for Group That Fights White Supremacy." *Huffpost*, August 15, 2017. Accessed March 2019. https://www.huffpost.com/entry/katharine-gorka-life-after-hate_n_59921356e4b09096429943b6.

Schwarz, Wendy. "Anti-Bias and Conflict Resolution Curricula: Theory and Practice." ERIC/CUE Digest No. 97. New York: ERIC Clearinghouse on Urban Education, 1994 (ED 305 135). https://www.ericdigests.org/1995-2/bias.htm.

Scott, Eugene. "Most Americans Say Race Relations Are a Major Problem, but Few Discuss It with Friends and Family." *Washington Post*, May 31, 2018. Accessed March 2019. https://www.washingtonpost.com/news/the-fix/wp/2018/05/31/most-americans-say-race-relations-are-a-major-problem-but-few-discuss-it-with-friends-and-family/?utm_term=.f38c85269baa.

Simon, Sidney B., Leland W. Howe, and Howard Kirschenbaum. *Values Clarification*. New York: Hart Publishing Company, 1972.

Singer, Jenny. "Mark Zuckerberg Argues that Holocaust Denial Is a Freedom of Speech Issue." *Forward*, July 18, 2018. https://forward.com/schmooze/406062/mark-zuckerberg-argues-that-holocaust-denial-is-a-freedom-of-speech-issue/.

Sofoluwe, G. O., ed. *Principles and Practice of Public Health in Africa*. Volume 2. Nigeria: University Press, 1996.

Soundarya, S. "Corporate Social Responsibility: A Contemporary Approach Towards Sustainable Development." *IOSR Journal of Business and Management*, no date, 40–43. Accessed June 14, 2019. http://www.iosrjournals.org/iosr-jbm/papers/NCCMPCW/P007.pdf.

Souris, Elena, and Spandana Singh. "Want to Deradicalize Terrorists? Treat Them Like Everyone Else." Foreign Policy, November 23, 2018. Accessed March 2019. https://foreignpolicy.com/2018/11/23/want-to-deradicalize-terrorists-treat-them-like-everyone-else-counterterrorism-deradicalization-france-sri-lanka-pontourny-cve/.

Southern Poverty Law Center. "New Brand of Racist Odinist Religion on the March." Accessed March 2019. https://www.splcenter.org/fighting-hate/intelligence-report/1998/new-brand-racist-odinist-religion-march.

———. "Ten Ways to Fight Hate: A Community Response Guide." August 14, 2017. Accessed March 2019. https://www.splcenter.org/20170814/ten-ways-fight-hate-community-response-guide.

Stanton, Gregory, et al. "The Precautionary Principle: Environmental Epidemiology's Gift to Genocide Prevention." Poster distributed at Seventh Biennial Meeting, the International Association of Genocide Scholars, July 2007, Sarajevo, Bosnia.

Steele, Jennifer, Y. Susan Choi, and Nalini Ambady. "Stereotyping, Prejudice, and Discrimination: The Effect of Group Based Expectations on Moral Functioning." No date. Accessed March 27, 2007. http://www.atkinson.yorku.ca/~jsteele/files/MoralityChapterFinal.doc.

Steinberg, Annie, MD, Jane Brooks, MEd, and Tariq Remtulla , BA. "Youth Hate Crimes: Identification, Prevention, and Intervention." *American Journal of Psychiatry* 160 (2003): 979–89.

Stern, Kenneth. *Antisemitism Today: How It Is the Same, How It Is Different and How to Fight It*. New York: American Jewish Committee, 2006.

Taber, Jay. "Forms of Resistance." *Skookum*. April 8, 2006. Accessed March 2019. http://skookumgeoduck.blogspot.com/2006/04/forms-of-resistance.html.

———. "Research as Organizing Tool." *Skookum*, June 1, 2005. http://skookumgeoduck.blogspot.com/2005/06/research-as-organizing-tool.html.

———. *Salvaging Democracy: Selected Works*. iUniverse, 2003.

Tavernise, Sabrina. "Survey Finds Rising Perception of Class Tension." *New York Times*, January 11, 2012. Accessed March 2019. https://www.nytimes.com/2012/01/12/us/more-conflict-seen-between-rich-and-poor-survey-finds.html.

Teitelbaum, Benjamin R. "Saga's Sorrow: Femininities of Despair in the Music of Radical White Nationalism." *Ethnomusicology* 58, no. 3 (Fall 2014): 405–30. https://www.jstor.org/stable/10.5406/ethnomusicology.58.3.0405?seq=1#page_scan_tab_contents.

Thompson, A. C. "An Atomwaffen Member Sketched Map to Take the Neo-Nazis Down. What Path Officials Took Is a Mystery." *Frontline*, November 20, 2018. https://www.pbs.org/wgbh/frontline/article/an-atomwaffen-member-sketched-a-map-to-take-the-neo-nazis-down-what-path-officials-took-is-a-mystery/.

Thompson, A. C., and Jake Hanrahan. "Ranks of Notorious Hate Group Include Active-Duty Military." ProPublica. May 3, 2018. Accessed March 2019. https://www.propublica.org/article/atomwaffen-division-hate-group-active-duty-military.

Un-Bias Guide Series by Deborah Levine. Accessed March 2019. https://americandiversityreport.com/diversity-resources/un-bias-guide-series/.

U.S. Conference of Catholic Bishops. "Confronting a Culture of Violence: A Catholic Framework for Action: Pastoral Message of the U.S. Catholic Bishops." 1994. Accessed March 2019. http://www.usccb.org/issues-and-action/human-life-and-dignity/violence/confronting-a-culture-of-violence-a-catholic-framework-for-action.cfm.

U.S. Department of Education. "Preventing Youth Hate Crime." Accessed March 2019. http://www.ed.gov/pubs/HateCrime/page5.html.

U.S. Department of Justice. "Community Relations Service." Accessed March 2019. https://www.justice.gov/crs.

U.S. Holocaust Memorial Museum. "Information for Students." No date. Accessed March 2019. https://www.ushmm.org/learn/students.

Ury, William. *Getting to Peace*. New York: Penguin Group, 1999.

Valasik, Matthew, and Shannon Reid. "White Nationalist Groups Are Really Street Gangs, and Law Enforcement Needs to Treat Them that Way." The Homeland Security News Wire, December 5, 2018. Accessed March 2019. http://www.homelandsecuritynewswire.com/dr20181205-white-nationalist-groups-are-really-street-gangs-and-law-enforcement-needs-to-treat-them-that-way.

Vice. "Get to Know the Memes of the Alt-Right and Never Miss a Dog-Whistle Again." https://www.vice.com/en_us/article/ezagwm/get-to-know-the-memes-of-the-alt-right-and-never-miss-a-dog-whistle-again.

Weingarten, Kaethe. "Compassionate Witnessing and the Transformation of Societal Violence: How Individuals Can Make a Difference." 2003. Accessed March 2019. http://www.witnessingproject.org/articles/CompassionateWitnessing.html.

———. "Restorative Justice Seminar Series, Seminar 2: The Wounded Witness." *Police, Lawyers, Judges and Community*, May 12, 2003. Accessed March 2019. http://www.brc21.org/resources/restore_justice/connorweingarten.html.

Weiss, Jessica. "Dozens of Hate-Fueled Attacks Reported at Walmart Stores Nationwide." *UnivisionNews*, March 26, 2018. Accessed March 2019. https://www.univision.com/univision-news/united-states/dozens-of-hate-fueled-attacks-reported-at-walmart-stores-nationwide.

Westervelt, Eric. "Is There a Cure for Hate?" *NPR*, November 6, 2018. Accessed March 2019. https://www.npr.org/2018/11/06/663773514/is-there-a-cure-for-hate.

Wikipedia. "Atomwaffen Division." No date. Accessed March 2019. https://en.wikipedia.org/wiki/Atomwaffen_Division.

———. "Organized Crime in California." Accessed March 2019. https://en.wikipedia.org/wiki/Organized_crime_in_California.

———. "White Power Music." Accessed March 2019. https://en.wikipedia.org/wiki/White_power_music.

Wood, Thomas. "Racism Motivated Trump Voters More Than Authoritarianism." *Washington Post*, April 17, 2017. Accessed March 2019. https://www.washingtonpost.com/news/monkey-cage/wp/2017/04/17/racism-motivated-trump-voters-more-than-authoritarianism-or-income-inequality/?utm_term=.fbe2b5dccc9c.

Ziv, Stav. "Two New Efforts Launched to Require Holocaust Education Nationwide, One Triggered by Spicer." *Newsweek*, May 1, 2017. Accessed March 2019. https://www.newsweek.com/two-new-efforts-launched-require-holocaust-education-nationwide-one-triggered-592671.

Index

AAC&U. *See* American Association of Colleges and Universities
AB. *See* Aryan Brotherhood
Abdulazeez, Muhammad Youssef, 1
Abolition of the Statute of Limitations on War Crimes and Crimes against Humanity, 4, 48
Aboud, Frances E., 72
accountability, 29–30, 221
Act for America, 151
action pathways, 151
active shooter protocols, 46–47, 169
Adam and Eve, 19
addiction, 15
ADL, 169, 169–170, 174
African Americans, 3, 37, 50, 109
Against Violent Extremism Network, 84, 170
Agenda 21, 151–152
AJC. *See* American Jewish Committee
Albany High School, 112–113
alcohol, 118
Alexa, 148
Allen, Ethan, 176
alternatives, in schools, 123
alt-right, 17, 27, 108
Amazon, 147, 148
"America First", 152
American Association of Colleges and Universities (AAC&U), 170
American Dream, ix, 15, 67, 102, 103, 141–142, 142
American Front, 20
American Jewish Committee (AJC), 170, 176
American National Socialism, 185–189
American Psychological Association, 170
American terrorists, vii
anarchists, 164
Anne Frank Center, 130–131
Anne Frank Webguide, 170
Anti-Bias Curriculum, 173
anti-bullying laws, 124
anti-Christian propaganda, 114
anticipatory action, 71–72
Anti-Defamation League, 2, 14, 31, 34, 169, 195
anti-discrimination, 222
anti-environmental, 167
antifa, 152
anti-gay hate crimes, 40
anti-gay propaganda, 113
anti-globalism, 17
anti-government, 161
anti-immigration rhetoric, in schools, 123
anti-mask laws, 58
anti-Muslim, 13, 113, 145, 183
anti-Nazi revolution, 195–196
anti-Semitism, ix, 3–5, 31, 45, 70, 128, 130; Christianity and, 129; church and, 131; definition of, 153; graffiti, 6; New

241

Index

Anti-Semitism, 160; rise of, 6, 7; secondary, 5. *See also* Holocaust
Anti-Semitism Today (Stern), 128
anti-terrorism, 49
anti-white propaganda, 114
apartheid, 43
apology, 93
Apple, 147
apps, 47
Arizona Hammerheads, 20
Armond, Paul de, 71, 180
arson, 43
artificial intelligence, 104, 147–148, 172
Aryan Brotherhood (AB), 20, 21–22
Aryan Circle, 20
Aryan Congress, 13–14, 19
Aryan Nations, 11, 13, 14, 19
Aryans, 3, 19
Aslinger, Kevin, 131, 131–132
assimilation, culture and, 146
Atomwaffen Division, 153
Auschwitz, 127, 128
Australia, 145
autonomy, 90

Banda, Hastings, 216
Bandura, Albert, 170–171
banking, 19
Baraboo, Wisconsin, 117
Bazelon, David L., 39
BDI. *See* Building Democracy Initiative
Beach, Henry, 161–162
Beierle, Scott Paul, 37
Bell, Devon, 46
beneficence, 90
Bennett, Rab, 128, 213
Berke, Andy, 1–2
best practices, 142
bias, ix, 33, 110; crime indicator, 153; in faculty, 126; hate crimes and, 42, 111, 200; prejudice and, 111; in school curriculum, 114–115; in schools, 126; in students, 126; theory and practice, 110–112; unconscious, 111–112
Bias, 178
bias incident response protocol, 199–200; case-coordinating protocol, 201, 204; circumstances that initiate, 200; definition of, 200; diversity and, 203; documentation in, 202; evidence in, 202; frontline respondents, 201; investigations, 202, 203; law enforcement and, 201; procedural steps, 201–204; reporting in, 200–201, 202; suspects in, 202; team for, 203–204
Bible, 18
Big Data, ix
bigotry, ix, 42, 108, 110
Billings, Montana, 63, 65, 96, 196
Bingham, Tyler Davis, 21
bitcoin, 164
BJA. *See* Bureau of Justice Assistance
Blee, Kathleen, 82–83
Blood and Honor (28), 151
Blood and Soil, 153
"Blood Money", 28
Bolshevik Revolution, 6
bomb threats, 227–230
Boston Marathon bombers, 148
Bowers, Robert, 37
Bowling Alone (Putnam), 85
boycotts, 66
boys, addressing needs of, 80–81
Boys Project, 81
British National Front, 14
Brooks, Jane, 181
Building Democracy Initiative (BDI), 171
bullying, 38
Bureau of Justice Assistance (BJA), 171, 180
Bush, George W., 42
businesses, 186
Butler, Richard, 13, 13–14

Call to Action (Hirabayashi, Yasui, & Korematsu), 181–182
Canada, hate crimes in, 42
Carmel, Jason, 171–172
Catholicism, 214, 214–215
cell phone apps, 47
censorship, 29
Center for American Progress, 172
Center for the Prevention of Hate Violence, 172
Charlottesville tragedy, 66, 69, 153, 172
Chattanooga, 1, 131–132
childhood, 118
children, 72, 96–97, 110–111, 118

Children and Prejudice (Aboud), 72
Christchurch massacre, 25
Christian Identity, 17, 18–20, 154, 165; genocide and, 19; holy war of, 20; intermarriage and, 19; Jews and, 19; Second Coming in, 19–20; slavery in, 19
Christianity, viii, 129, 214
Christian Patriots, 17
church, 131, 214–216
Church of the Creator, 154, 163
citizenship, 123, 129, 151, 185, 215
civic education, 15, 119–120
civic engagement, community building, 63–65
civic life, 89
civic reinvention, 85
civil asset forfeiture, 58
civil rights, vii, 207
Civil Rights Movement, 48, 66, 121
Civil Rights Policy Planning Center, 169
Civil War, 70, 121
clergy, 137
coalitions, ix, 70, 209
coded messages, 154
Cogan, Jeanine, 49
Coincidence Detector, 155
Colcom Foundation, 12
Cold War, 158, 218
Color of Justice (Ogawa), 43
combat risk factors, hate groups, 23
communication, 77, 93, 94–95, 208
communism, 19
community, ix, 214; building, 63–65; capacity building, 76; cohesion, 154; communication, 77; consensus, 74; cooperation in, 64–73; crowdfunding, 76; democracy and, 86–87; in Europe, 86–87; funding and resources, 75–76; goals, 73; groups, 74, 222; hate crimes and, 43; leaders, 85; minorities and, 65; monitoring, 65, 74; neo-Nazis and, 65, 67; networks, 64; in New Zealand, 148; organizing, 64, 75; planning, 8; preparation gaps, 65–66; projects, 75–76; racially mixed, 64; recommendations for, 73–77, 85–87; risk of, 72; schools and, 114; security of, 86–87; service, 94; service delivery in, 65; social marketing for, 76–77; values, 15, 67, 90–91; Walmart and, 53
Community Relations Service (CRS), 172, 181, 205; best practices, 207; conciliation and, 205; education and, 206; event contingency planning, 206; hate crime training curriculum of, 207; law enforcement and, 207; racial and ethnic tensions and, 207; schools and, 206; training and, 205–206
compassionate witnessing, 92–93
complacency, 145
conciliation, 205
Confederate monuments, 70
Conference of Mayors, U.S., 2
conflict, 95
conflict resolution, 124
Conner, Cheryl L., 16n10
conspiracy theories, 15, 27, 79–80
Constitution, U.S., 2, 27, 142, 147, 161
constitutionalists, 154
constitutional sheriffs, 155
Contra Costa County Boyz, 20
conversion, 82–85
Coolidge, Calvin, 141–142
Cooper, McShon, 37
coordination, 155
Cop in the Hood (Moskos), 45
corporations: diversity of, 113; hate speech and, 54; policies of, 54–56, 60; politics and, 53; recommendations for, 59–60; responsibility of, 53–56; social responsibility and, 54; strategies for dealing with hate for, 54; terms of service, 55–56
corrective actions, for schools, 121–122
counteracting neo-Nazis, 59
Countering Violent Extremism (CVE), 22–23
counter-narratives, hate groups and, 23–24
counterterrorism, 57
county supremacy, 155
Crazy White Boyz, 20
creativity, 96
credit card companies, 147
critical thinking, 27
crowdfunding, 76
CRS. *See* Community Relations Service
crucifixion, 3

cruelty, 89
"cuckservative", 155
culture, assimilation and, 146
culture, religion and, 135
Curry, Marshall, 176
CVE. *See* Countering Violent Extremism

data collection and usage, in schools, 122
David Horowitz Freedom Center, 13
dehumanization, 89
democracy, ix, 86–87, 96, 119, 164
demographic changes, in U.S., 100–102
De-Nazification, 4–5
Department of Defense, 80
Department of Homeland Security, 22, 48, 149, 182, 227–230
Department of Justice, U.S., 69, 171, 172–173, 173, 181
depression, 118
deradicalization, 82–85, 142
Derman-Sparks, L., 173, 175
deterrence, 148
"Development of Children's Racial Awareness and Intergroup Attitudes", 175
Devil, 107
Dickson (chief justice), 42
dignity, 90–91
diplomacy, 70–71
DIRN. *See* DuPage Interfaith Resource Network
disability bias, 39–40
disciplinary actions, for schools, 122
discrimination, vii, 39, 54, 109, 124
disillusionment, 82
disparities, 99–100
diversity, 54, 72, 97, 113; awareness of, 112; bias incident response protocol and, 203; of corporations, 113; genocide and, 191; intersectionality, 96; leadership, 115; religion and, 135; in schools, 122
documentation, in bias incident response protocol, 202
dog whistle, 156
domestic spying, 50
domestic terrorism, 48, 84
Donors Capital Fund, 13
Donovan, Jack, 27

drugs, 118
Dumpson vs. Ade, 56–57
DuPage Interfaith Resource Network (DIRN), 136–143

The Early Years (Siraj-Blatchford), 178
Ecce Homo (Nietzsche), 26
echo, 155
economics, 81; conflict, 103; extremism and, 99; hate crimes and, 43; marginalization and, 100; racism and, 101; recommendations for, 104–105; social tensions and, 103–104; terrorism and, 101–102
education, ix, 2, 8, 66–67, 119, 187–188, 211; civic, 15, 119–120; CRS and, 206; hate crimes and, 91; Holocaust, 126; public, 120. *See also* Holocaust education
Ehrlich, Howard, 177
8chan, 25
88 ("Heil Hitler"), 151
Eisenhower, Dwight, 158
elections, 28, 119–120, 120
electronic communications, 47
empathy, 33, 94, 112, 113, 119
equality, 27, 96, 185
equity, ix
ethics, Holocaust and, 128, 213–219
ethnoviolence, 39
eugenics, Nazis and, 3
Europe, 5–8, 86–87
European Convention on Human Rights, 4, 48
event contingency planning, 206
Evergreen State College (TESC), 199–200
Everyday Antiracism (Pollock), 177
evidence, in bias incident response protocol, 202
evil, 107
exiting, 82–85
EXIT USA, 173
expendable category of people, 217
exposure, 66–67
extremism/violent extremism, 1–2, 8; counter-narratives, 23–24; CVE, 22–23; definition of, 156; economics and, 99; European context of, 5–8; global context of, 3; internet and, 27;

narratives of, 22; religion and, 135; youth and, 45
Extremist Crime Database, 14, 174

Facebook, 25, 28, 104, 147
Facing History and Ourselves, 173–174, 179
facts, 95
faculty, bias in, 126
faith-based communities, 225–226
fake news, 95, 123
fascism, 3, 7, 152, 214
Fatal Five, 1
Federal Bureau of Investigation (FBI), 1, 22, 34, 39, 48, 57, 166, 174, 207, 211
Federal Reserve Bank, 27
feminism, 27
FIJA. *See* Fully Informed Jury Association
financial pressure, 66
Finkelstein, Joel, 174
Fioretto, Federico, 7
First Amendment, 41, 56, 69, 117
"Five Eyes" system of intelligence, 148
focused deterrence, law enforcement and, 46
forced sterilization, of African American women, 3
Forgiveness Project, 84
4chan, 151, 154
14/88, 151
Fourteenth Amendment, 69
Fourth Reich, 20
Frankl, Viktor, 67
Franklin, Benjamin, 142
freedom of speech, 29, 56–57, 58, 122, 130, 156, 195, 222
Freemasons, 5–6
Fresnecks, 20
Fully Informed Jury Association (FIJA), 156
funding, 12, 28

Gab, 156
Gale, William Potter, 161
gangs, 15, 87. *See also* prison gangs
Gargan, Edward, 215
"gas the kikes, race war now.". *See* GTKRWN
GDL. *See* Goyim Defense League

gender, 27, 103
Geneva Convention, 4, 47, 48
genocide, 19, 157, 214
geographic location, of hate groups, 38
George Washington University, 177
German Institute on Radicalization and De-Radicalization Studies, 175–176
Germany, 218
Gillis, Roy, 49
globalism, 7
globalization, 99–100, 215, 218
Global Survivors Network, 84
goals, community, 73
God, 91
Goffman, Erving, 82
Google, 28, 76, 147, 148
Google Chrome, 155
government, 46, 48, 59, 69–70, 80, 207–208, 222
Goyim Defense League (GDL), 157
graffiti, 32
Great Depression, 103
"the greatest story never told.". *See* #tgsnt
GTKRWN ("gas the kikes, race war now"), 157
gun control laws, 145, 148, 155
guns, 70

Hamm, Mark S., 81
Hammerskins, 20, 157
harassment, 84
Harris, David, 176
hate, ix, 1, 85
hate crimes, ix, 8, 49; accountability for, 221; acknowledgment and condemnation of, 221; anti-gay, 40; bias and, 42, 111, 200; in Canada, 42; community and, 43; CRS training curriculum, 207; definition of, 39–40, 42, 50, 109, 197; economics and, 43; education and, 91; FBI and, 48, 49; FBI definition of, 39; government and, 222; hate groups and, 41; hate speech and, 41; indicators of, 41–42; integrated neighborhoods and, 101; international cooperation on, 222–223; intervention against, 91; investigation of, 210–211; law enforcement and, 41, 221; laws, 40, 41, 50, 59, 207–208, 221; LGBTQ, 40;

malicious harassment and, 43; as messages, 37; monitoring, 222; motivation for, 38–39, 83; multijurisdictional task forces and, 211; office inquiries into, 222; origin of, 84; plan for combating, 221–223; policy sample, 197–198; preventing, 209; race and, 37, 101; randomness of, 37; recommendations for dealing with, 50; reporting of, 45–47, 49, 50, 123, 210–211, 222; rise of, 40; social media and, 44; surveys, 222; targets of, viii; types of, 44; unresolved, 208; victim assistance services of, 49; youth and, 44–45, 91

Hate Crimes Statistics Act, 39, 41

Hate Crime Unit, 207

hate groups, 114; combat risk factors, 23; conflict, 38; counter-narratives, 23–24; definition of, 11; examples of contemporary, 13–14; funding of, 12; geographic location of, 38; hate crimes and, 41; internet and, 25; leaders of, 38; literature of, 38; monitoring, 124–125; name changes of, 12; in Oklahoma, 127; phenomenon, 11–13; preparation for, viii; prison gangs and, 20; recruitment, 38; rise of, vii; rise of European, 6; violence and, 14–15

hate incidences, ix

hate-initiatives, in schools, 118–121

hate prevention policy, for schools, 121

hate speech, 41, 53, 54, 122, 172

Hatley, James, 91

hatred, 108–112

healing relationships, 94

health care, 186

health standards, 188

Heimbach, Matthew, 166

Heller, Brittan, 174

Herek, Gregory M., 49

Highly Insane Criminals, 20

Hinton, Wade, 2

Hirabayashi, Jay, 181–182

historical revisionism, vii

Hitler, Adolf, 3, 4, 26, 28, 31, 101, 127, 151

Hohensee, J. B., 175

holidays, 139

Holocaust, viii, 3, 5, 15, 26, 31; death toll, 132; denial, 29, 127–128, 129–131, 130; ethics and, 128, 213–219; extermination camps, of Nazis, 217; forced labor, of Nazis, 218; human rights and, 214–216; morality and, 128; neutralization of people and, 217; survivors, 91, 128, 133; Zyklon B gas used in, 6

Holocaust Commission, U.S., 128

Holocaust education, 126, 128; achievements possible through, 128–129; Anne Frank Center and, 130–131; as elective, 131–132; options for, 131; recommendations for, 132–133; states that mandate, 129

Holocaust Museum, 91, 133

Hope Not Hate, 175

HRC. *See* Human Rights Commission

Hubbard, Jvonne, 85

human dignity, 197, 214, 218–219

human rights, 47–48, 214–216

Human Rights Commission (HRC), 208

Human Rights First, 221–223

Humboldt County Gangsters, 20

humiliation, 84

humor and memes, Nazis, 31–32

iCivics, 119, 175

identitarianism, 157

identity formation, of students, 118

immigration, 3, 5, 7, 123, 186

Imperial eagle, 31

Implementing an Anti-Bias Curriculum in Early Childhood Classrooms, 175

Improving Security by Democratic Participation (ISDEP), 175

impulsive hate offenses, 157–158

incel rebellion, 158

inclusivity, 158

income, 186

inequality, 7, 102, 103

Instagram, 28

integrated neighborhoods, hate crimes and, 101

integration, 122, 154

Intelligence Project/ Report, 178

interfaith, 135; case study, 138; organizations, 137; scheduling

strategies, 139; schools and, 139–140. *See also* DuPage Interfaith Resource Network
Interfaith Conference of Greater Milwaukee, 137
Interfaith Restorative Practices Coalition, 138
intermarriage, 19
international cooperation, on hate crimes, 137, 222–223
internet, 22, 25, 27, 29–30, 33–34, 147–148
interracial relationships, 191
intervention, 125, 158
intolerance, 222
investigation, of hate crimes, 210–211
Iraqi war, 217
Irving, David, 127–128
ISDEP. *See* Improving Security by Democratic Participation
Islamic Society of North America (ISNA), 176
Islamic State, recruitment of, 83
Islamophobia, 158
ISNA. *See* Islamic Society of North America
Israel, 5, 129, 149
Italy, 7

Jayapal, Pramila, 164
JBS. *See* John Birch Society
JD Journal for Deradicalization, 175
Jenkins, Alan, 176
Jesus Christ, 3, 18–19
Jews, 3, 6, 18–19, 25–30, 96. *See also* anti-Semitism
Jim Crow, viii, 66
John Birch Society (JBS), 2, 158
John F. Kennedy School of Government, 180–181
Josephson Institute of Ethics, 175
Jung, C. G., 107
justice, 90, 93–94

Katz, P. A, 175
Kaufman, George W., 67
Keller, Craig, 164
Kerry, John, 2
Khan, Deeyah, 182–183

Kidwell, Ronald Lee, 37
Kill All Normies (McDougald), 108
Kill All Normies (Nagle), 180
King, Martin Luther, Jr., 121
King, Rodney, 43
Koehler, Daniel, 83, 175
Koplin, Steven Z., 170
Korematsu, Karen, 181–182
Krieger, Larry, 67
Krieger Verwandt, 20
Ku Klux Klan, 14, 18, 31, 48, 56, 58, 83, 85, 159, 206

land reform, 187
land-use laws, 155
Lane, David, 151
language, 129
law enforcement, 6; active shooter protocols, 46–47; African Americans and, 50; bias incident response protocol and, 201; civil asset forfeiture of, 58; CRS and, 207; extreme response by, 46–47; focused deterrence and, 46; hate crimes and, 41, 221; investigation of hate crimes, 210–211; neo-Nazis and, 45–46, 50, 124; in New Zealand, 146, 149; relationships with, 50; reporting and, 45–47; right-wing extremism and, 50; schools and, 122, 124, 209–210; special responsibility of, 45–46
laws: anti-bullying, 124; anti-mask, 58; discrimination and, 109; freedom of speech and, 58; genocide and, 214; hate crimes, 40, 41, 50, 59, 207–208, 221; immigration, 123; internet and, 147–148; against Ku Klux Klan, 58; neo-Nazis and, 66; paramilitary, 59; RICO, 57–58
Lawyers' Committee for Civil Rights Under Law, 179
The Lawyer's Guide to Balancing Life & Work (Kaufman), 67
leaderless resistance, 158
leadership, 38, 85, 113–114, 115
League of the South, 159
legitimacy, ix, 46
Leibovitz, Alison, 2
Levant, Ezra, 13
Levine, Deborah, 11

Levitas, Daniel, 161
LGBTQ hate crimes, 40
liberalism, 214
The Liberator's Daughter (Levine), 11, 179
Liberty, USS, 167
Lieberman, Michael, 169
Life Against Hate, 181
lightning rod events, 70
Lindbergh, Charles, 152
listening, 94
literature, of hate groups, 38
local action, communication and, 208
lone wolf, 158

mafia, 57
malicious harassment, hate crimes and, 43
Manson, Charles, 21
Man's Search for Meaning (Frankl), 67
marginalization, 100
Marjory Stoneman Douglas High School, 120
marketing, values and, 31
Marr, Wilhelm, 3
Maryland Public Information Act (MPIA), 226
mass murder, 38
mass shooting, 25, 145, 148
The Matrix, 163
McCabe, Andrew, 57
McCarthy years, viii
McCord, Mary, 58
McDougald, Park, 108
McElhiney, Michael, 21
McInnes, Gavin, 162
McVeigh, Timothy, 80
media, 19, 23, 79–80, 82, 210
mediation, 124, 205
Mein Kampf (Hitler), 26, 28
mental health, 22, 118
mental illness, racism and, 107–108
Mercer, Robert, 13
messaging with values, 95–97
Mexican Mafia ("La Eme"), 21
Mexico, 163
Microsoft, 147
middle class, 187
military, 59, 80
militia movement, 159

Miller, Mike, 64
Mills, Barry Byron, 21
minorities, 7, 43, 65, 109, 141
Minutemen, 159
misogyny, 159
mobility, 96, 102–103
monitoring, 65, 124–125, 222
Montana Human Rights Network, 179
moral disengagement, 89
morality, 89–91, 128
Moskos, Peter, 45
motivation, 38–39, 83
mourning, 92–93
Movimiento Estudiantil Chicano de Aztlan, 163
MPIA. *See* Maryland Public Information Act
Mud People, 19, 160
multiculturalism, 27, 160
multijurisdictional task forces, 211
music, 32–33
Muslim Brotherhood, 160
Muslim Jewish Advisory Council, 176
Muslims, 113

Nagle, Angela, 180
name changes, of hate groups, 12
National Alliance, 14, 20
National Association of Student Personnel Administrators Diversity on Campus, 180
National Center for Hate Crime Prevention, 180
National Consortium for the Study of Terrorism and Responses to Terrorism, 14
National Fact-Finding, 169
national history, right-wing extremism and, 12
national intelligence agencies, in New Zealand, 148
nationalism, vii, 12, 17
National Socialist Movement (NSM), 160, 191, 195
National Socialist White People's Party, 20
National Threat Assessment Center (NTAC), 178
National Workshop on Christian-Jewish Relations, 136

Native Americans, 70, 127, 152–153, 160
The Nature of Prejudice (Allport), 110
Nazi Low Riders (NLR), 20
Nazis, vii, 26, 63, 152; alphanumeric code symbols of, 31; Aryan Nation and, 13; Aryan race, 3; church and, 214–216; culture of, 218; defeat of, 4; De-Nazification, 4–5; eugenics and, 3; extermination camps of, 217; fascism and, 3, 7; forced labor, 218; freedom of speech and, 122, 195; history of, 15; human rights and, 214, 215; ideology of, 8, 14; immigration and, 3, 5; memorabilia, 28; message of, 195; mission of, 118; neo-Nazis and, 26; Nietzsche and, 26; NSM and, 160; peaceful stand against, 196; personal responsibility and, 218; policies of, 4, 47; principles of, 3; reeducation and, 4–5; right-wing extremism and, 26; social networking of, 28–29; students as, 117; symbols, 87, 118; Third Position, 166; traditional symbols of, 31; victims of, 213; visibility of, 90; witnessing and, 91
negotiation, 70–71
neighborhood associations, 63
neo-Confederates, 160
neo-fascists, 7
neo-Nazis, viii, ix, 5, 11, 18, 23, 27, 28, 50, 96, 141, 182; Atomwaffen Division, 153; community and, 65, 67, 73–77; conversion of, 82; counteracting, 59; emerging symbols of, 31–32; freedom of speech and, 56, 156; Holocaust denial and, 130; humor and memes, 31–32; law enforcement and, 45–46, 50, 124; laws and, 66; military and, 80; music of, 28; Nazis and, 26; NVC and, 93; online strategies against, 33–34; parents and, 33; propaganda, 32, 83; public health model and, 71–72; recruitment, 79–80, 118; risk assessment and analysis of, 68–70; school shootings and, 117; social infrastructure and, 80; social media and, 56; stepwise progression of responses to, 67–68; Strausserism, 166; targeting by, 34; (((triple parentheses))), 167; violence of, 65; white supremacy and, 17; ZOG, 168
Network Contagion Research Institute, 174
Network of Associations of Victims of Terrorism, 84
neurological pathways, 112
neutralization of people, Holocaust and, 217
The New American (TNA), 2
New Anti-Semitism, 160
New Code of the West, 160
newspapers, 188–189
New Testament, 91
New World Order, 159
New Zealand, 145–149
Nicholas II (Tsar), 26
Nietzsche, 26
A Night in the Garden, 176
9/11. *See* September 11th, 2001 attacks
NLR. *See* Nazi Low Riders
No-Hate process, 114
nonmalevolence, 90
Non-Violent Communication (NVC), 93, 94–95
nonviolent incidents, at schools, 117
Not in Our Town, 63, 65, 96, 180, 196
NSM. *See* National Socialist Movement
NTAC. *See* National Threat Assessment Center
La Nuestra Familia, 21
Nuremberg Tribunal, 4, 47–48
NVC. *See* Non-Violent Communication

oath keepers, 161
Odinism, 161
offenders, 211–212
Office for Victims of Crime (OVC), 212
official systems, 48–49
Ogawa, Brian, 43
Oi!, 32
Oklahoma, 127
Oklahoma City Bombing, 11
One World Government, 19
online. *See* internet
The Opportunity Agenda, 33, 176
"The Organizational Dynamics of Far-Right Hate Groups in the United States", 173

Organization of Chinese Americans, 176–177
OVC. *See* Office for Victims of Crime

Palestine, 5
panic buttons, 47
paramilitary laws, 59
parents, 33, 72, 123
Parkland High School, 117
Parliament of the World's Religions, 135–136
Parrott, Matt, 166
participation, ix
partnerships, ix, 121
Patriot Movements, 18, 161
Pawlikowski, John, 128, 129
PayPal, 28
Peckerwoods, 20
Pepe the Frog, 32
Persian Gulf War, 43
personal responsibility, 218
physical abuse, 39
physical mobility, 102–103
The Pianist, 132
Picciolini, Christian, 181
Pierce, William L., 177
Pitcavage, Mark, 169
Pittsburgh, 37. *See also* Tree of Life Synagogue
Pius XII (pope), 216

El Plan Espiritual de Aztlán, 163

police. *See* law enforcement
policies, 54–56, 209
politics, 18, 53
Pollock, Mica, 177
Posse Comitatus, 18, 161, 165
Pound, Ezra, 7
precautionary principle, 68–69
prejudice, ix, 3, 33, 72, 108–112
The Prejudice Institute, 177
premeditated hate episode, 162
press, 188–189
prison gangs, 20–22
profiling, 146–148
Program on Extremism, 177
Promising Practices Against Hate Crimes, 171–172

propaganda, 23, 25, 32, 83, 132
Protocols of the Elders, 3
The Protocols of the Learned Elders of Zion, 5, 26
Proud Boys, 162
psychiatric approaches, 107–108
psychology, 107
Public Enemy Number One, 20
Public Good Project, 180
public health model, 71–72
Putin, Vladimir, 25–26
Putnam, Robert D., 85

race, 37, 65, 80, 101, 120, 162, 185
racial and ethnic tensions, 207, 209
racial healing, 115
"Racial Holy War.". *See* RAHOWA
racialism, 162
racialization, 167
racial mixing, 64
racial purity, 3–5
racism, viii, ix, 27, 31, 66, 108–112, 112; in children, 110–111; economics and, 101; institutional, 101; media and, 82; mental illness and, 107–108; stigma and, 82–83; Trump and, 101; xeno-racism, 167
racist groups, leaving, 83
Racketeer Influenced and Corrupt Organizations. *See* RICO
racketeering, 57–58
radicalization, 22, 79–80, 81, 86, 86–87, 108, 123, 163
Radicalization Awareness Network (RAN), 177
RAHOWA ("Racial Holy War"), 163
RAM. *See* Rise Above Movement
RAN. *See* Radicalization Awareness Network
reactive hate episodes, 163
reconquista, 163
recruitment, 79–80, 86–87, 114; boys needs and, 80–81; hate groups, 38; of Islamic State, 83; neo-Nazis, 79–80, 118; of students, 118
red pill, 163
Red Terror, 6
reeducation, Nazis and, 4–5
Regnery, William, 12

rehumanizing the enemy, witnessing and, 193–194
relationships, healing, 94
religion, 18, 20, 107, 129, 189, 214, 215; culture and, 135; diversity and, 135; expression of, 138; extremism/violent extremism and, 135; schools and, 139–140; stereotypes of, 138; in workplace, 138–139. *See also* interfaith
Religious Diversity at Work (Levine), 178
Religious Diversity in Our Schools (Levine), 178
Remtulla, Tariq, 181
reporting: in bias incident response protocol, 200–201, 202; of hate crimes, 45–47, 49, 50, 123, 210–211, 222; law enforcement and, 45–47; in schools, 124–125
respect, 90, 112
Respect Washington, 164
Responding to Hate at School, a Guide for Teachers, Counselors and Administrators, 178
"Responding to Hate Crimes", 171
Responding to Hate Crimes and Bias Motivated Incidents on College and University Campuses, 173
restorative justice, 93–94, 211
restorative practices, 138
RICO (Racketeer Influenced and Corrupt Organizations), 57–58
rights, equality of, 185
right-wing extremism, vii; definition of, 164; law enforcement and, 50; national history and, 12; nationalism and, 12; Nazis and, 26; social media usage, 147–148; violence and, 37–38
right-wing libertarian anarchist community, 164
riots, 43
Rise Above Movement (RAM), 164–165
risk: assessment and analysis of neo-Nazis, 68–70; of community, 72; mitigation resources for active shooter, 169
rites of passage, 82
Rogers, Diana, 17
Rogers, Richard, 17
Roman edict law, 187
Rosenberg, Marshall, 93

Rothstein (justice), 42
Royal Canadian Mounted Police, 178
rumors, 210
Russia, 25–26, 28
Russian Orthodox Church, 26
R vs. Keegstra, 42

Sacramaniacs, 20
safe spaces, 86
Sahakian, David, 21
Sander, Thomas, 181
Saskatchewan Human Rights Code, 42
Satan, 19
Scaife, Cordelia, 12
Scaife, Richard Mellon, 12
Scaife Foundation, 13
scheduling strategies, interfaith, 139
Schloss, Eva, 132
schools, 43; alternatives in, 123; anti-immigration rhetoric in, 123; bias and curriculum in, 114–115; bias in, 126; community and, 114; corrective actions for, 121–122; cost of, 99; CRS and, 206; data collection and usage in, 122; disciplinary actions for, 122; diversity in, 122; hate-initiatives in, 118–121; hate prevention policy for, 121; hate speech in, 122; integration of, 122; interfaith and, 139–140; intervention in, 125; law enforcement and, 122, 124, 209–210; monitoring of, 124–125; nonviolent incidents at, 117; partnerships with, 121; programs for white teenage boys, 81; race and, 120; recommendations for, 124–126; religion and, 139–140; reporting in, 124–125; shootings, 117, 125; staff training, 119; storytelling in, 126; student training in, 119–121; threat assessment in, 125
SCM. *See* Sovereign Citizen Movement
SCN, 2
Second Amendment, 56
Second Coming, 19–20
Secret Service, U.S., 125, 178
security, of community, 86–87
security operating grants, 225–226
self-medication, 118
self-radicalization, 29, 79

self-reflection, 193
September 11th, 2001 attacks (9/11), 27
service delivery, in community, 65
sexism, 112
sexual abuse, 39
sexual orientation, 113
shadow, 107
shame, 84
shaming, 112
Shrinky Dinks, 165
significance quest theory (SQT), 83
Silent Aryan Warriors, 20
Simcox, Chris, 159
Simon Wiesenthal Center, 181
Siraj-Blatchford, I., 178
skinheads, 11, 14, 20, 38. *See also* Aryan Nation
slavery, 19, 70
small hats, 165
social change, 96, 101
social cohesion, ix
social Darwinism, 164
social deprivation, 84
social desirability bias, 165
social infrastructure, neo-Nazis and, 80
socialism, 19, 185–189
social justice, ix
social marketing, 30–31, 76–77
social media, viii, 28, 44, 56, 147–148
social mobility, 102–103
social networking, of Nazis, 28–29
social responsibility, 54, 113
social tensions, 103–104
Soldiers of the Aryan Culture, 20
South Africa, 193, 216
Southern Brotherhood, 20
Southern Poverty Law Center, 178, 195
Sovereign Citizen Movement (SCM), 165
SPEAK, 45
Spencer, Richard, 137, 182
SQT. *See* significance quest theory
staff training, in schools, 119
State Department, 2
Steinberg, Annie, 181
stereotypes, 114, 138
Stern, Kenneth, 128, 170
stigma, racism and, 82–83
Stockholm Declaration, 153
Stop Hate Project, 179

storytelling, in schools, 126
strategic frames, 165
Strausserism, 166
street gang, 166
Strong Cities project, 2
student-led initiatives, 112–113
students: bias in, 126; identity formation of, 118; as Nazis, 117; recruitment of, 118; training in schools, 119–121
suffering, 93
Supreme Court, 58
surveillance cameras, 148
suspicious package signs, 227–228
sustainability, 72, 75
Swastika, 31, 112
symbols, ADL directory of, 169–170

Tactical Community Policing for Homeland Security, 182
talking with children, 96–97
Tallahassee, 37
targeted harassment and violence, 166
targeting, 34, 70
Teaching Tolerance, 178
technology, vii, 29, 148
Teitelbaum, Benjamin R., 33
10 Ways to Fight Hate on Campus, 181
terrorism, 1, 84, 101–102, 141, 148, 166
Terrorism and Violent Extremism Awareness Guide, 178
TESC. *See* Evergreen State College
#tgsnt, 157
Third Position, 166
The Threat (McCabe), 57
threat assessment, in schools, 125
Thus Spoke Zarathustra (Nietzsche), 26
TNA. *See The New American*
tolerance, 108, 191
Toolkit on Juvenile Justice, 81
Topenkopf, 31
Traditionalist Worker Party, 166
training, CRS and, 205–206
trauma, 92, 124
Tree of Life Synagogue, 37, 135
(((triple parentheses))), 167
trolling, 25, 31
Trump, Donald, vii, 23, 100–101, 152
turbokike, 167
Turner Diaries (Pierce), 177

28 (Blood and Honor), 151
Twitter, 25, 28

Un-Bias Guide for Educators (Levine), 179
Un-Bias Guide for Leaders (Levine), 179
Under the Shadow of the Swastika (Bennett), 128, 213
unemployment, 209
Unforgiven, 20, 167
UN Genocide Convention, 48
United Aryan Brotherhood, 20
United Nations, 2
United Nations Genocide Convention, 4
United States (U.S.), 28, 47, 100–102, 104
Universal Declaration of Human Rights, 4, 48
U.S. *See* United States

values, vii, ix, 15, 31, 67–68, 90–91, 95–97
vandalism, 32, 43
Vanguard America, 167
VCPI. *See* Virginia Center for Policing Innovation
victims, 49, 211–212, 213
Vietnam war, 217
violence, vii, ix; of AB, 21; aftermath of, 93; definition of, 14; ethnoviolence, 39; forecasting, 148; language and, 129; motivation for, 38–39, 83; mourning and, 92–93; of neo-Nazis, 65; performative, 38; religion and, 129, 215; right-wing extremism and, 37–38; strategic, 38; types of, 38
violent extremism. *See* extremism/violent extremism
Virginia Center for Policing Innovation (VCPI), 182
Volksfront, 20
voting, citizenship and, 185

wage inequality, 102, 103
Wall Street, 147
Walmart, 53
Washington State Human Rights Commission, 182, 195–196
wealth inequality, 102
Weingarten, Kaethe, 172, 193
Wessler, Steve, 172
White American Youth (Picciolini), 181
White Aryan Resistance, 14, 20
white ethnostate, 167
Whitefish, Montana, 137
white power, 20, 27, 32–33
White Race, 18
white supremacy, 17, 137; anti-Muslim, 145; apartheid and, 43; funding of, 28; music of, 32–33; neo-Nazis and, 17; politics and, 18; in prison gangs, 20–21; religion and, 18; social media and, 28; youth subculture of, 27, 44
Wisconsin vs. Mitchell, 41
"wise use" or "multiple use" anti-environmental movement, 167
witnesses, 211–212
witnessing, 91–94, 193–194
The Witnessing Project, 183
women, 3, 141, 158, 159
workplace: leadership study, 113–114; religion in, 138–139
World Church of the Creator, 20
World Columbian Exposition, 135
world-view, challenging, 27
World War II, vii, 4, 7, 8, 127, 152, 166

xeno-racism, 167

Yahweh, 19
yarmulkes, 165
Yasui, Holly, 181–182
Young Americans Foundation, 69
youth, 27, 44, 44–45, 45, 81, 91, 120
"Youth Hate Crimes: Identification, Prevention, and Intervention", 181
youth work, 168
YouTube, 25, 28

Zionism, 5, 5–6, 161
ZOG ("Zionist Occupation Government"), 168
Zuckerberg, Mark, 29
Zyklon B gas, 6

About the Authors

Marc Brenman served as the executive director of the Washington State Human Rights Commission from 2004 to 2009 and senior policy advisor for civil rights at the U.S. Department of Transportation from 1995 to 2004, where he was a co-author of the department's Environmental Justice Order. He was previously with the Office for Civil Rights at the U.S. Department of Education, from investigator to division director, working on national civil rights policy. He served on the Diversity Standards Task Force for the Society for Human Resources Management and on the Board of Advisors for the City Project in Los Angeles, where he was on a team that produced guidance on reducing minority racial disparities in health funded by the California Endowment. He has worked on environmental justice, race issues, limited English proficiency, disability, sex discrimination, LGBT rights, culturally appropriate alternative dispute resolution, corporate social responsibility, and international human rights. He is the co-author of *The Right to Transportation* on social equity and *Planning as If People Matter: Governing for Social Equity* with Professor Tom Sanchez. He is the editor and writer of three chapters in *Religious Diversity in the Workplace*, edited by Deborah Levine, and has a book in press called *Community Response to Neo-Nazis and Extreme Rightwing Groups* with Rowman & Littlefield. He has taught graduate courses on civil rights history, human rights, public policy development, advocacy, and strategic planning and has a master's degree from the Public Administration and Tribal Governance Program at Evergreen College in Olympia, Washington, and the Young African Leadership Initiative, USAID program in Nairobi, Kenya. He is the author of many articles, op-eds, and policy and research papers on social equity, including on transportation equity history for the American Bar Association, and is a member of the Environmental Justice and Social Equity Committees, Transportation Research

Board. He has presented and keynoted on transportation equity, diversity metrics, and other topics at many conferences, including EEOC EXCEL Conference, Rural Transportation Conference, American Planning Association, IBBTA, Housing Land Advocates, Texas Health and Human Services Conference, Association for Conflict Resolution, Mediators Beyond Borders, Intercultural Management Association, Seattle Race Conference, and Harvard Law School. He consults, teaches, writes, and has his own firm, IDARE LLC. In 2010, he assisted Public Advocates, Inc., in winning the first civil rights case under ARRA, the federal stimulus law, for $70 million. In 2012, he won first prize in the Americans for Democratic Action Education Fund essay contest, discussing what Reverend Martin Luther King Jr. would say to President Obama. In 2013, he consulted on a major civil rights complaint that achieved bus services for African Americans at a large midwestern shopping center.

Deborah J. Levine has thirty-three years of experience in speaking, consulting, and coaching around cultural diversity for healthcare organizations, universities, professional associations, and international industries including Volkswagen, Nissan, and International Paper. Born in Brooklyn and brought up in Bermuda, she has lived, worked, and studied across the United States, acquiring advanced degrees in cultural anthropology, religion, and urban planning. Deborah is a community leader and coalition builder, having created the Women's Council on Diversity, the DuPage/Chicago Interfaith Resource Network, and the Youth Multicultural Video Contest. She was the Tulsa Jewish Federation's community/media liaison shortly after the Oklahoma City bombing and currently leads the Media Task Force of Chattanooga's Council Against Hate while also serving as the education director of an International Rotary e-Club. An award-winning author of thirteen educational books, Deborah is the founder of the AmericanDiversityReport.com and has been its editor-in-chief for the past dozen years. Her classroom guide, *Teaching Curious Christians about Judaism*, won a national press association award and was taken to the Vatican as a gift for Pope Francis. That guide and her workplace manual, *Religious Diversity at Work*, demonstrate her broad knowledge of the interfaith world. Her memoir, *The Liberator's Daughter*, ushered her into Holocaust education as it includes the World War II letters of her father, a U.S. military intelligence officer assigned to interrogate Nazi prisoners of war. Her *Matrix Model Management System* is a copyrighted cognitive technology for thought leadership and is the basis for her work in cross-cultural communication and unconscious bias training. Deborah's articles on cultural diversity have been published in academic journals: *Harvard Divinity School Bulletin*, the *Journal of Ecumenical Studies*, and the *Journal of Public Management and Social Policy*. In addition to her writing, Deborah has given cultural diversity workshops and presentations for universities, corporations, government agencies, and community nonprofits. Her interactive, storytelling-based methodology is designed to engage diverse teams, promote inclusion, and improve emotional intelligence in decision making. Her clients include the National Association of Veterinarian Universities, National Park Service/SE Region, First Tennessee Bank, Erlanger Medical Center, Alabama University Medical College, Metropolitan Ministries/Chattanooga, Birmingham International Center, Tulsa Public Schools, and Alabama Fulbright Fellows.